ON LAMBETH MARSH

ON LAMBETH MARSH

The South Bank
and
Waterloo

Graham Gibberd 19.5.92

Graham Gibberd

British Library Cataloguing in Publication Data

Gibberd, Graham
On Lambeth Marsh: The South Bank and Waterloo

I. Title
942.1

ISBN 0 9518920 0 2

All rights reserved.
No part of this book may be copied, reproduced, reprinted, stored in any retrieval system, or transmitted in any form or by any means, without the prior permission in writing of the author. The illustrations in this book are copyright and may not be reproduced, copied, scanned or reprinted without permission in writing of the author and the copyright holders.

© 1992 Graham Gibberd

Printed by
BAS Printers Ltd,
Over Wallop, Hampshire

Published by Jane Gibberd,
at 20 Lower Marsh, London SE1 7RJ

LONDON

I wander thro' each charter'd street,
Near where the charter'd Thames does flow,
And mark in every face I meet
Marks of weakness, marks of woe.

In every cry of every Man,
In every Infants cry of fear,
In every voice; in every ban,
The mind-forg'd manacles I hear

How the Chimney-sweepers cry
Every blackning Church appalls,
And the hapless Soldiers sigh
Runs in blood down Palace walls

But most thro' midnight streets I hear
How the youthful Harlots curse
Blasts the new born Infants tear
And blights with plagues the Marriage hearse

William Blake   *23 Hercules Row [Road]*

CONTENTS

	List of illustrations and maps	viii
	Acknowledgements	xii
	Preface	xiii
	Introduction	1
1	Locations	6
2	The Island Village	40
3	The Rise and Fall of Industry	54
4	Landlords	67
5	Rural Life till 1820	76
6	The Change to Urban Living	101
7	The Marsh Lives On	143
	Appendix	
	John Evelyn	146
	Wenceslas Hollar	148
	Gilbert White	149
	William Blake	153
	Culpeper Family Tree	156
	Notes	158
	Bibliography	162
	Index	166

ILLUSTRATIONS AND MAPS

ILLUSTRATIONS

COVER
                                                                                 page
Lambeth Marsh by Paul Sandby

INTRODUCTION
1.	Lambeth Marsh located in London	3
2.	Lambeth Marsh administrative boundaries	4
3.	Locations [w1.1] to [w1.15]	7
4.	Location of Tradescant's house [w1.15]	8
5.	Vauxhall Manor and Escheat	8
6.	Locations [w1.16] to [w1.25]	11
7.	Locations [w2.1] to [w2.12]	12
8.	Locations [w2.13] to [w2.21]	15
9.	Locations [w2.22] to [w2.41]	17
10.	Locations [w2.42] to [w2.55]	19
11.	Locations [w3.1] to [w3.16]	21
12.	Locations [w3.17] to [w3.32]	23
13.	Locations [w3.33] to [w3.46]	24
14.	Cuper's Gardens shown on the Rocque map	24
15.	Hungerford pier and rail bridge before 1864	27
16.	Locations [w4.1] to [w4.15]	28
17.	Locations [w4.16] to [w4.21]	30
18.	Locations [w4.22] to [w4.30]	32
19.	Locations [w4.31] to [w4.41]	34
20.	Locations [w4.42] to [w4.52]	37
21.	Locations [w4.53] to [w4.60]	39

THE ISLAND VILLAGE
22.	The River Neckinger derived from Roque maps	41
23.	Lambeth Marsh ground features	42
24.	Standard ferry fares, W. Roades 1731	44
25.	Labelye's final design, Westminster Bridge	46
26.	Rebuilding the collapsed pier 1750 by Canaletto	47
27.	Blackfriars bridge under construction by Edward Rooker	48
28.	A woman mudlark at Blackfriars Bridge by Munby	48
29.	Waterloo Bridge demolition drawings	49
30.	Photograph of Hungerford Bridge 1850 by Roger Fenton	49
31.	Hungerford Bridge under construction in 1844	50
32.	Hungerford Bridge chains being removed, Whistler 1861	50
33.	Building the first Waterloo Station, 1848	51
34.	Waterloo Station expansion, 1848-1991	52

Illustrations and maps

THE RISE AND FALL OF INDUSTRY

35.	Boatyards at Stangate	55
36.	Riverside Breweries in 1806	56
37.	Horn Brewery and Windmill, The Cut 1804	57
38.	Carlisle House site in 1840	58
39.	Coade stone plaques demolished 1959, Blackfriars Road	59
40.	'Architecture' from Coade's catalogue	59
41.	Type foundry 1842 of William Clowes	61
42.	Trussons' and Collinge's advertisements	64
43.	Dog and Pot coal hole	65
44.	Pedlar's Acre window in Tradescant Museum	66

LANDLORDS

45.	1785-6 survey of Kennington Manor land	68
46.	1806 Enclosure Survey of Lambeth Manor land	70
47.	Paris Garden Manor in 1566	74
48.	St George's Fields, Cary 1787	75

RURAL LIFE TILL 1820

49.	Bonner's House prior to demolition	79
50.	Tradescant's and Captain Bligh's tombs	81
51.	The Camberwell Beauty butterfly	81
52.	Morgan's map 1782	82
53.	Hollar's map before the Fire	82
54.	Hollar's engraving of insects	84
55.	Gardens open to the public	85
56.	The Dog and Duck sign	87
57.	The Folly	87
58.	Curtis's London Botanic Garden by Sowerby	89
59.	The London Botanic Garden located	91
60.	Restoration Garden 1755	92
61.	Stockdale's map 1797	93
62.	Painting of Lambeth Marsh by Paul Sandby	96
63.	A View from a Gentleman's Seat in Lambeth Marsh	97
64.	Features of the view from a Gentleman's seat	99

CHANGE TO URBAN LIVING

65.	Sala's interior of the Coburg tavern	103
66.	View in the New Cut	105
67.	Signor Calpi's Acts in 1771	107
68.	Astley's Westminster Bridge Road entrance	107
69.	Hercules and the horses of Diomedes	108
70.	Ticket for Sanger's Circus	108
71.	The Canterbury in the 1870's	109
72.	The Ring in the 1920's	110
73.	The Ring's destruction in 1942	111
74.	A 1916 programme of Surrey Theatre	113
75.	Amateur theatre by Cruickshank	114
76.	The Festival of Britain site	114
77.	Cut-out characters from toy theatres	117

78.	Chevalier D'Eon's dual at Carlton House	119
79.	Morley College 1992	122
80.	Bethlem Hospital portico and Coade stone crest of 1815	124
81.	Bethlem Hospital in the 1870's	125
82.	Freemasons' School for Girls	126
83.	Charity School for Boys, drawing by R. B. Schnebbelie	128
84.	George Reynold's drawing of his new school	128
85.	Coade stone statue of Charity Boy	129
86.	A Magdalen Girl in 1766	129
87.	The Magdalen Hospital in St George's Fields	129
88.	General Lying-in Hospital 1751	131
89.	General Lying-in Hospital 1992	132
90.	The Royal Waterloo Hospital	133
91.	St Thomas's Hospital nurse's home, site of Astley's	133
92.	St Thomas's Hospital in 1871	134
93.	The Philanthropic Society by Rowlandson	136
94.	Archbishop Temple School, now Marine Society	136
95.	Surrey Institute	137
96.	St Mary Lambeth	139
97.	Christ Church Blackfriars	139
98.	Christ Church and Upton Chapel	140
99.	St George's Cathedral	140
100.	St John's Waterloo 1992, by Capa.	141
101.	St John's Waterloo bombed in 1941	142

THE MARSH LIVES ON

102.	The Oxo building redeveloped	144

Illustrations and maps

MAPS showing LAMBETH MARSH, referenced or illustrated

1572 Braun & Hagenburg (Stilliard)
1593 Norden: London and Southwark
1593 Norden: Westminster
1666 Hollar: London after the Fire
1681 T. Jonas Hill, Vauxhall Manor
1682 William Morgan (Morden and Lea)
1696 Jacobus de la Feuille
1720 John Strype (Thorold)
1720 After 1682 Morden and Lea
1731 Robert Hulton (Spring Garden)
1746 Rocque all scales
1755 St Mary Lambeth
1755 Stow, St Olave Bermondsey
1755 Clowes (1920) of 1755 Morden and Lea
1760 Road plan after Morden and Lea
1765 Robert Sayer
1766 Rocque: large scale with environs
1769 Rocque: small scale
1785 Hodskinson & Middleton, Kennington Survey
1785 Clowes version of Hodskinson & Middleton
1785 Gibberd version of Hodskinson & Middleton
1787 Cary: Westminster Bridge, milk house
1793 Cary: Westminster Bridge, Apollo Gardens
1797 Stockdale
1797 Fairburn
1797 Wallis
1799 Horwood
1805 Civil War forts after Hollar
1806 Enclosure Survey map
1807 Horwood
1819 Horwood
1828 Wyld
1830 Greenwood, Kennington, 3/4 inch to 1 mile
1832 Greenwood, London
1860 Post Office directory
1862 Stanford, 6 inches to 1 mile
1865 SLAS map of entertainment
1872 Ordnance Survey
1980 Lambeth Potteries

ACKNOWLEDGEMENTS

Robin Densum and his colleagues from the London Museum and their earlier Southwark and Lambeth Archaeological Excavation Committee have provided information over the years concerning the local archaeological digs and this book might never have happened had it not been for Robin Densum's interest in the nineteenth century steam baker's oven found on my premises in Lower Marsh.

I would like to thank Michael Bruce for his patience over the years and the inspiration I received from his slide/sound show *The Story of Waterloo*, that was shown at the South Bank.

I am grateful to all my friends in the Southwark and Lambeth Archaeological Society (SLAS) and in particular to George Young, Roy Edwards and Brian Bloice. The members of the two Archive Libraries and the Councils of Lambeth and Southwark deserve special thanks and acknowledgement for the use of their material. I would also like to thank John Bridges, Keeper of Maps and Prints at the Greater London Records Office, for his help in my work on William Capon's painting of Lambeth Marsh. I would also like to thank the residents of the Marsh for the various conversations I have had with them concerning their own histories.

Susan Shaw of Merrion Press should be thanked for her invaluable help in the production of this book.

Most important to thank is my wife, Jane, for her readings and for tolerating my 'going-on' for so long.

Illustrations
The following are the sources of illustrations acknowledged with thanks:
Greater London Record Office: Ills. 37, 63, 83, 93.
Guildhall Library, The Corporation of London: Ill. 57.
London Borough of Lambeth Archives Department: The Cover, Ills. 4, 5, 14, 22, 24, 36, 38, 45, 46, 48, 49, 52, 62.
Southwark Local Studies Library: Ills. 47, 60, 61.
The British Library: Ills. 40, 53.
Trustees of the British Museum: Ills. 32, 88.
The Battle of Waterloo Road 1941: Photograph by Capa, Ill. 100.
The Magdalen Hospital Trust: Ills. 86, 87.
Trinity College, Cambridge: Ill. 28.
Alan Godfrey Maps: Ill. 34.
Royal Society of Literature: Ill. 84.
Victoria and Albert Museum: Ill. 27.
By courtesy of the Trustees of Sir John Soane Museum: Ill. 25.
Windsor Castle, Royal Library. © 1992 Her Majesty The Queen. Ill. 29.
Author's collection: Ills. 15, 29, 30, 31, 33, 34, 39, 41, 42, 44, 56, 58, 59, 61, 64, 65, 66, 67, 68, 69, 70, 71, 75, 76, 77, 79, 80, 81, 82, 83, 85, 91, 92, 94, 95, 96, 97, 98, 99, 102, and artwork 1-21, 36, 45, 46, 55 redrawn by the author from small portions of: – Bartholomew's 1940 Greater London atlas, pre-1950 Ordnance Surveys or earlier road maps and surveys.

PREFACE

Few of the millions of people who pass through Waterloo station, who visit the South Bank or who walk along The Cut, could locate these places on a map. Although most people would say that the area is south of the Thames or part of South London, they would find it hard to believe that it is situated due east of Knightsbridge and at London's geometric centre, in a loop in the Thames. Waterloo, the South Bank and The Cut are historically part of a single area of London that from the fourteenth century until 1888 was called Lambeth Marsh.

Many residents of Lambeth Marsh were famous for political, professional or historical reasons and have their own biographies or are quoted in the histories of Lambeth, Southwark or Surrey. However, like any other 'place', Lambeth Marsh is a living organism whose character is more than the sum of its parts and deserves a history of its own. This history reinstates Lambeth Marsh on the map of Central London, where it resides between the Cities of Westminster and London. Today, books and television tell of the area's famous people, theatres and music-halls but refuse to be precise about their exact locations, as if anywhere south of the Thames must be far from Central London, almost in a foreign land, or in a best-forgotten slum.

We should never forget that people are only one part of the environment and that localities, however nondescript, interact with people quite as much as people do with each other. As an example of the interaction of place and people, consider William Blake's poem *London*, quoted in the frontispiece, that in fact refers not to London in general but specifically to Hercules Road in Lambeth Marsh, where he lived happily with his wife in a small terraced house and where they could sun-bathe in the nude in their private back garden. With this information about the poet's home, the poem appears differently and should raise new questions for those with an interest in William Blake's writings.

By emphasising the character-of-place this history may be told in just one volume, rather than by taking the many volumes that would be necessary if repeating the biographies of those already published or by telling the stories of the millions who have known The Marsh.

Essential to the understanding of any place is how it looks, and for Lambeth Marsh a wealth of maps, engravings and paintings is available. The few paintings and engravings discussed and illustrated here were chosen for their photographic accuracy, without artistic licence or historical error. Detailed location maps and lists are given in chapter one and are cross referenced to the later chapters.

Sources

The manor records that cover Lambeth Marsh need to be viewed with particular caution as they often listed tenants who were absent, who illegally sublet, or who claimed the land belonged to others. In this anarchic situation it was nothing new that tax collecting was difficult and the recent Poll tax, along with most others before it, still fails to raise taxes from the poor. Many buildings in Lambeth Marsh contained businesses or residents who were never listed, were unknown to the landlords, or who were squatting.

Records have always been made by those in power for the purposes of tax collection, listing as many names of people as they could possibly get hold of. In Lambeth Marsh records are more extensive than anywhere else in the country with the two landowners, the Archbishop of Canterbury and the Duchy of Cornwall, keeping lists of copyholders, leases, tenants and court cases almost continuously from Domesday. After 1810, with the breakdown of the parish administrative system, many more new records were made; doctors, such as Lister at the Lying-in Hospital, kept them to prove the causes of disease, and reformists and trade associations did so to prove the cause of poverty.

Most of the records may be found at one or more of the following record offices:

Duchy of Cornwall Estate Office, Buckingham Palace Road
Minet Library, Lambeth Council Archives
Archbishop of Canterbury records at Lambeth Palace and Canterbury

Cuming Museum, Southwark Council, Walworth Road
Curtis Museum, Alton
Greater London Record Office
Guildhall Library
Southwark Local Studies Library
Horniman Museum
Imperial War Museum
Livesey Museum
London Museum, Southwark & Lambeth Archaeological Unit
Royal Horticultural Society Library
Somerset House
Soane Museum

INTRODUCTION

PLACE NAMES

The South Bank (1951)

This name was first used in 1951 for the Festival of Britain that was held on the river front between Waterloo Bridge and County Hall. The name now refers to the area along the Thames from Westminster to Blackfriars Bridges and inland to York Road/Stamford Street or the line of the railway.

The Cut or New Cut (c. 1797)

Strictly speaking the name refers to the actual road The Cut (earlier The New Cut) that runs from the Old Vic to Blackfriars Road. The short length of road is first drawn dotted on Cary's 1787 map and was first labelled 'New Cut' in 1797 on Wallis' and Fairburn's maps but with no record of how it acquired the name. It was, however, a short cut from Lambeth Marsh village [Lower Marsh] across the fields to some earlier housing development in the neighbouring manor of Paris Garden in Southwark and that also crossed a major administrative boundary; criminals often being chased by 'Runners' from Southwark into the sanctuary of rural Surrey.

The name also refers to The Cut market that around the 1900s ran for two miles from Blackfriars Road along The Cut road, over the crossing into Lower Marsh; it then went on across Westminster Bridge Road, along Carlisle Lane, over Lambeth Road to Sail Street and became continuous along the Lambeth Walk until it reached Vauxhall. The market was London's most notorious, written about by Dickens, Mayhew and numerous others. Today The Cut market is very much reduced being licensed only in Lower Marsh and The Cut itself and relying mainly on lunchtime trade from office workers.

Waterloo (1817)

The first reference to Waterloo in the area was the bridge, named to commemorate the victory at the Battle of Waterloo (1815) and that opened in 1817. Waterloo station when built in 1848 received its name from the bridge and road. Today Waterloo refers to the area around the station and Waterloo Road, and includes the Waterloo roundabout and its large area of pedestrian underpass.

North Lambeth (1900)

This name is an administrative area referring to all the borough north of Vauxhall; it includes Lambeth Marsh. This name should not be confused with Lambeth North underground station opposite the Lincoln Tower in Westminster Bridge Road that is within the area of Lambeth Marsh.

South Lambeth (1263)

South Lambeth, between Vauxhall and Stockwell, is a village name, still used, that predates even Vauxhall. South Lambeth and South Lambeth Road are not, as people assume, the southern part of the modern Borough of Lambeth that goes as far as Norbury but are relics of the old Manor of South Lambeth.

Surreyside (1800)

Surreyside was another name that was in use from 1800 with the rise of the entertainment business and was given to Lambeth Marsh. The name Surreyside derived from the fact that until 1889 the area was still part of Surrey, the Surrey side of the Thames.

Transpontine (1858)

Transpontine was the rather pompous Latin name for 'across the bridge', where the many Transpontine theatres or music-halls thrived in Lambeth Marsh.

Water Lambeth (Lambhythe 1086)

Water Lambeth, more often known just as Lambeth, was a village spread out on the Thames waterfront south from St Mary Lambeth and the Archbishop's Palace. Lambeth High Street still exists as the road parallel to the Albert Embankment behind the fire station and starting at Lambeth Road. This village is not part of Lambeth Marsh and was always referred to separately.

Lambeth Marsh (1332 Lay subsidy returns)

Lambeth Marsh was the name given to the road, the village and the surrounding marshes. John Norden's 1615 survey of Kennington Manor states: '... which leads from the Town of Lambeth Marsh to the Marshes of Lambeth north-west, and by that lane [Cornwall Road] to the River Thames' and later '... many tenements lying dispersed within the Town of Lambeth Marsh'. Lambeth Marsh lost its name in 1889 with the coming of the Borough of Lambeth whose ratepayers wished to forget the less salubrious part of their new-found borough. The word 'Lambeth' was dropped from the Marsh and Road and the road name was changed to Upper and Lower Marsh.

The area covered extends as a wedge shape in the bend of the Thames from Lambeth to Blackfriars Bridges, with its radius centred at St George's Circus. It is important to remember throughout that the Thames at Westminster travels north-south, so that County Hall is due east of Parliament (the east end of Westminster Abbey) but south of the Royal Festival Hall. The area crosses the eastern manor boundaries of the Marsh, into Paris Garden Manor and St George's Fields.

The story of Lambeth Marsh starts with neolithic finds showing man's settlement on a sand-bank, habitable as a piece of ground above the normal tidal levels of the river. The island is still visible in the road levels that slope away on all sides along Upper and Lower Marsh, and is reconfirmed by the bore holes drilled for every new building.

For centuries the marsh ensured the rural existence of a green and pleasant oasis close to London's centre, but then suddenly within a single life span it all changed. Between 1780 and 1820 Lambeth Marsh turned into the scourge of civilised society to be written about by each new generation, such as Dickens,

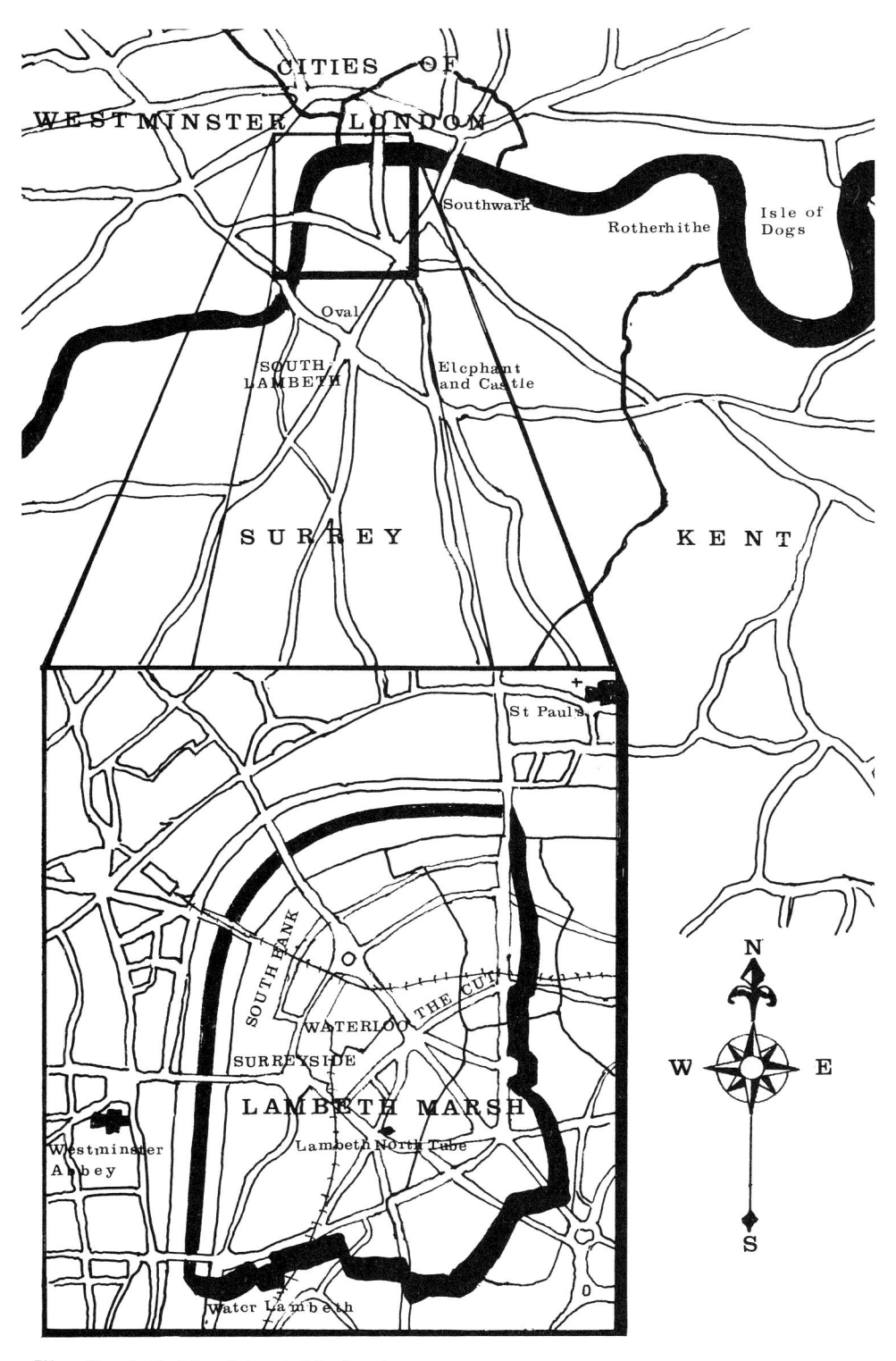

Ill. 1 Lambeth Marsh located in London

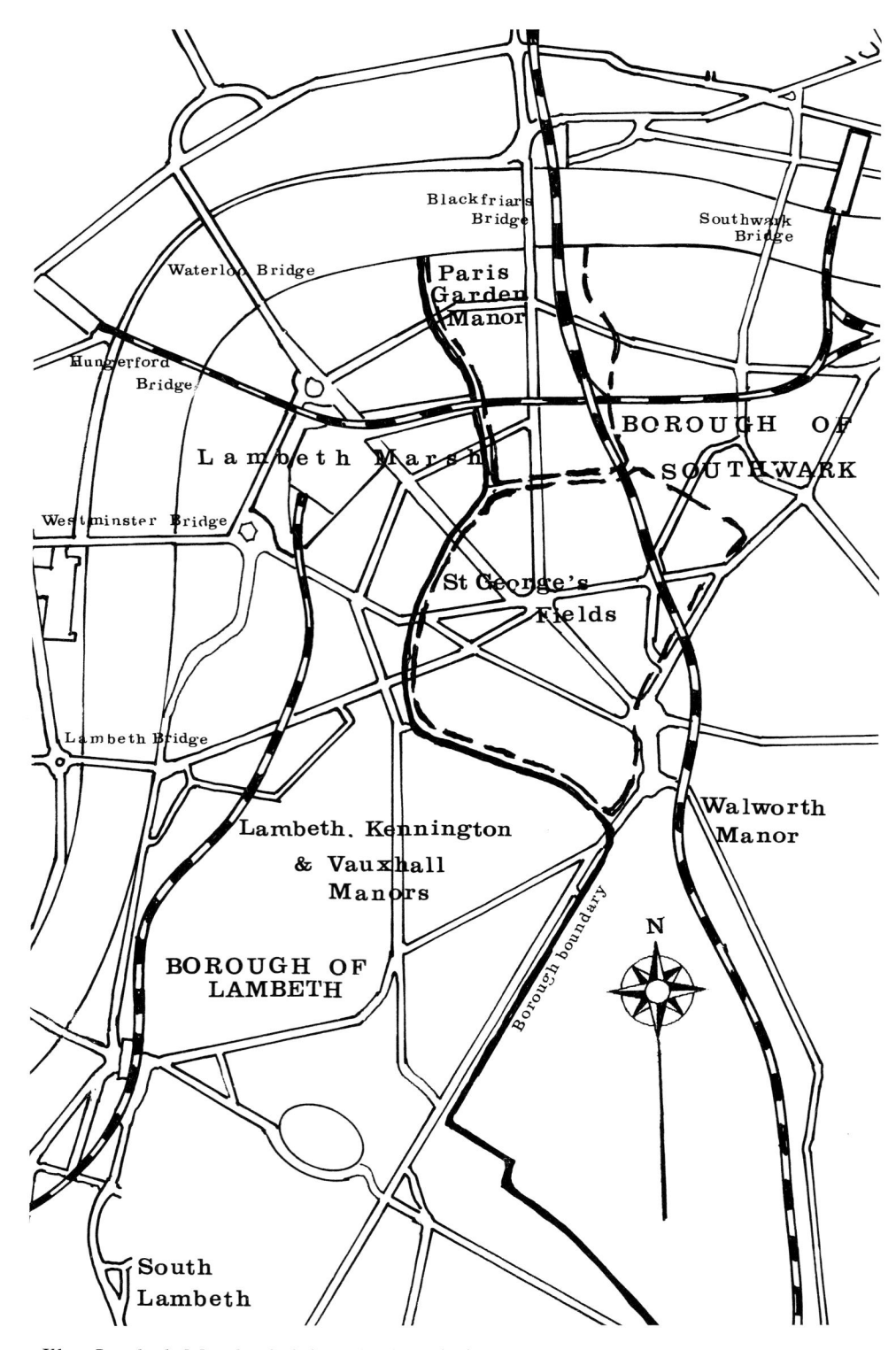

Ill. 2 Lambeth Marsh administrative boundaries

Mayhew and Booth, as an example of the worst poverty and deprivation that man could produce. In the early nineteenth century, London, never one of Britain's major industrial cities, saw Lambeth become the centre for light industry with a population explosion fed by mass immigration from the countryside and from Ireland, a change more usual in England's northern heartland. Lime kilns, potteries, blacking factories, lead, iron and printing works, were all planted among houses that had no proper drainage or water.

Lambeth Marsh has seen it all, from the battles between the monarchy and church, the hardships of immigrants and minorities, the trade unions versus industry, the struggles of the artisan, of Reformists and Radicals, and of the Lambeth Irish and the Lambeth Co-operative Society. Lambeth Marsh saw the riots between Catholics and Protestants that later resolved to make it a centre of religious freedom with Rowland Hill's Surrey Chapel, the Upton Chapel, Methodist and Non-conformist Chapels, the Roman Catholic Cathedral, the Spurgeon Tabernacle and many others. New ways of teaching and reform were often instigated within institutions in Lambeth Marsh, with Dr Bell's system, Emma Cons' Morley College and many schools for the disabled. Lambeth Marsh was also a haven for those caught 'down on their uppers', where the long arm of powerful exploiters was ineffective. Millions of people in their own way knew the area, but most preferred to forget their past in the Marsh and at a later date those more famous left out that part of their lives in recollections.

Lambeth Marsh has always had a reputation as London's entertainment centre, first with gardens and taverns, then with theatres and music-halls, continuing today with concert halls, film and television theatres and art galleries. Why this should have happened in Lambeth Marsh, of all places, is due to just two factors.

Firstly there is the geography that places it between the Cities of London and Westminster in a marsh that remained a green haven long after the rest of London's urbanisation.

Secondly, the Marsh was in Surrey beyond the laws of the two Cities and was not exploitable by them. The landlords north and south of the river were very different; north of the river they were dukes and earls whilst in Lambeth Marsh the landlords never changed, being the Archbishop of Canterbury and the Duchy of Cornwall. North of the river the landlords exploited their land with speculative developments but in Lambeth Marsh the two ground landlords never built; only tenants ever built and these were always small developments. Poverty, the plague and cholera did visit the Marsh, more as a result of neglect, ignorance and the anarchy of the laws of the jungle than from the misuse of power and exploitation by the rich. Politicians pass laws to prove their power and commerce tries to control the purse strings, but as each new power group adds to the previous all their powers become diluted; so diluted that now the lack of exploitation has led to neglect and Lambeth Marsh enjoys a breathing space.

1
LOCATIONS

– A drive around the environs –
– Lambeth Marsh to St George's Circus –
– South Bank to St George's Circus –
– County Hall to Lambeth Bridge –

Chapter one gives maps and numbered entries [w1.1 to w4.60] in four sequenced routes that may be used as tours or walks. CAPITAL letters denote entries still visible in 1992.

Subsequent chapters refer to these numbered entries for location purposes. Where applicable entries in chapter one are also cross referenced to later pages for more detail.

[w1.] **A drive round the environs to places connected to Lambeth Marsh.**

[w1.1]   WESTMINSTER ABBEY (see p. 2).

[w1.2]   ST PAUL'S CATHEDRAL (see p. 92).

[w1.3]   ST BRIDES, FLEET STREET (see p. 92).

[w1.4]   Pye Gardens.

[w1.5]   OCTAVIA HILL'S RED CROSS HALL AND HOUSING (see p. 123).

[w1.6]   Finch's Grotto, FINCH'S ROW (see p. 88).

[w1.7]   OCTAVIA HILL'S SUDREY STREET HOUSING (see p. 123).

[w1.8]   Surrey Music-hall, now the WINCHESTER PUB (see p. 110).

[w1.9]   South London Music-hall, called the 'Sarf', previously the first Catholic Chapel after 1788 Reform Act (see p. 110).

[w1.10] ELEPHANT AND CASTLE. SPURGEON'S TABERNACLE.

[w1.11] Surrey Zoological Gardens, Walworth Manor (see p. 134).

[w1.12] LAMBETH HOSPITAL and workhouse, MASTER'S HOUSE RESTORED.

[w1.13] Lambeth Wells (see p. 87).

[w1.14] Vauxhall Gardens (see p. 77).

[w1.15] Tradescants' House, the Vauxhall Escheat and Wenceslas Hollar.

Locations 7

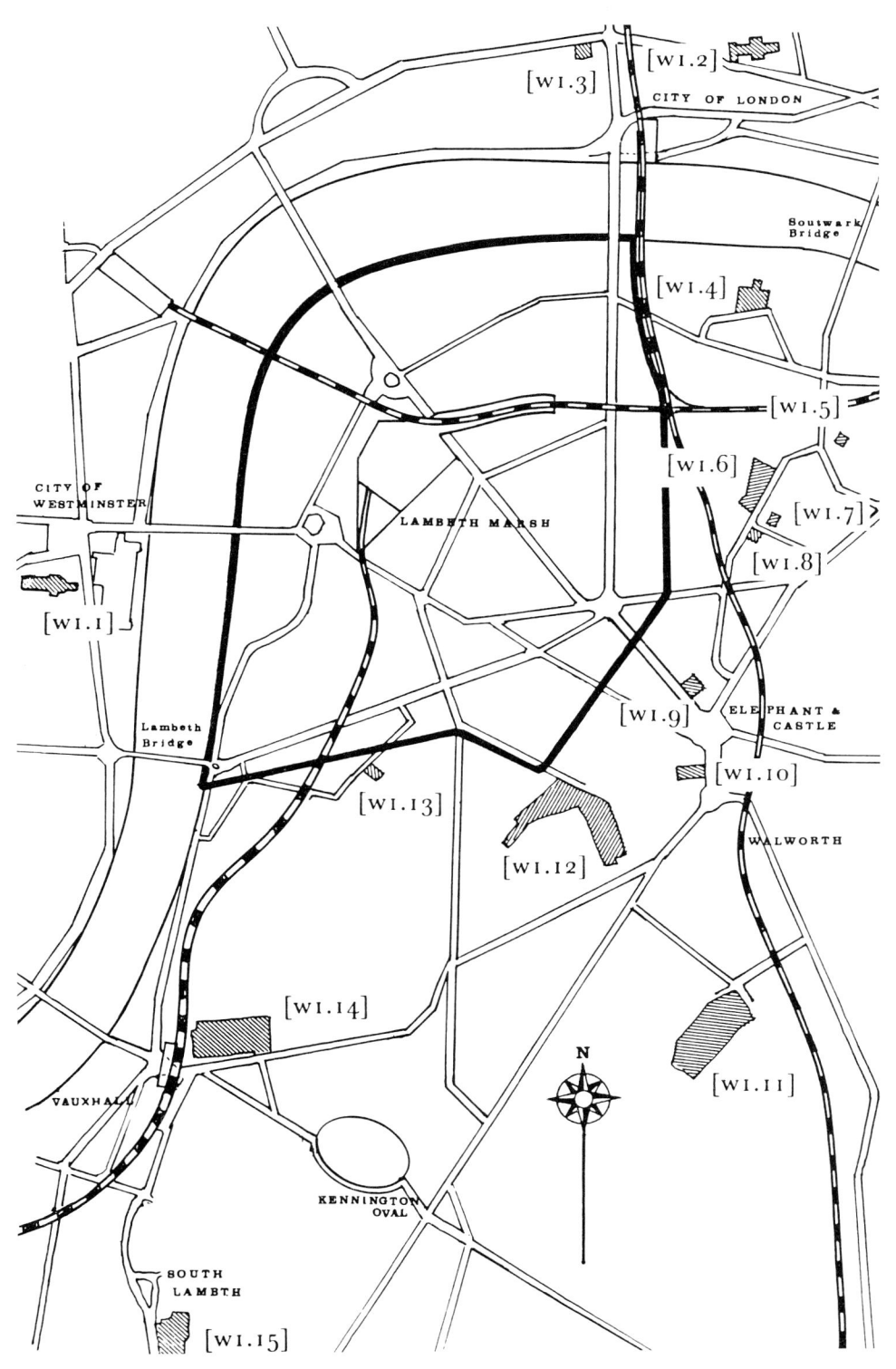

Ill. 3 Locations [wi.i] to [wi.i5]

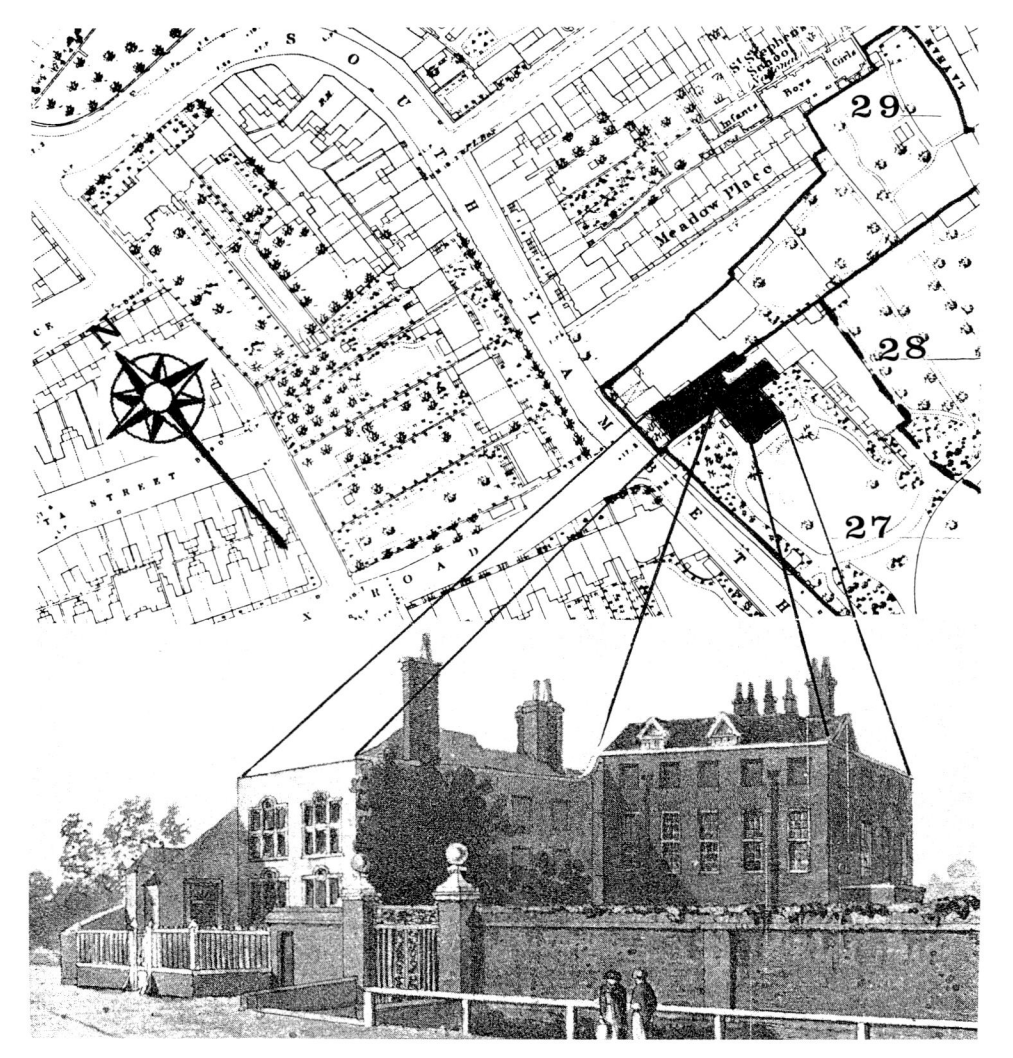

Ill. 4 Location of Tradescant's house [WI.15]

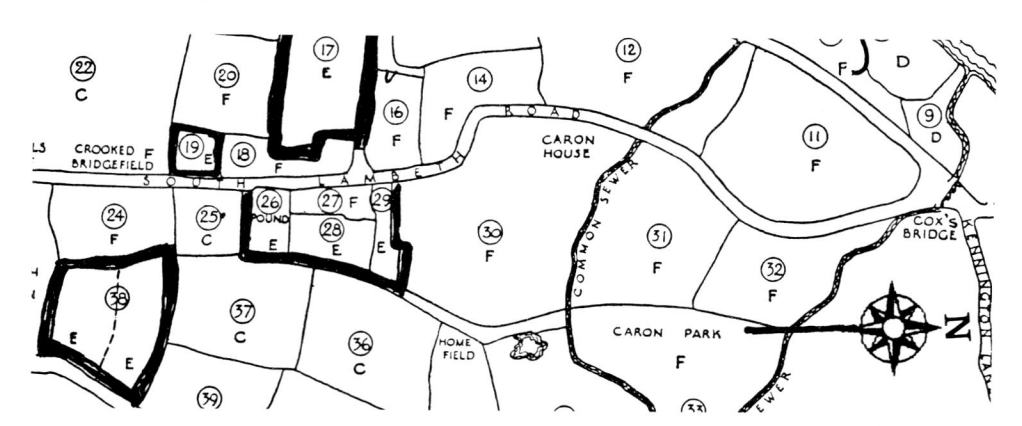

Ill. 5 Vauxhall Manor and Escheat

HOUSE WALL VISIBLE AS BACK GARDEN WALL IN STAMFORD BUILDINGS (see p. 80).
The following is a compilation of tenants of the plot of land off South Lambeth Road. The house on the site links the name of important people connected with the history of Lambeth:

Sir William Caron, Tradescant, Ashmole, Ducarel and Thomas and Gilbert White.

(An escheat is a smaller portion of land that is leased, sold or given off from a manor.)

1592	Property to Lawrence Palmer, grandfather to Catherine Foster, 'messuage, barn, orchard and garden'.
1618	Sir William and Catherine Foster to Caron.
1624	Caron dies.
1629	Tradescant records his plants at Lambeth (plot 29).
1632	Caron house estate settled, reverts to Canterbury. Foster portions named the Vauxhall Escheat.
1652	Ashmole's catalogue of Tradescant's collection at plot 29. *see* also biographical notes on Hollar.
1657	Evelyn's visit to plot 29.
1661	Leases of all the Vauxhall Escheat let for 21 years 'the moiety of a messuage, garden and orchard', deed 5993.
1661	Pepys dined at Ashmole's, plot 27.
1662	Tradescant the Younger died.
1664	Lease conditionally granted to Ashmole plot 27.
1674	Ashmole purchased plot 27 from Frances Bowyer, widow.
1674	Widow Tradescant hands over lease of plot 29 (landlord Mr Bartholomew).
1678	Widow Tradescant drowns in pond.
1679	Ashmole describes the 30 species left of the 1,800 in Tradescant's garden.
1681	Vauxhall survey with plot numbers, Vauxhall Escheat 17, 19, 26, 28, 29, 38.
1681	Front of Tradescant's house let to Mr Jones.
1683-5	Caron House demolished.
1687	Evelyn dines at Ashmole's, 9 July.
1692	Ashmole dies.
1695	Aubrey describes garden.
1749	Watson describes garden.
1773	Ducarel describes garden.
1774	Ducarel (historian) occupies Tradescant's and Ashmole's house.
1774	Ben White (G. W.'s brother) takes lease of Vauxhall Escheat for brother Thomas.
1794	Ben White dies and leaves estate in trust.
1810	New building lease to Ben White Trust.
1820	Ben White Trust sells out.
1821	Stamford House School starts.
1826	Canterbury survey of Vauxhall manor property, John Roupell has plot 17.
1830	Captain Woodgate buys plots 27 and 28.

1847	St Michael's School started on adjacent ground plot 27 or Old Caron House.
1867	Captain Woodgate bought plots 26 and 28.
1871-5	Tradescant House and Ashmole's houses detailed on Ordnance Survey.
1879	Stamford House School closed and Tradescant's house demolished.
1879	Frederick Snelling bought plot 29 and built on land.
1988	BUTCHER'S YARD PLOT 29 CONTAINS THE REMAINS OF A WHEELWRIGHT'S SHOP.

[w1.16] John Evelyn's House, Sayes Court, Deptford.

[w1.17] THE HALFWAY HOUSE, Now BRADY'S opposite PLOUGH WAY, LOWER ROAD, ROTHERHITHE (see p. 77).

[w1.18] REDRIFF STAIRS, CHERRY GARDEN PIER AND MANOR HOUSE.

[w1.19] William Curtis's first garden, CURTIS STREET (see p. 88).

[w1.20] Neckinger to Jacob's Island, NECKINGER, a road (see p. 40).

[w1.21] BERMONDSEY ABBEY, EXCAVATIONS VISIBLE (see p. 40).

[w1.22] Samuel Pepys' London residence, Seething Lane (see p. 76).

[w1.23] ST MARGARET PATTENS, ROOD STREET (see p. 98).

[w1.24] THE MONUMENT (see p. 98).

[w1.25] ST MICHAEL, CORNHILL (see p. 98).

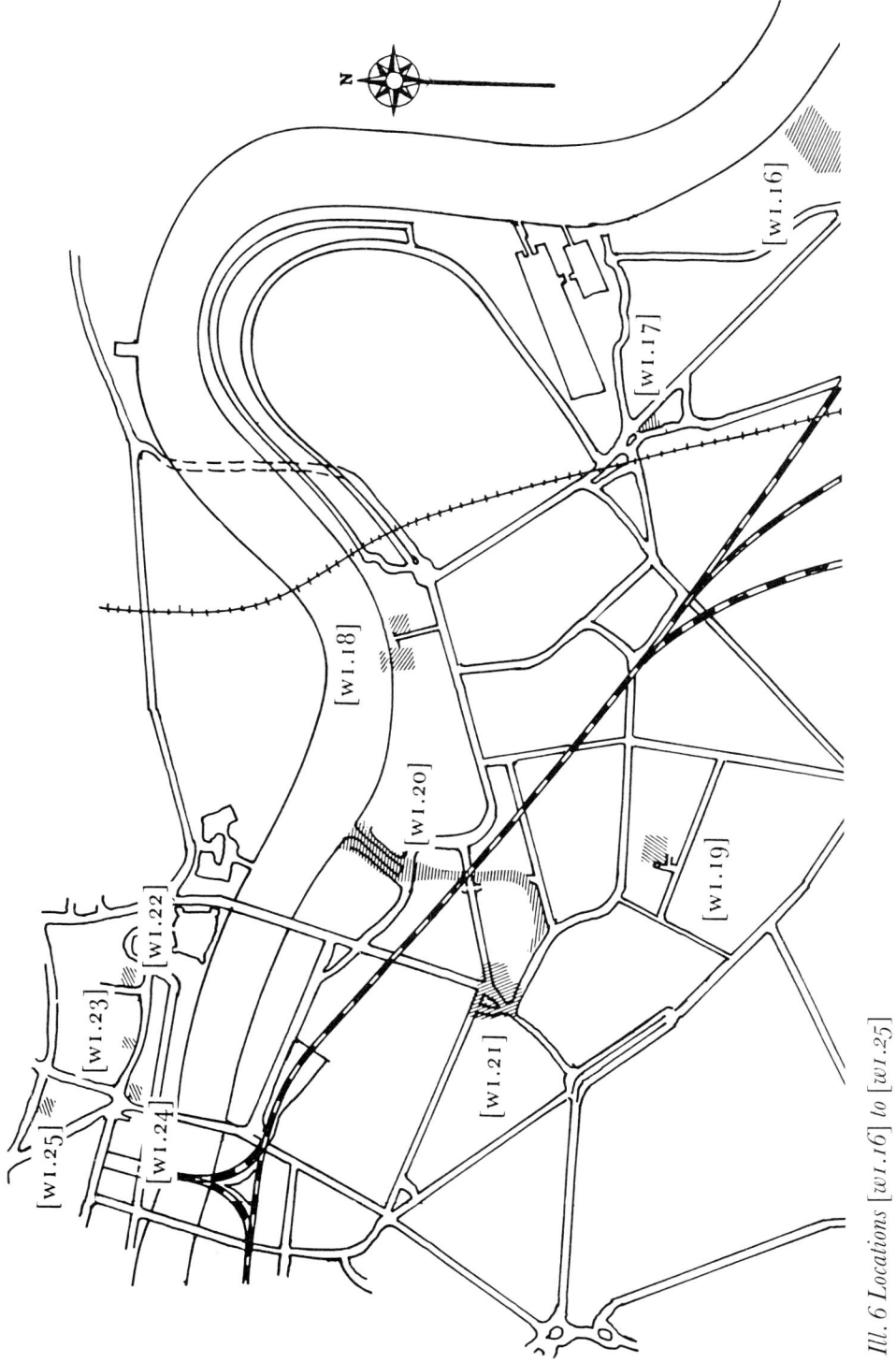

Locations

Ill. 6 Locations [w1.16] to [w1.25]

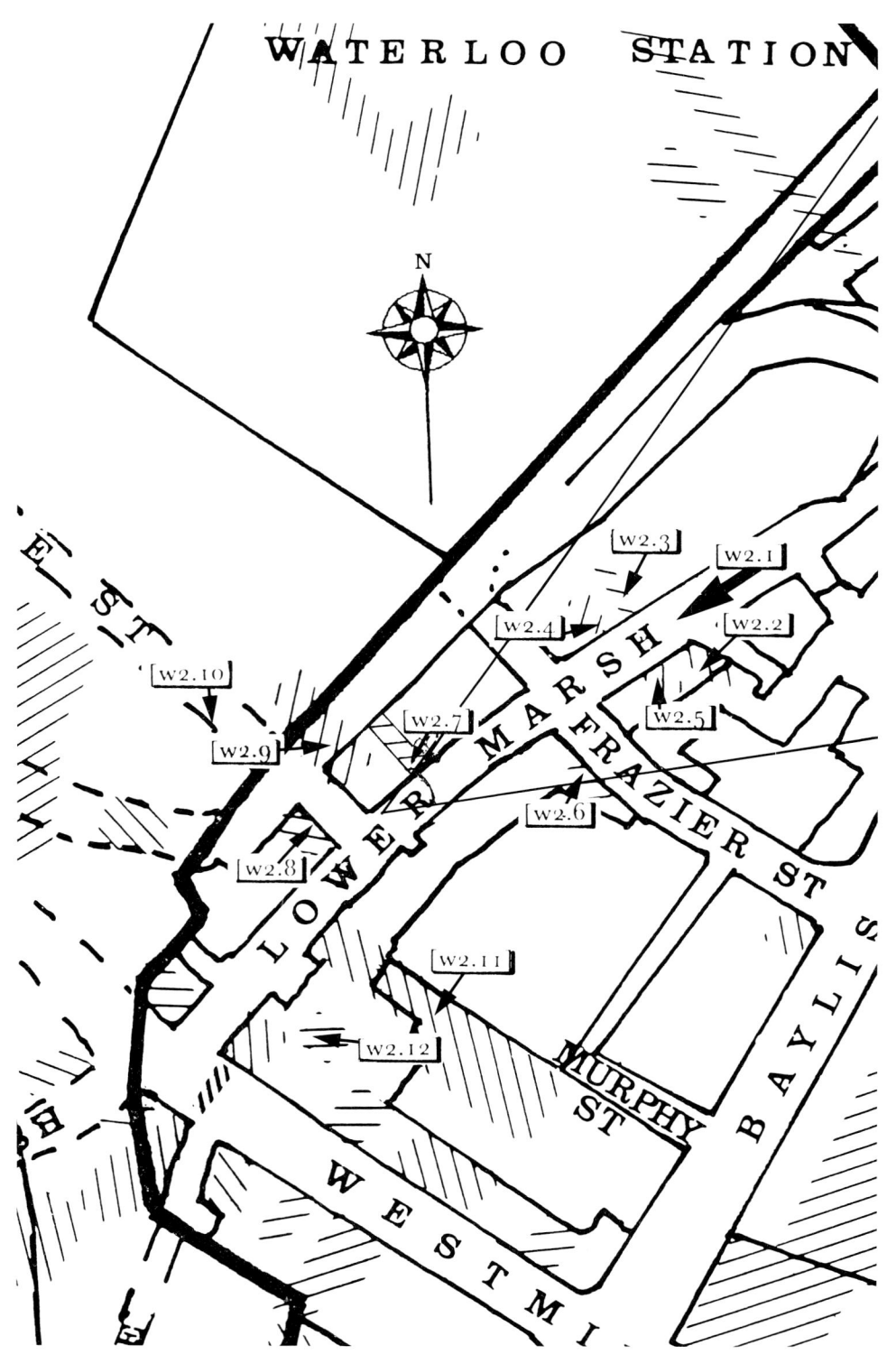

Ill. 7 Locations [w2.1] to [w2.12]

Locations 13

[w2.] **Lambeth Marsh to St George's Circus.**

[w2.1]   LAMBETH MARSH (NOW UPPER AND LOWER MARSH) first mentioned 1377, a village on high ground in the Marsh of the same name. Mixed up in both Lambeth and Kennington Manors.

[w2.2]   THE SPANISH PATRIOT.

[w2.3]   The Black Bull 1615, the Bull 1697.

[w2.4]   The White Hart 1662-85, Three Compasses 1806.

[w2.5]   TRUSSONS, menswear shop 1866 (see p. 64).

[w2.6]   FRAZIER STREET and Frazier's penny gaff. Mayhew's London, Street Markets on a Saturday Night: '. . . you hear the sound of music from Frazier's Circus, on the other side of the road, and the man outside the door of the penny concert, be*see*ching you to 'Be in time-Be in time' (see p. 113).

[w2.7]   GRANBY PLACE, and LAMBETH MARSH painted by Paul Sandby with dancing outside the public house in 1770, the Artichoke 1789-1980, now STREETS (see p. 98).

[w2.8]   OIL JARS.

[w2.9]   All Saints Church and school built 1846, demolished 1899 in Leake Street (see p. 141).

[w2.10] LEAKE STREET. A rural lane with cows PAINTED BY CAPON 1804. The first London Necropolis Railway station 1780 (see p. 98).

[w2.11] The Bell till 1785 (see p. 77).

[w2.12] Bishop Bonner (see p. 79):
   1539   Elected bishop of London.
   1549   Imprisoned in the Marshalsea for Catholic preaching by Edward VI.
   1553   Released by Queen Mary.
   1559   Imprisoned by Elizabeth I.
   1569   Died in the Marshalsea.

   Bonner's house:
   1664   '. . . and over to the old house in Lambeth Marsh and there ate and drank . . .' Samuel Pepys, 23 July.
   1780   'Bishop Bonner's house in 1780' (Guildhall drawing).
   1806   Enclosure map; site numbered 971, scheduled 'Bonner's House'.
   1823   'Ancient Building Lambeth Marsh prior to demolition', Thomas Allen, *History of Lambeth* (1829), p. 303, illustration and text:

   'memorials to Cranmer in the chapel of my lord the Bishop of London in the Lower Marsh London, more

>   correctly Henry Holbeach suffragan Bishop of Bristol was consecrated March 24 1537 here by Hilsey the prelate (Dennes Addendum to History of Lambeth p. 224).'

1890   Guildhall drawing published with the following text in William Walford, *Old and New London*, quoting Allen's history:

> 'in Lambeth Marsh stood, until the beginning of July 1823, when it was pulled down, an ancient fragment of a building called Bonner's House, though much mutilated and altered from what it appeared a few years before. This is traditionally said to have been part of the residence of Bishop Bonner, which extended a considerable way further in front. 'There is nothing in the history of the place to prove that it belonged to any of the Bishops of London.'

1872-1940   The site was rebuilt as the Lambeth Swimming Baths.

1988   Excavation by the Museum of London. The engravings were proved by the excavation to have been accurately drawn although the foundations were seventeenth-century; further evidence of an earlier building was found in the ground. In spite of the lack of verified evidence, the house was known for many years as BONNER'S HOUSE, by Pepys as 'the Old House', in 1696 the 'Watch House', and by others as 'the house with the Turret'.

[w2.13] THE RED LION. Ye Flower Pot: Mr Higgins 1693; Lady Cooke 1730-40; Red Lion 1989. 'Ye Flower Pot' before Westminster Bridge Road existed.

[w2.14] The Rose 1615-63.

[w2.15] MARSHGATE, a tollgate in 1760, now pedestrian crossing (see p. 46).

[w2.16] THE OLD DOVER CASTLE public house (Dover Castle 1715 survey).

[w2.17] Crown and Cushion 1785-1893, Cock (Dunghill Cock) 1615-1785.

[w2.18] THE NEW CROWN AND CUSHION, 1893 (see p. 85).

[w2.19] THE LONDON NECROPOLIS RAILWAY 1870, EXISTING BUILDING 1903; private railway for funeral trains to the NECROPOLIS CEMETERY beyond Woking, first in Leake Street (see p. 53).

[w2.20] SKETCHES BY BOZ, chapter III, houses still standing (see p. 65).

[w2.21] Temple of Flora, by the hoardings 1789-96 (see p. 86).

Locations

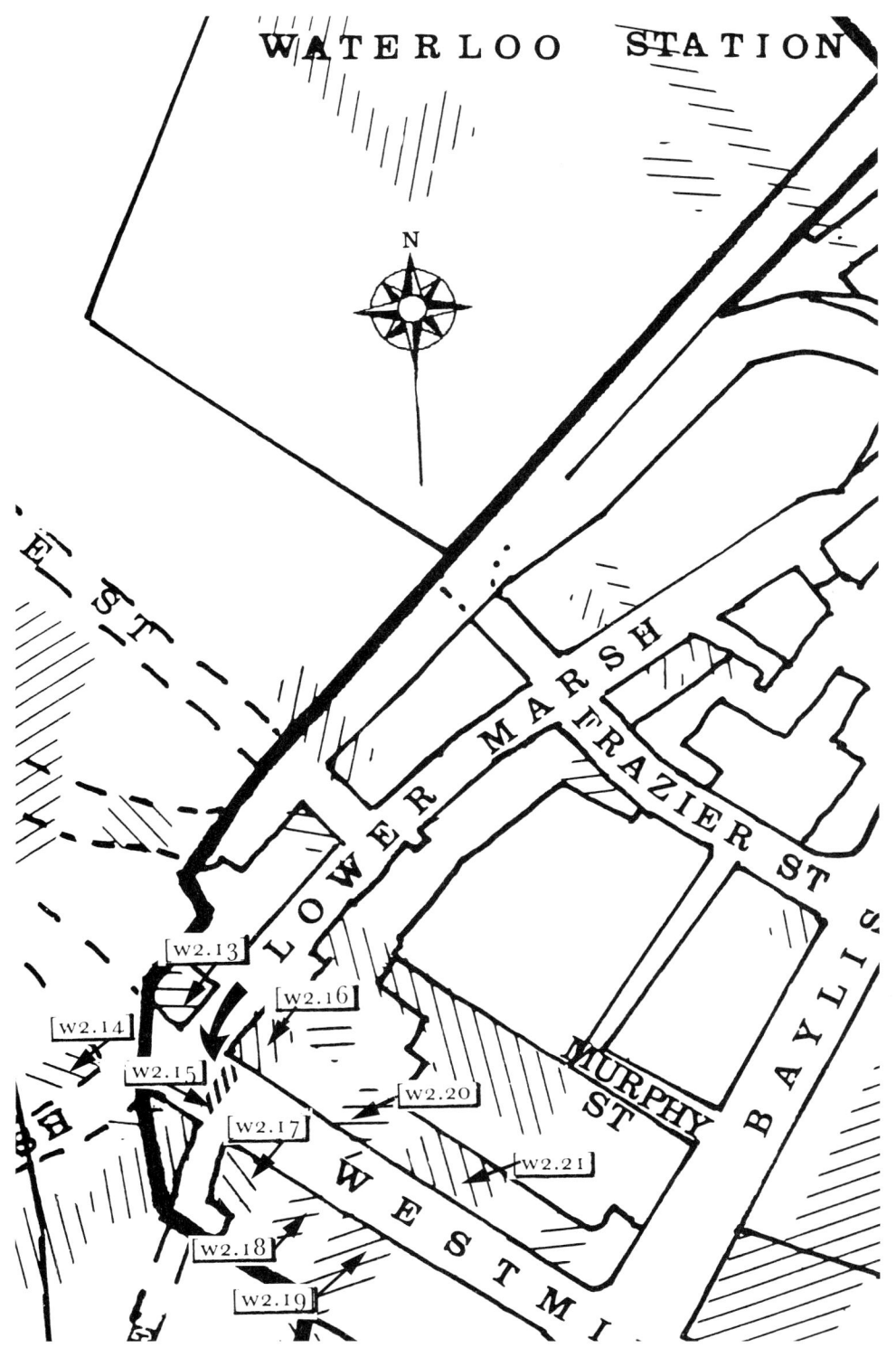

Ill. 8 Locations [w2.13] to [w2.21]

[w2.22] Roman pottery and neolithic arrow heads (see p. 54).

[w2.23] HORSE AND GROOM, 1660.

[w2.24] Oakley Arms public house 1732. In 1802 Colonel Edward Despard and Irish followers were arrested, tried and hanged for treason (see p. 138).

[w2.25] Union Brewery 1806, Union Street [Frazier Street] (see p. 58).

[w2.26] Apollo Gardens 1788-93, now Pearman Street houses (see p. 85).

[w2.27] St Thomas's Church and vicarage 1856-1940.

[w2.28] The Tower public house 1872-1940.

[w2.29] Freemasons' School for Girls 1788, north side of Westminster Bridge Road. School moved in 1852 and later St Paul's Church built on the south side (see p. 126).

[w2.30] ST GEORGE'S CATHOLIC CATHEDRAL, architect Pugin built 1841, bombed 1941, rebuilt not as original. ST GEORGE'S TAVERN (see p. 141).

[w2.31] School for Indigent Blind (1811-1901), now Bakerloo tube terminal yards (see p. 134).

[w2.32] ST GEORGE'S FIELDS, Manor of Walworth, disputed ownerships, including Bridge House Estates; Gordon and his rioters set out from here (see p. 74).

[w2.33] OBELISK. First in the middle of ST GEORGE'S CIRCUS 1771, then in its present position, the wrong way round (see p. 47).

[w2.34] Philanthropic Society: its chapel rebuilt as ST JUDE'S CHURCH and the NOTRE DAME SCHOOL (see p. 135).

[w2.35] The Lactarium and the Civil War forts (see p. 76).

[w2.36] CHARLOTTE SHARMAN SCHOOL 1867-1929 (see p. 122).

[w2.37] King Edward's School.

[w2.38] ST GEORGE'S CIRCUS with radial views to bridges, 1769 (see p. 47).

[w2.39] The Surrey Theatre, 1816. At first the Royal Circus and Equestrian Philharmonic Society 1782. Cinema 1920. (see p. 112) Demolished 1934 for the extension to:-

[w2.40] THE EYE HOSPITAL (see p. 134).

[w2.41] The Magdalen Hospital 1772-1868 (see p. 129).

Locations

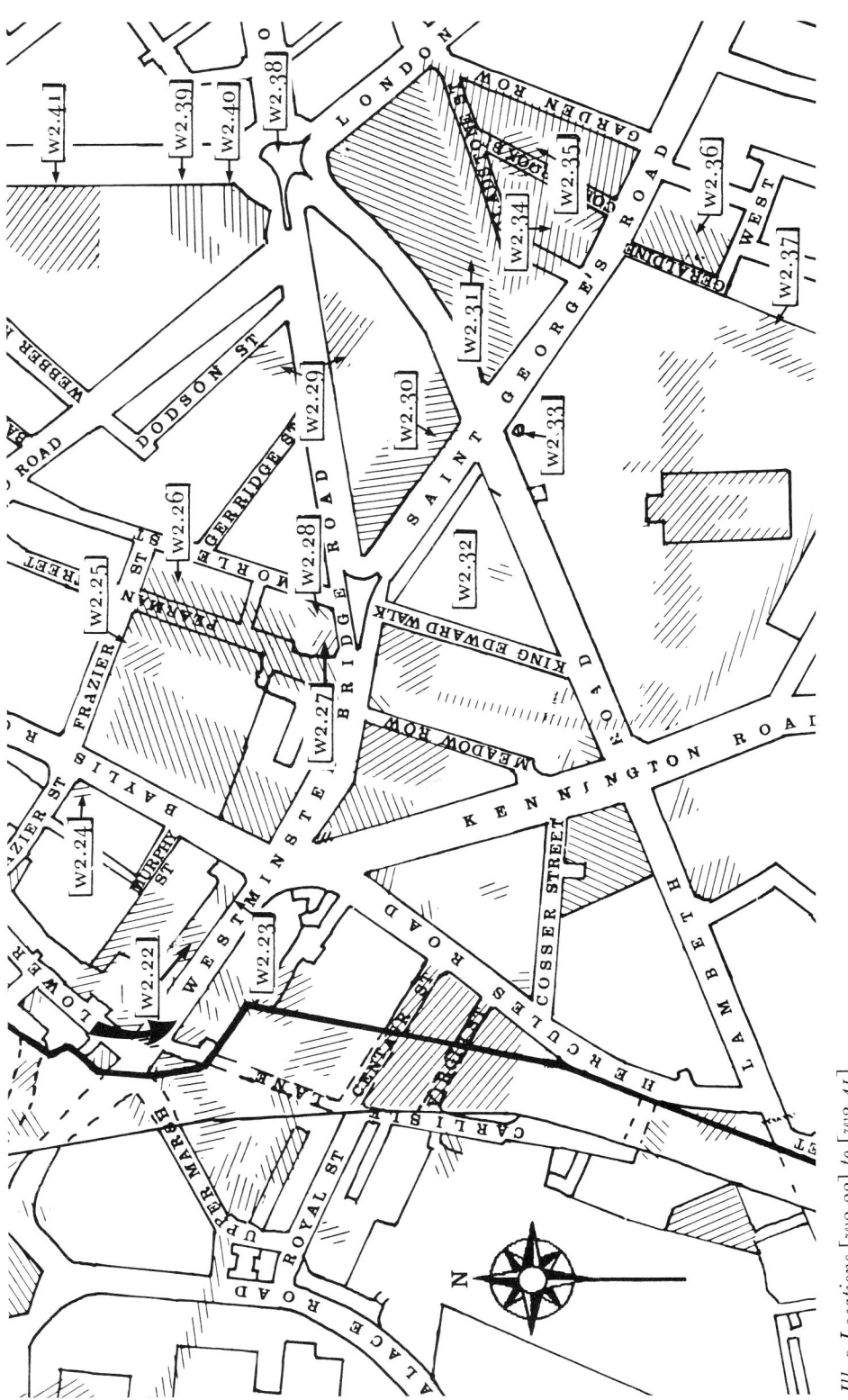

Ill. 9 Locations [w2.22] to [w2.41]

[w2.42]   THE OLD KING'S HEAD (see p. 78).

[w2.43]   BOUNDARY ROW and dyke (see p. 73).

[w2.44]   Paris Garden Manor, first mentioned 1113. Water-mill and boundary ditch water flowing into Thames at Barge House Stairs. In 1660 the Manor House was Holland's Leaguer, a brothel (see p. 73).

[w2.45]   The Surrey Chapel of the Reverend Rowland Hill 1782. Later The Ring run by Bella of Blackfriars, a boxing ring. The Ring was destroyed by a V2 bomb and is commemorated with a plaque on the new office building. The present pub named in 1920 THE RING is on a site opposite it (see p. 110).

[w2.46]   Dog and Pot iron foundry (see p. 64).

[w2.47]   Christ Church Workhouse, now SOUTHWARK INSTITUTE (see p. 123).

[w2.48]   YOUNG VIC THEATRE (see p. 106).

[w2.49]   THE WINDMILL 1799-1857 of Horn's Brewery. TAPHOUSE PUB in THE CUT (see p. 58).

[w2.50]   THE UPSTREAM THEATRE, and Mission Hall.

[w2.51]   William Curtis's London Botanic Garden 1779-89. Formerly a Lazar (leper) hospital, then Spring Gardens 1731, Restoration Gardens 1755 (see pp. 88, 92).

[w2.52]   The Halfway House, now STAGE DOOR public house 1983. Pepys' diary 27 November 1665 (see p. 78).

[w2.53]   THE OLD VIC:
    1816   Royal Coburg Theatre, foundation stone.
    1818   Theatre opened.
    1833   The Victoria Theatre.
    1834   Paganini farewell performance.
    1871   Theatre auctioned.
    1879   Emma Cons (1838-1912) the Royal Victoria Coffee Hall.
    1884   First Morley lectures in the OLD VIC.
    1912   Emma Cons dies, OLD VIC directed by Lilian Baylis (1874-1937).
    1914   First Shakespeare season.
    1940   Bombed. See photographs by Capa in *Battle of Waterloo*.
    1950   Reopened (see p. 104).

[w2.54]   GAS LAMP 1856, recently moved from Kennington Cross.

[w2.55]   NORTH LAMBETH LIBRARY, now community centre.

Locations 19

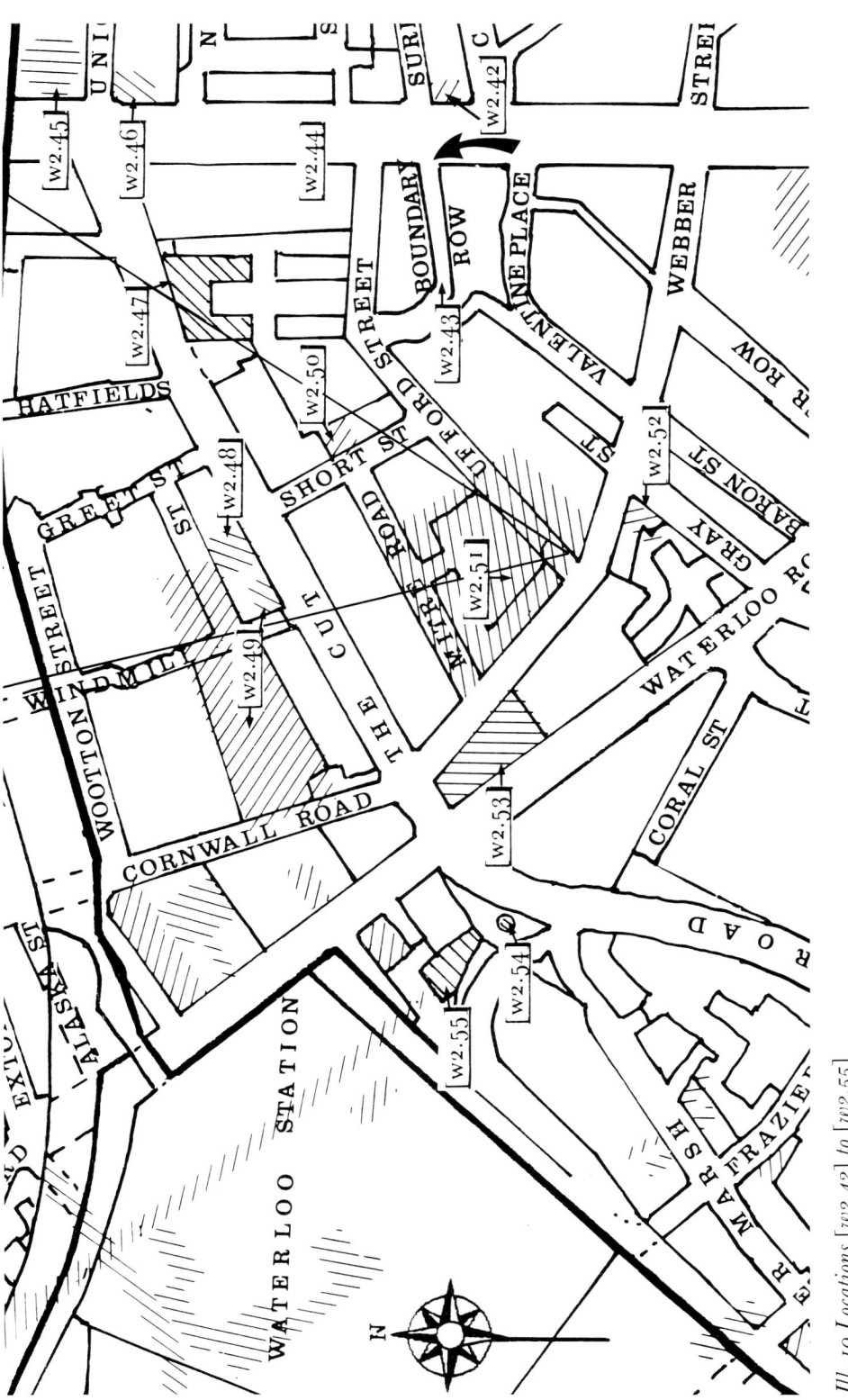

Ill. 10 Locations [*w2.42*] *to* [*w2.55*]

[w3.] **South Bank to St George's Circus.**

[w3.1] CORNWALL ROAD. Called Vineyard in 1755.

[w3.2] Bible Christian Chapel, 1872.

[w3.3] LONDON FIRE BRIGADE FIRST FIRE STATION 1889.

[w3.4] Zion Methodist Chapel, Wesleyan 1872.

[w3.5] UNION JACK CLUB, first built in Waterloo Road 1907-9 for members of the armed forces to stay, new tower block 1980 (see p. 53).

[w3.6] WATERLOO STATION. First line opened 1848. Rail link to east over present footbridge 1864. Station rebuilt as War Memorial 1922 (see p. 51).

    1799-1819   Belvidere Brewery in Vine Street. Croggon moved to the Lion Brewery (see p. 57).

The Pear Tree, now BRITISH RAIL CLUB under the station.

[w3.7] ST JOHN'S CHURCH 1824. Roupell family and an American Indian Princess buried here (see p. 141).

[w3.8] THE ROYAL WATERLOO HOSPITAL FOR WOMEN AND CHILDREN, 1823; present building 1903-5. Faced with unique Doulton tiling (see p. 132).

[w3.9] HMSO BUILDING, during 1914-18 war St George's Military Hospital (see p. 133).

[w3.10] St Andrew Coin Street, 1856 (see p. 142).

[w3.11] UNITARIAN CHAPEL, 1821.

[w3.12] BENEVOLENT SOCIETY OF ST PATRICK, 1820; later the London School of Printing; now the Seamen's Mission School (see p. 62).

[w3.13] ROUPELL STREET. Developed by William Roupell, a scrap-metal merchant, Member of Parliament and convicted embezzler (see p. 62).

[w3.14] Halfpenny Hatch of Mary Curtis 1780, and Hatch House Tavern 1749, now the WHITE HART. A halfpenny charged for access along a right of way (another in Bermondsey) (see p. 107).

[w3.15] WAREHOUSE, art deco. Unique concrete structure with no reinforcement in it.

[w3.16] CHRIST CHURCH 1671; spire 1695; collapsed into marsh; rebuilt 1738; bombed 1941. WATCH HOUSE STONE (see p. 138).

Locations

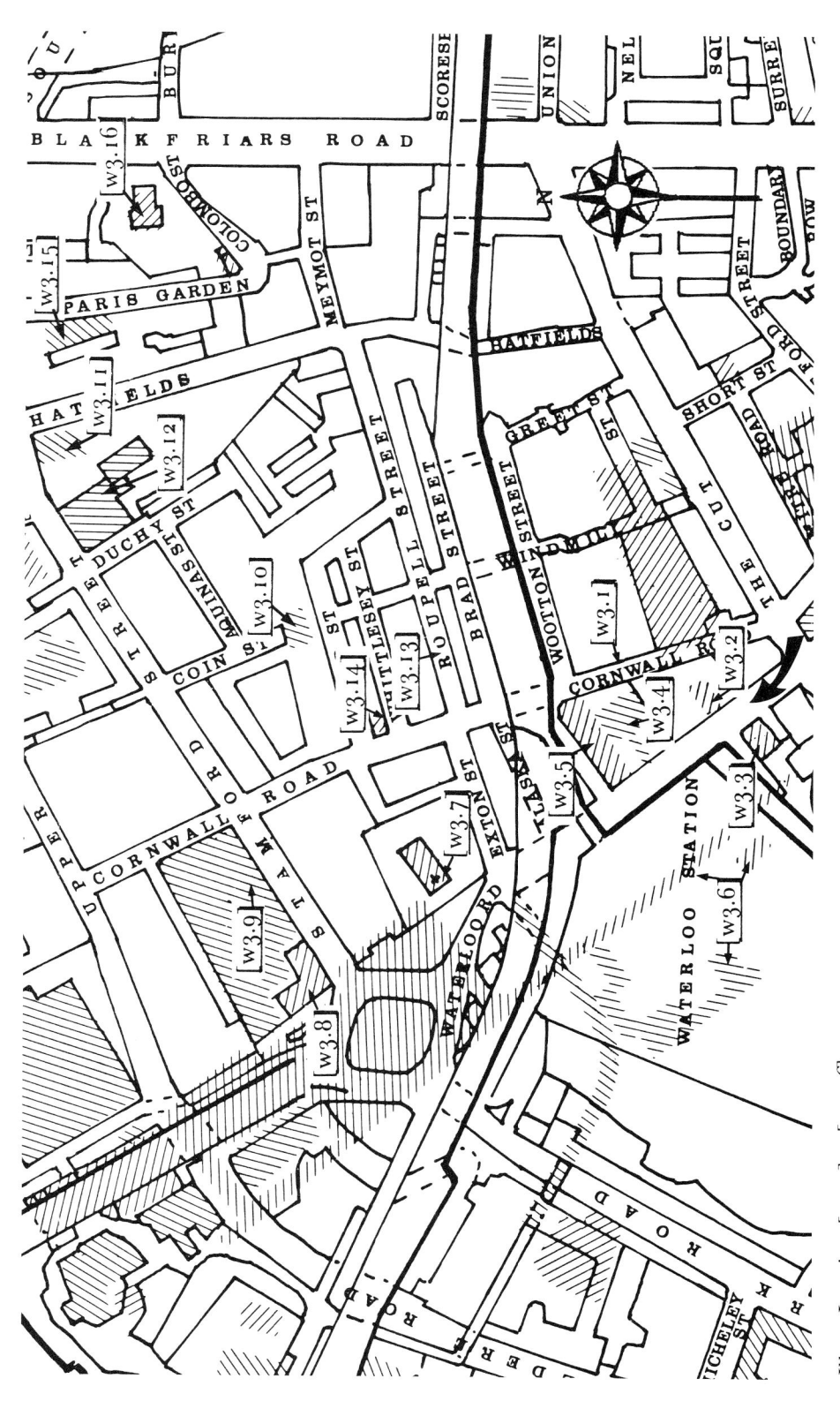

Ill. 11 Locations [w3.1] to [w3.16]

[w3.17] THE ROSE AND CROWN 1675.

[w3.18] Holland's Leaguer, brothel in Charles II's time, Paris Garden Manor House (see p. 88).

[w3.19] PLAQUE TO ROTUNDA 1788 for Captain Cook's collection; Surrey Institute 1806; closed 1852 (see p. 137).

[w3.20] The Albion Mills 1786. First steam-powered flour mill. Burned down 1791 (see p. 47).

[w3.21] BLACKFRIARS BRIDGE. First bridge: 1760 first pier; 19 Nov. 1766 completed for pedestrians; 1769 open for carriages. Second (existing) bridge opened 1869 (see p. 47).

[w3.22] DOGGET'S ARMS after Mr Doggett (1670-1721) an actor, who organised a watermen's river race, and a uniform and badge for the watermen.

[w3.23] NARROW WALL. Supposedly the Roman river wall (see p. 54).

[w3.24] BARGE HOUSE STAIRS. Refers to Henry VIII's barge house straddling the water-filled stream that was the boundary with Paris Garden Manor; later royal barge houses were at Stangate (see p. 55).

[w3.25] OXO TOWER, built as a decorative tower to avoid planning regulations on advertising on buildings 1937 (see p. 144).

[w3.26] Clowes Printing Works, 1825. Britain's largest printing works for eighty years. The story of nineteenth-century printing is that of Clowes. The first steam-powered book press and many other firsts. Bombed 1940. The Company still exists (see p. 60).

[w3.27] Stephens Ink factory and Bowaters factory and warehouse.

[w3.28] Applegarth and Cowper printing machine makers started 1819. Augustus Applegarth (1788-1871) was brother-in-law to Edward Cowper and lived at 239 Kennington Road (see p. 61).

[w3.29] Square Shot Tower, 1789-1937 (see p. 62).

[w3.30] LONDON WEEKEND TELEVISION CENTRE (see p. 116).

[w3.31] NATIONAL THEATRE 1976 (see p. 116).
    The Olivier Theatre.
    The Lyttleton Theatre.
    The Cottesloe Theatre.

[w3.32] WATERLOO BRIDGE. First bridge opened by The Prince Regent 1817 but started by the Strand Bridge Company. Present bridge opened 1942 (see p. 49).

Locations

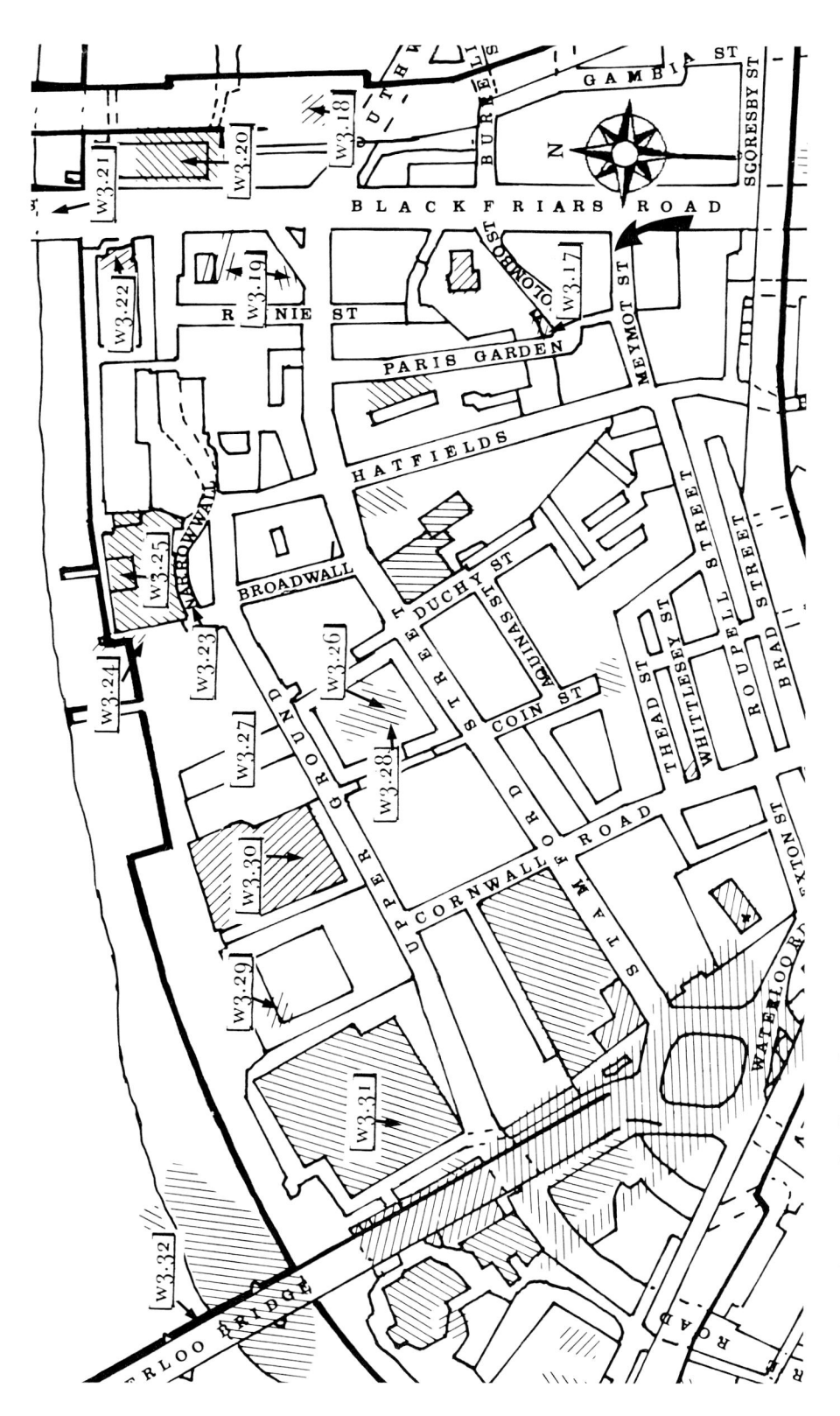

Ill. 12 Locations [w3.17] to [w3.32]

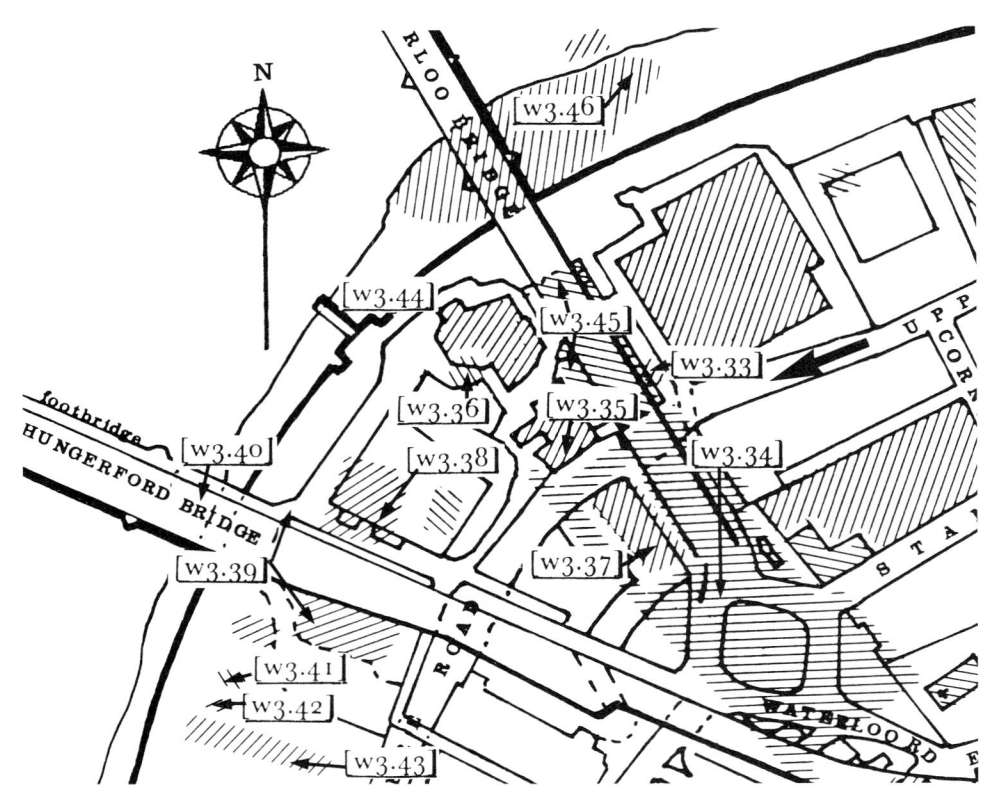

Ill. 13 Locations [w3.33] to [w3.46]

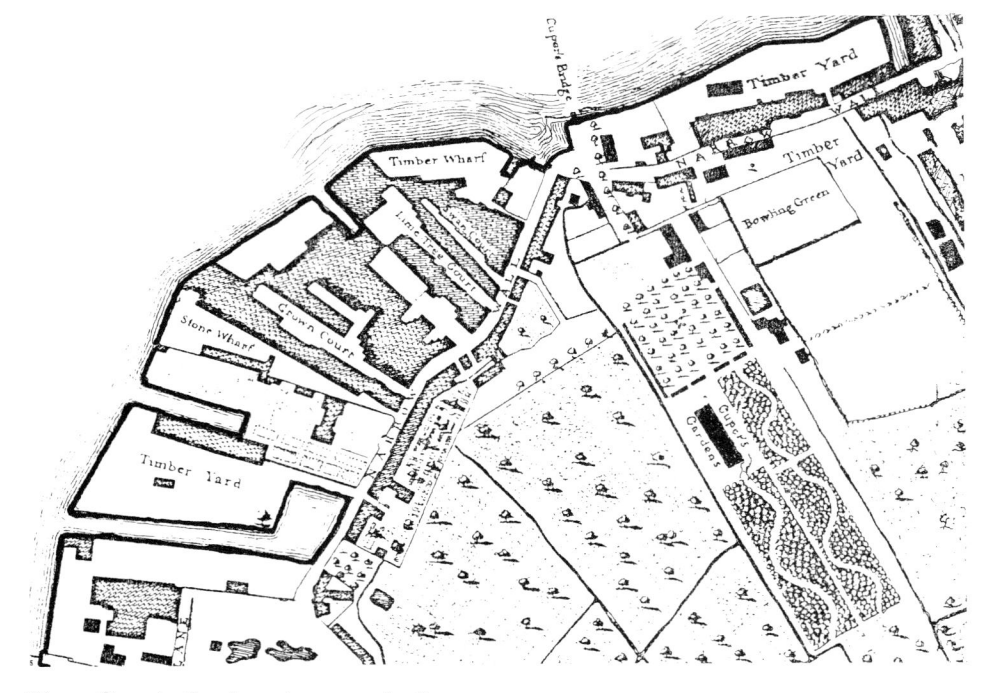

Ill. 14 Cuper's Gardens shown on the Rocque map

[w3.33] The Feathers public house 1691-1769; part of Cuper's Garden. 1752-9 run by Widow Evans separate to garden. 1759-1969 an independent pub on several levels. Still remembered by some as a place for courting (see p. 84).

[w3.34] Cuper's Garden 1691-1769 (see p. 83). 1769 Mark Beaufoy's Wine and Vinegar Works (see p. 58).

1559	Sold by Thomas, Duke of Norfolk, to Richard Garthe and John Dyster.
1572	Stilliard and Agas maps, no building, river walk but no road.
1589	Thomas Cure, gent, to Richard Humburie, goldsmith; Richard Love's tenant.
1634	Augustus Skinner, to Thomas Earl of Arundel: the tenant was Boydel Cuper.
1636	Manor of Kennington map and survey, Earl Arundel his garden.
1642	Earl (the Collector Earl) left England.
1644	Arundel made Duke of Norfolk. Died 1646.
1649	Parliament survey, no mention of plot.
1660	Harbord survey report, 7 acres to Boydel Cuper.
1670	John Arundel (an unknown relative), in dispute.
1680	Thomas Bedford in trust for Sir Lionel Jenkins.
1682	Morden and Lea map, no road but one building.
1685	Sir Liolin Jenkins to Jesus College.
1689	Cuper acquired 3 extra acres from Canterbury.
1690	De Feuille map: no road, no building. Cuper's stairs.
1700 & 3	A Captain Cuper paid rates.
1708	Hatton describes gardens and bowling green.
1718	Boyden Cuper died leaving garden to wife Elizabeth.
1738	Garden and the Feathers public house to Ephraim Evans.
1740	Ephraim dies, Widow Evans continues.
1746	Rocque map shows Cuper's Gardens.
1752	Last licence for Mrs Evans.
1753-9	Dinners by Mrs Evans at the Feathers.
1762	Beaufoy's Wine and Vinegar factory and Friends Row.
1785	Hodskinson and Middleton map and survey; no road, many buildings and waterways.

[w3.35] THE HAYWARD GALLERY (see p. 116).

[w3.36] Round Shot Tower. Operated 1829-1949. Used in Festival of Britain 1951, demolished 1962 (see p. 62).

[w3.37] Formerly site of Phelp's soap factory.

[w3.38] THE ROYAL FESTIVAL HALL, 1951. Belvedere House. The Lambeth Water Works. Belvedere Gardens 1781. The Red Lion Brewery 1836-1949 with five artesian wells and the COADE STONE LION, saved by George VI. North end was timber yard windmill (see p. 115).

[w3.39] COADE STONE GRINDING STONE 1769-1837 (see p. 59).

[w3.40] HUNGERFORD BRIDGE by Brunel (see p. 50).
- 1836 — Footbridge Act.
- 1844 — Bridge being built shown by Charles Evans *The Grand Panorama of London* (London, Charles Evans, The Pictorial Times, 1844).
- 1845 — Bridge opened.
- 1850 — Walford. *Old and New London*, vol. 3, p. 133, Engraving of *Walking on the bridge*.
- 1851 — Panorama, showing suspension bridge, Victoria and Big Ben towers with no tops.
- 1858-9 — Bridge chains in place. Big Ben tower structure in place still scaffolded, no clock face. Roger Fenton, *Houses of parliament under construction*.
- 1859 — Charing Cross railway authorised.
  - 31 May Big Ben clock and face fixed and working.
  - July the clock chime hung and rung and then broken.
  - 15 September Brunel dies. Clifton Suspension Bridge towers (Folly) left incomplete from 1830s.
- 1860 — Rail bridge started. Complete proposals including a seven foot wide footpath each side.
- 1861 — Whistler etching shows the tubular train-bridge piers completed and the pedestrian way and steamer pier both kept open with temporary timber walks. The suspension chains are intact but people are drawn dismantling them (British Museum).
  - Clifton Suspension Bridge work recommenced using chains from Hungerford Bridge to complete it as a memorial to Brunel.
- 1864 — Rail bridge formally opened, the footbridge never being closed during building.
  - 8 December Clifton Suspension Bridge opened.
  - Rail bridge with steam from train.
- 1864-70 — Victoria Embankment built.
- 1877 — Tolls ended.

[w3.41] Brewery at river front, 1799, north side of King's Arms stairs (and pub) and College Street.

[w3.42] FLAG POLE DONATED BY THE STATE OF BRITISH COLUMBIA to the Festival of Britain in 1951. First sited outside Festival Hall. The world's tallest unstayed flag pole.

[w3.43] Asparagus gardens and willow copses on reclaimed beaches in the seventeenth century (see p. 54).

[w3.44] QUEEN ELIZABETH HALL and PURCELL ROOM, two concert halls (see p. 116).

[w3.45] NATIONAL FILM THEATRE and MUSEUM OF THE MOVING IMAGE (MOMI) at Cuper's Bridge (see p. 115).

[w3.46] SAND-BANK and the Folly 1668-1780, moored on the South Bank (see p. 87).

Locations

Ill. 15 *Hungerford pier and rail bridge before 1864*

Ill. 16 Locations [w4.1] to [w4.15]

Locations

[w4.] **County Hall to Lambeth Bridge.**

[w4.1] D.Napier & Son (1808-1958) engineering works (see p. 65).

[w4.2] LEAKE Street. A rural lane with cows PAINTED BY CAPON 1804 (see p. 98).

[w4.3] THE GENERAL LYING-IN HOSPITAL founded by John Leake 1765 (see p. 131).

[w4.4] Congregational Chapel (the White Horse Club), built 1847-8, demolished 1950.

[w4.5] Addington Street primary school 1870-1940.

[w4.6] Fire engine manufactury, with pump emblem (building 1870-1990). Archaeological excavation 1990, neolithic finds (see p. 54).

[w4.7] 'Gentleman's seat'. Site of house for the view of Capon's Lambeth Marsh painting 1804 (see p. 98).

[w4.8] Gatti's-in-the-Road, music-hall and cinema till bombed 1940 (see p. 110).

[w4.9] Chevalier D'Eon (1728-1810), French spy and transvestite, lived at 33 Westminster Bridge Road (see p. 118).

[w4.10] The Crown 1723-37.

[w4.11] THE CANTERBURY ARMS 1780-1940, FISH TANKS VISIBLE (see p. 108).

[w4.12] The Queen's Head 1800.

[w4.13] The Bower Saloon 1838-79, or Duke's Head (see p. 109).

[w4.14] STANGATE and ferry. In 1357 owned by Bishop of Rochester: fights and burnings by ferrymen. Later became Carlisle House. Flaxman lived in Stangate, the road which now only exists by the tower block of flats named STANGATE (see p. 45).

[w4.15] Astley's 1769-1895 (see p. 106).
    1768   Philip Astley left army.
    1769   Opened at Halfpenny Hatch an open-air circus.
    1779   Partially roofed and called Amphitheatre Riding House built in Westminster Bridge Road.
    1783   Licensed for a stage. Royal Grove and Amphitheatre.
    1793   Called Royal Saloon, burnt down.
    1795   Rebuilt, called Amphitheatre of Arts, later Astley's Royal Amphitheatre, Directors Philip and son John.
    1804   Rebuilt.
    1805   John Astley's second theatre, the Olympic theatre, now the site of the Aldwych.
    1810   Visited by Reynolds family to *see The Battle*.

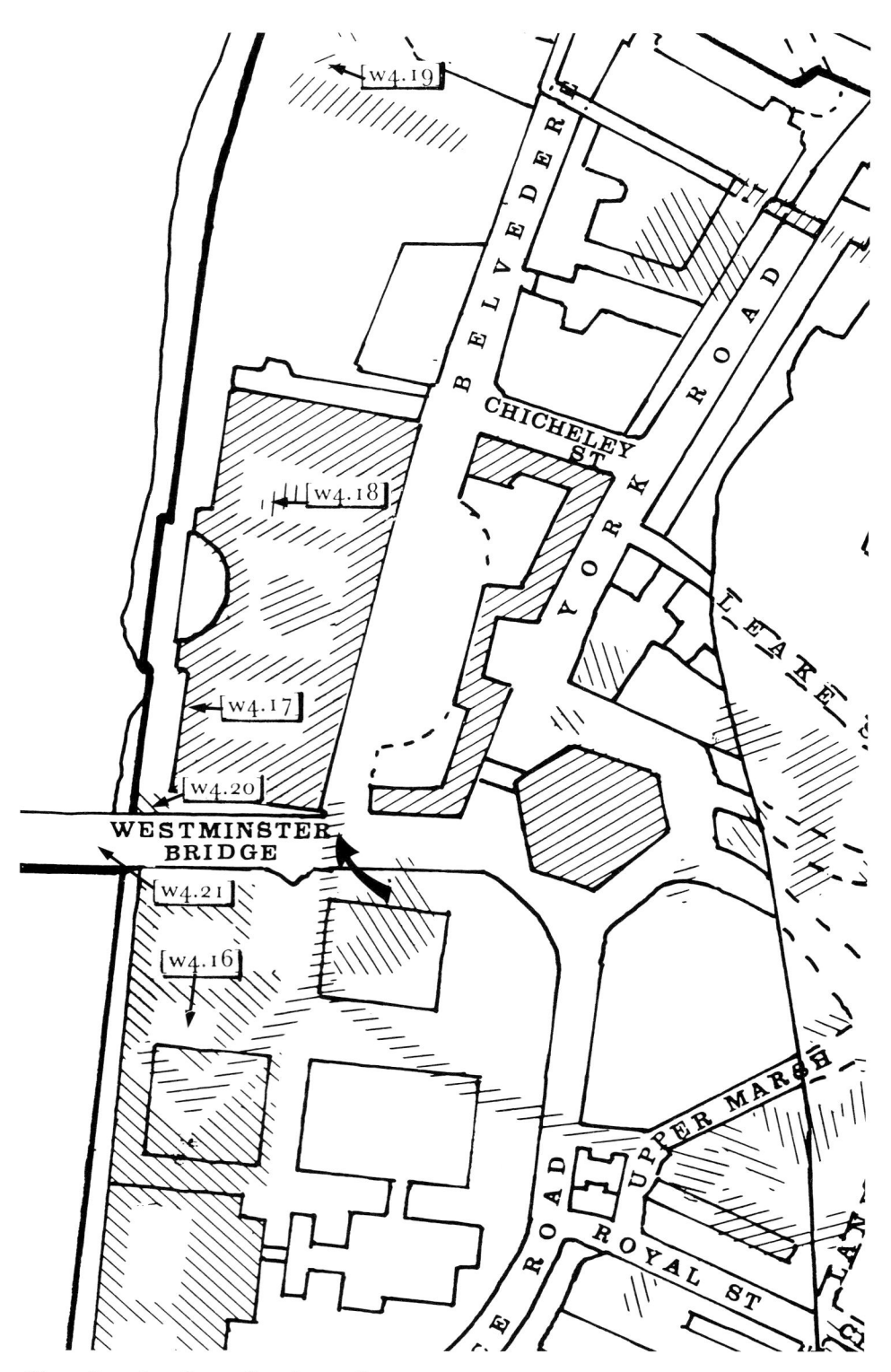

Ill. 17 Locations [w4.16] to [w4.21]

Locations

	1841	Burnt down. Andrew Ducrow proprietor.
	1843	Rebuilt as Astley's New Royal Amphitheatre of Arts, under William Batty.
	1871	Enlarged by Sanger.
	1893	Closed by LCC.

[w4.16] ST THOMAS'S HOSPITAL, founded 1173 at London Bridge by Edward VI, ORIGINAL STATUE. Florence Nightingale founded nurses' college and designed building 1871 (see p. 133).

[w4.17] COUNTY HALL. The Riverside building built 1909-22. A local resident still alive modelled for sculptures. York Road buildings 1938-51. Island Block built 1976 (see p. 66).

[w4.18] Roman boat found on site 1910 (see p. 54).

[w4.19] King's Arms 1764-1827.

[w4.20] COADE STONE LION (see p. 59).

	1731	Batty Langley advertised artificial stone products.
	1731	Richard Holt at King's Arms Stairs with patent.
	1769	Coade stone manufactury at King's Arms Stairs.
	1770	George Coade died.
	1796	Mrs Eleanor Coade (1) died, succeeded by daughter also 'Mrs' Eleanor.
	1799	New exhibition rooms, Westminster Bridge Road.
	1813	John Sealy (partner) died. William Croggon taken on; his books are complete until Mrs Coade(2)'s death.
	1821	Mrs Coade(2) died.
	1827	Watercolour with small lion over entrance.
	1828	William Croggon new lease. Still called Coade stone.
	1833	Bankruptcy, caused by non-payment for work on Buckingham Palace.
	1835	Croggon died. Son Thomas reopened business.
	1837	Work includes the Red Lion Brewery; 'South Bank Lion', 24 May.
	1837	Bought by Messrs Routledge and Lucas.
	1840	Final stock sold off to Blanchard.
	1855	Blanchard advertising Coade stone.
	1870	Finally out of business.

[w4.21] WESTMINSTER BRIDGE (see p. 45).
The first bridge, the rise:

	1736-7	Bridge Act and first lottery.
	1737	7 September. Mr Labelye's design 'he will be a proper person to be employed in case the commissioners proceed to the laying the foundation of a stone pier.'
	1738-9	Labelye appointed for the foundations.
	1739	Monday 29 January, first caisson in place.
	1739-40	Pile-driving machine with three horses starts work. The frost.
	1740	Lotteries 3 and 4. Labelye's bridge design accepted and final appointment made.
	1741-2	Stone in short supply.

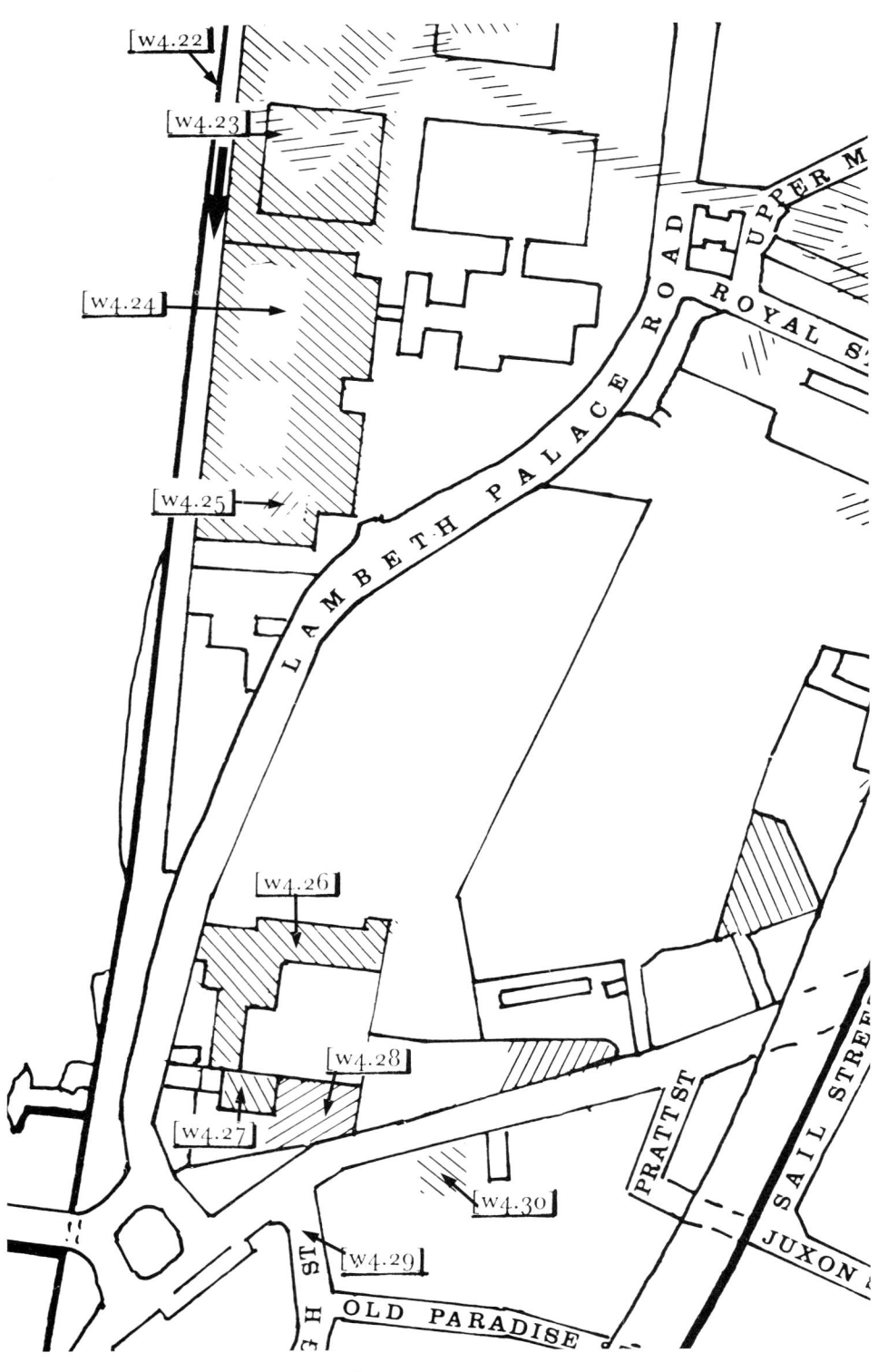

Ill. 18 Locations [w4.22] to [w4.30]

Locations

        1743   First centring struck.
        1744-5   Joints open. Cornice and balustrade, paving and causeway built.
        1746-7   Last centring struck. First signs of disaster. Sinking pier.
        1748   Schemes for repairing.
        1749   New contracts, two arches dismantled, pile driving and new foundations completed.
        1750   Repairs completed.
        1751   Labelye's payment.
        1746-52   The approaches. Lambeth Marsh and Westminster Square.

        Decline and fall:
        1759   Rumours on bridge safety.
        1823   Telford's report. No action taken.
        1834   Cubitt's report recommending new foundations and new superstructure. James Walker appointed and the need for a new bridge emphasised.
        1843   2000 tons removed from roadway of old bridge. The balustrade replaced by wooden fencing.
        1843-6   Plans by George Rennie and Charles Page published. Page's gothic iron bridge accepted.
        1854   New bridge work starts.
        1860   Half width of new bridge opened to the public.
        1862   QUEEN VICTORIA OPENED THE EXISTING BRIDGE ON 1 MARCH at 3.45 AM, TO CELEBRATE THE PRECISE MOMENT OF HER BIRTH.

[w4.22] EMBANKMENT built 1866-70. WILLIAM DOULTON'S CAST-IRON SEATS. DATED DOLPHIN LAMPS.

[w4.23] Stangate Ferry, the Mitre (painting 1801) demolished for embankment (see p. 45).

[w4.24] Barge houses and boatyards 1700-1871; King's Livery barge houses and Searle's boatyard (see p. 55).

[w4.25] John By (1779-1836), founder of Ottawa and canal builder (see p. 55).

[w4.26] ARCHBISHOP of CANTERBURY'S PALACE from 1197. The Horseferry (see p. 55).

[w4.27] ST MARY LAMBETH 1087 founded by Bishop of Rochester (see p. 139).

[w4.28] THE TRADESCANT TRUST, BLIGH AND TRADESCANT TOMBS (see p. 80).

[w4.29] LAMBETH HIGH STREET and apothecaries' windmill.

[w4.30] Norfolk House, NORFOLK ROW. Katherine Howard. 1990 excavation (see p. 71).

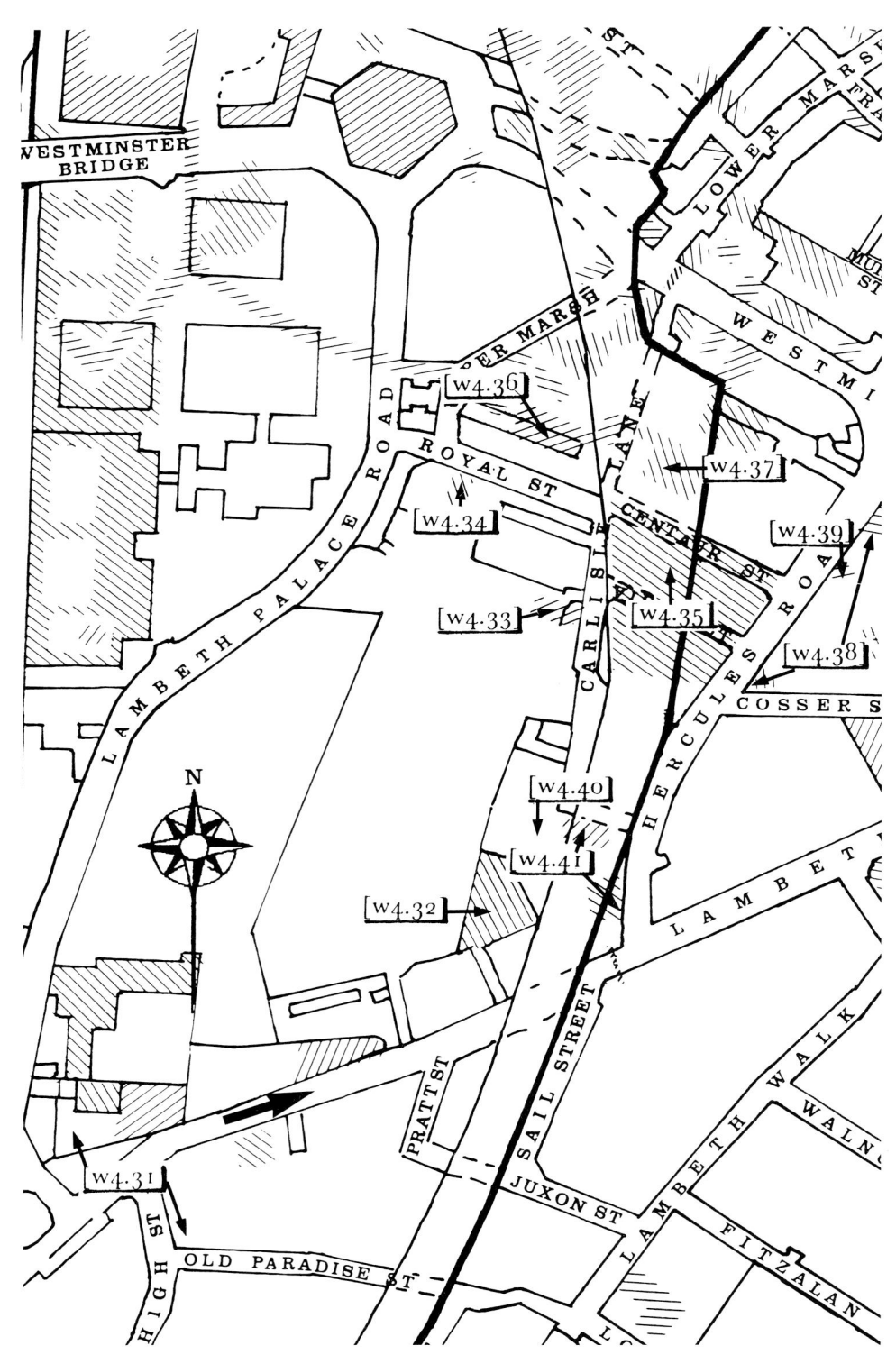

Ill. 19 Locations [w4.31] to [w4.41]

Locations

[w4.31] ARCHBISHOP TENISON'S SCHOOL 1715, rebuilt when combined with Parochial School for girls in 1816.

[w4.32] ARCHBISHOP TEMPLE SCHOOL founded 1715, present building 1904, with niche for COADE STONE BOY (see p. 126).

[w4.33] Holy Trinity, Carlisle Lane 1839-1950.

[w4.34] ROYAL STREET, Grimaldi (1779-1837) brought up here and returned to the cherry orchard throughout his life. The Royal George public house demolished 1990 (see p. 117).

[w4.35] Carlisle House, La Place, in CARLISLE LANE:
- 1197   First built by Bishop of Rochester.
- 1539   Second built by Bishop of Carlisle.
- 1690   Part of site became a pottery.
- 1730   A tavern.
- 1739   Carlisle Academy of Young Gentlemen.
- 1827   Old buildings demolished, housing built.
- 1848   Railway demolished all except a ROW OF HOUSES IN HERCULES ROAD (see p. 71).

[w4.36] Candle Factory, Carlisle Lane 1870.

[w4.37] Field's Soap factory, Carlisle Lane 1806.

[w4.38] THE PINEAPPLE public house, built by Astley, with the York and THE HERCULES on the other corners.

[w4.39] WILLIAM BLAKE PLAQUE. Poet and painter lived here 1793-1800 (see p. 127 and Appendix p. 157).

[w4.40] Lambeth Green 1750-1848 (see p. 126).

[w4.41] Charity Boys' School (see p. 126).
- 1671   Richard Lawrence gave to the parish, for the purpose of a free school in Lambeth, the field known as the 'dog house field', called later Lambeth Green.
- 1672   Thomas Rich (died 1672). Foundation started.
- 1706   Lawrence Charity School at Lambeth Green.
- 1708   Rich foundation school was in the yard of the Bear and Ragged Staff.
- 1751   Rich foundation subscription was regularised by the Mercers' Company.
- 1753   Combined (i) Thomas Rich's Grammar School, (ii) Richard Lawrence's charity for the clothing and education of twenty poor boys of Lambeth Marsh, and (iii) a subscription parochial school. Roger Harrison, headmaster 1751-70.
- 1785   Coade stone boy and girl purchased from Mrs Coade.
- 1808   School rebuilt on Lambeth Green. Illustrated in *Survey of London* and George Reynolds' letter (head 1805-17). Reynolds also taught at Asylum for Female Orphans.

	1847	Called Lambeth Parochial School.
	1848-51	Rebuilt by railway to make way for railway widening. Reynolds also took in Parochial School in Lambeth High Street.
	1885	Altered by railway widening. Top floor added and Coade boy moved to new niche facing Hercules Road.
	1902-4	Renamed Archbishop Temple School on land donated by him. Coade stone boy given new niche. Niche still exists. Coade stone boy and girl from Asylum for Girls buried in the second world war in Archbishop's gardens and recovered afterwards.
	1976/7	SCHOOL COMBINED AND MOVED TO ST MICHAEL'S SCHOOL, WYNDHAM ROAD, RENAMED ARCHBISHOP RAMSEY'S CHURCH OF ENGLAND SCHOOL. COADE STONE BOY MOVED AND FIBREGLASS MOULDED REPLICA MADE FOR DISPLAY.

[w4.42] Lambeth Road turnpike.

[w4.43] LAMBETH CHAPEL (WESLEYAN METHODIST). First built 1808, bombed in the 1939-45 war. Rebuilt and combined with the parish church of St Mary when the parish church became the Tradescant Museum.

[w4.44] SURREY LODGE (see p. 106):
	1787-97	Shield Nursery.
	1806	Surrey Lodge, became Sir James Wyatt's house.
	1884	Emma Cons and Lilian Baylis built workers' lodge and also lived there: the London Dwellings Company 1879.

[w4.45] TRUSTEE SAVINGS BANK founded 1818 on Lambeth Green.

[w4.46] THREE STAGS. Coaching inn between the horseferry and London Bridge.

[w4.47] Dog and Duck 1642-1799. Also known as St George's Spa 1773-91 (see p. 86).

[w4.48] The Verulam Chapel.

[w4.49] THE TOWER CLINIC AND CENTRE, 1975.

[w4.50] River Neckinger, open ditch in 1806 flowing to Thames at Cuper's Bridge and back behind BROOK DRIVE (see p. 40).

[w4.51] Rules of the King's Bench. Large area within 'The Rules' for the debtors' prison including private houses. 1373 in Borough High Street, 1758-1879 in St George's Fields. Dickens visited his father here as a boy (see p. 135).

[w4.52] CAPTAIN BLIGH (of the Bounty) lived here 1794-1814, died 1817, buried ST MARY LAMBETH (*see* TOMB) (see p. 101).

Locations

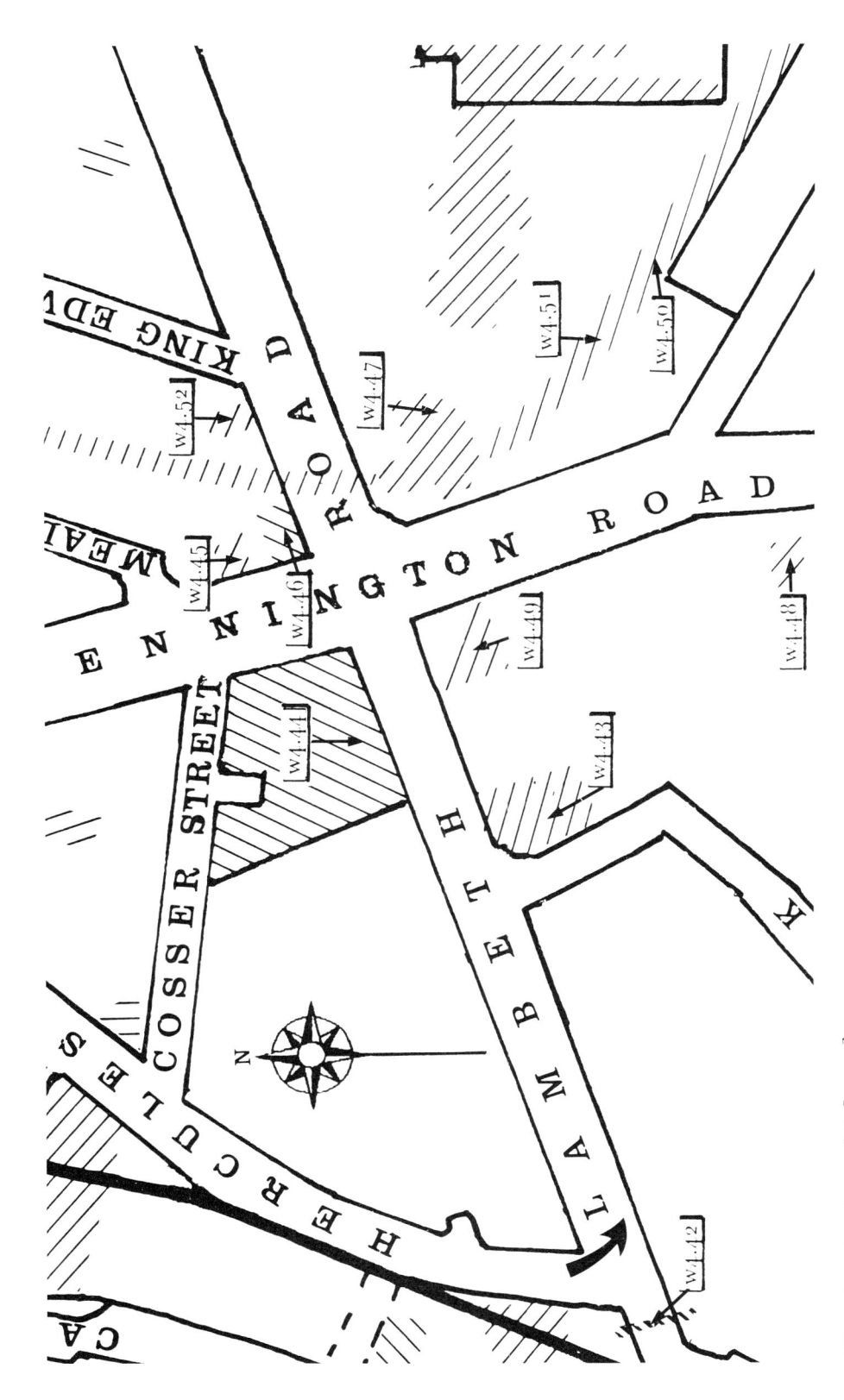

Ill. 20 Locations [w4.42] to [w4.52]

[w4.53] Upton Chapel, now CHURCHILL CLINIC 1980, on the corner LONDON DISPENSARY 1865.

[w4.54] BETHLEM HOSPITAL. First in Bishopsgate then in Moorfields. 1812 in St George's Fields, gave rise to word BEDLAM for mad house. 1926 turned into THE IMPERIAL WAR MUSEUM and the MARY HARMSWORTH PARK (see p. 124).

[w4.55] MORLEY COLLEGE. First lectures in the OLD VIC 1884. College founded 1881; present site 1923, which previously was the Yorkshire Society's School for Boys, founded here 1812 (see p. 121).

[w4.56] Sowerby's House 1810. No. 2 Meads Place, Westminster Bridge Road, demolished 1880. Famous botanic illustrator. Worked for William Curtis. (see p. 93).

[w4.57] 1755 a turnpike at the corner.
Lambeth Asylum for Girls 1758-1960 (see pp. 73, 131, 138):

1758	Founded by Sir John Fielding to look after fatherless or orphaned girls. A house on the site of Hercules tavern.
1764	Built on new site [the Lincoln Tower site]. Entry for girls between seven and ten, placed in domestic service at fourteen. Designed to house 200 girls.
1808	Coade stone girl purchased.
1824	Rebuilt to the design of L. W. Lloyd.
1866	Moved to Beddington Park, in Surrey.
1873	Old site purchased by J. Oakey for the manufacture of emery paper and called the Wellington Mills, where the mill-stone was found during excavations in the 1970s, before the present Wellington Mills housing was built.
1876	Remainder purchased and CHRIST CHURCH Westminster Bridge Road with LINCOLN TOWER built, Methodist and Upton chapel, headquarters with Hawkstone Hall. Lincoln Tower with stars and stripes on steeple.
1897	Known as Beddington but officially titled the Royal Female Orphanage by patron Queen Victoria.
1939	Evacuated to Cornwall.
1943	Moved to small house at High Wycombe. Encouraged children to train for careers.
1960	Only five children. Closed and girls then sent to foster homes.

[w4.58] HERCULES TAVERN built with Hercules Hall by Astley 1799 (see p. 106).

[w4.59] Flora Tea Gardens 1796-7 or Mount Gardens [behind the New Crown and Cushion] (see p. 85).

[w4.60] Henry Maudslay's Iron Works 1810-1900 (see p. 64). Famous engineer, machine-tool, and screw-thread inventor.

Locations

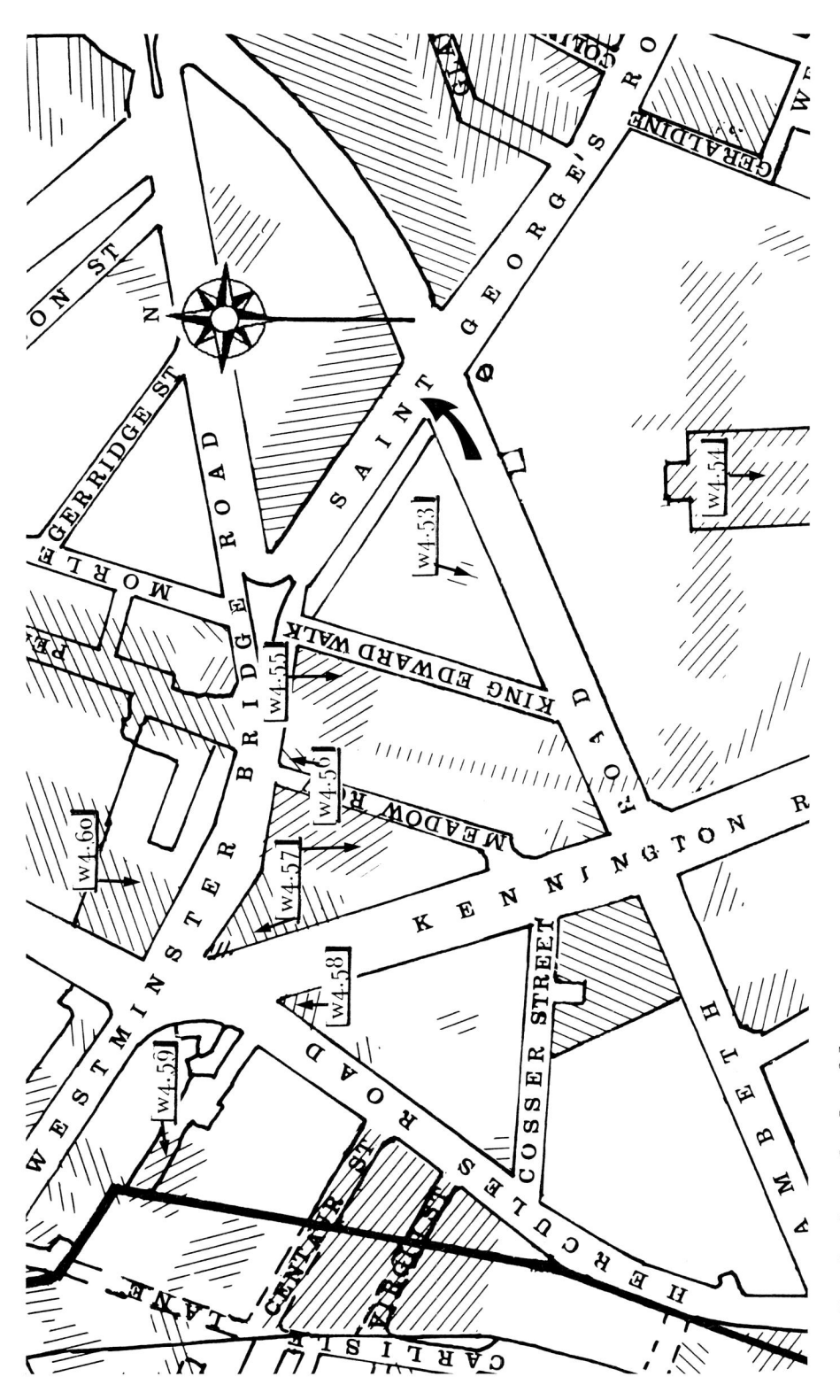

Ill. 21 Locations [w4.53] to [w4.60]

2
THE ISLAND VILLAGE

– Sand-banks and rivers – river transport – road transport –
– Westminster Bridge – Blackfriars Bridge – Waterloo Bridge –
– Hungerford Bridge – the railway –

SAND-BANKS AND RIVERS

Lambeth Marsh is in the north-west corner of a large loop of the Thames, a flood plain that extends from Vauxhall in the west through Peckham to Deptford in the east. This flood plain was drained naturally by just one small stream, the Neckinger. There is little evidence to show where the Neckinger rose but if it was in the only hill around, the Crystal Palace hill, it must at some time have joined the 'Earls Sluice', although in historical times this had its own outlet into the Thames at Deptford whilst rising near Denmark Hill.[1] References to the Neckinger's whereabouts over the plain appear contradictory but could be compatible if we accept that such a small meandering river was easily channelled, divided into a delta, ditched or blocked, all of which would hide or destroy the evidence of its course before man's intervention. Alternatively, the Neckinger may have been the last drainage channel of an ox-bow lake left behind at some previous ice age when the Thames changed its course and so never drained from a hill.

Bermondsey Abbey [w1.21] from 1300 to 1500 had a main branch of the Neckinger that passed down a road still called 'Neckinger', entering the Thames at Jacob's Island [w1.20]. The Abbey, covering a large area around Bermondsey market, was extensively excavated in the 1980s and the lavitarium built over the river was found. The low-lying land east of the Abbey had another branch that was flooded in the nineteenth century to form the Surrey Docks and canal that entered the Thames at Rotherhithe [recently remade as a leisure canal].

To the west, in Lambeth Marsh itself, William Curtis relates in 1778 that all the ditches had clean water good for bog plants which flowed into the Thames under Cuper's Bridge [now under Waterloo Bridge].[2] Maps, particularly those of Rocque, show the ditches in the Marsh coming from the ponds of the Dog and Duck [Mary Harmsworth Park w4.54] that then went upstream along the back of Brook Drive to the Elephant and Castle and New Kent Road where the delta joined into the other pieces of the river. In 1984 waterways were excavated on the Campbell building site [Baylis Road]; some were found to be very large, with water two or three metres wide and over one metre deep.[3]

Down the Thames from Lambeth Marsh towards Southwark another branch of the Neckinger formed an enclosing dyked perimeter to the small manor of Paris Garden, at its east along Broadwall [Hatfields], to the south with St George's Fields along Boundary Row and to the west to Southwark along Gravel Lane [Great Suffolk Street]. Agas' map of London labels Paris Garden Manor and shows a water-mill and mill pond on the surrounding dyked stream which is shown on the Rocque maps connected to the Dog and Duck ponds.

The Island Village

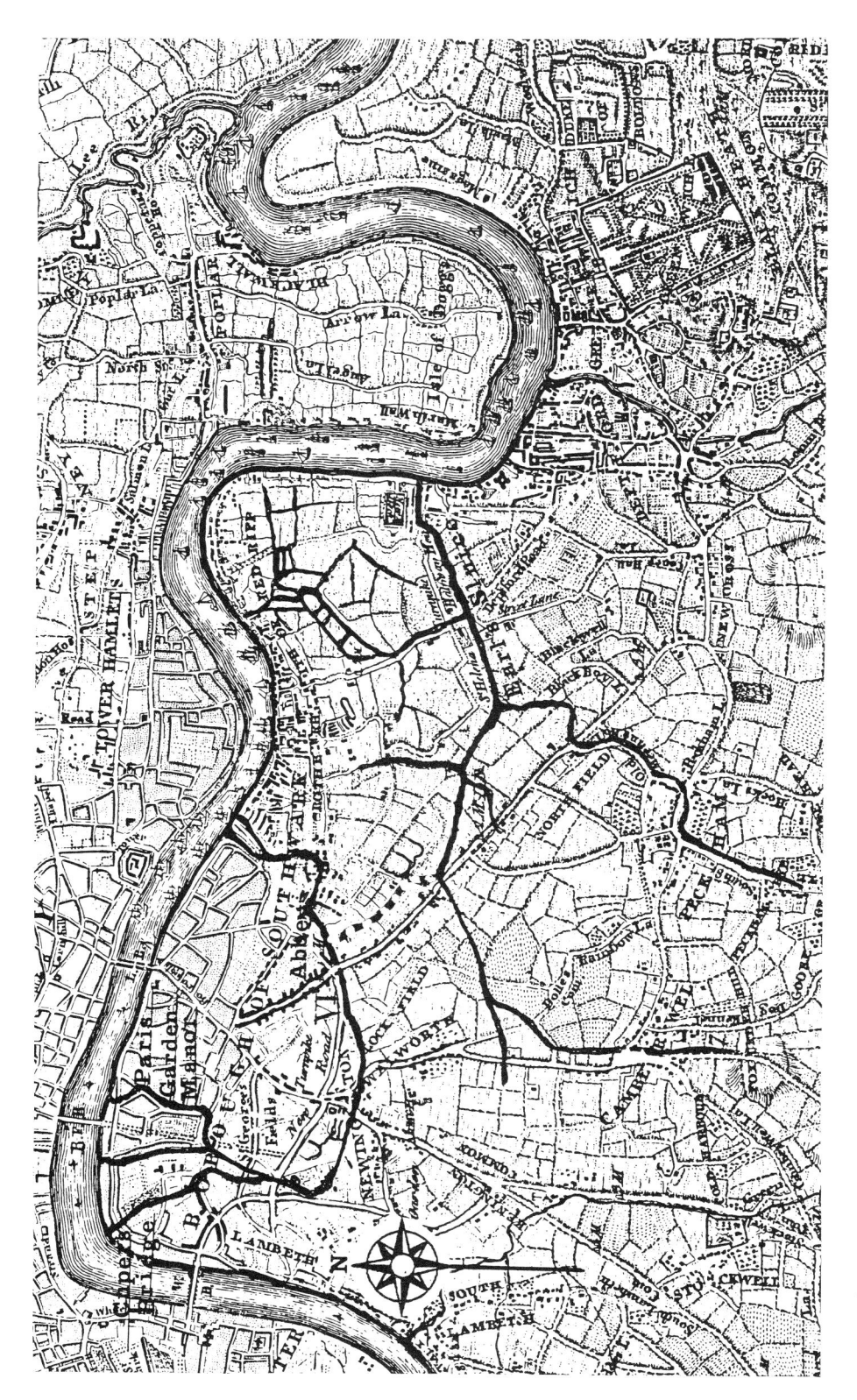

Ill. 22 *The River Neckinger derived from Rocque maps*

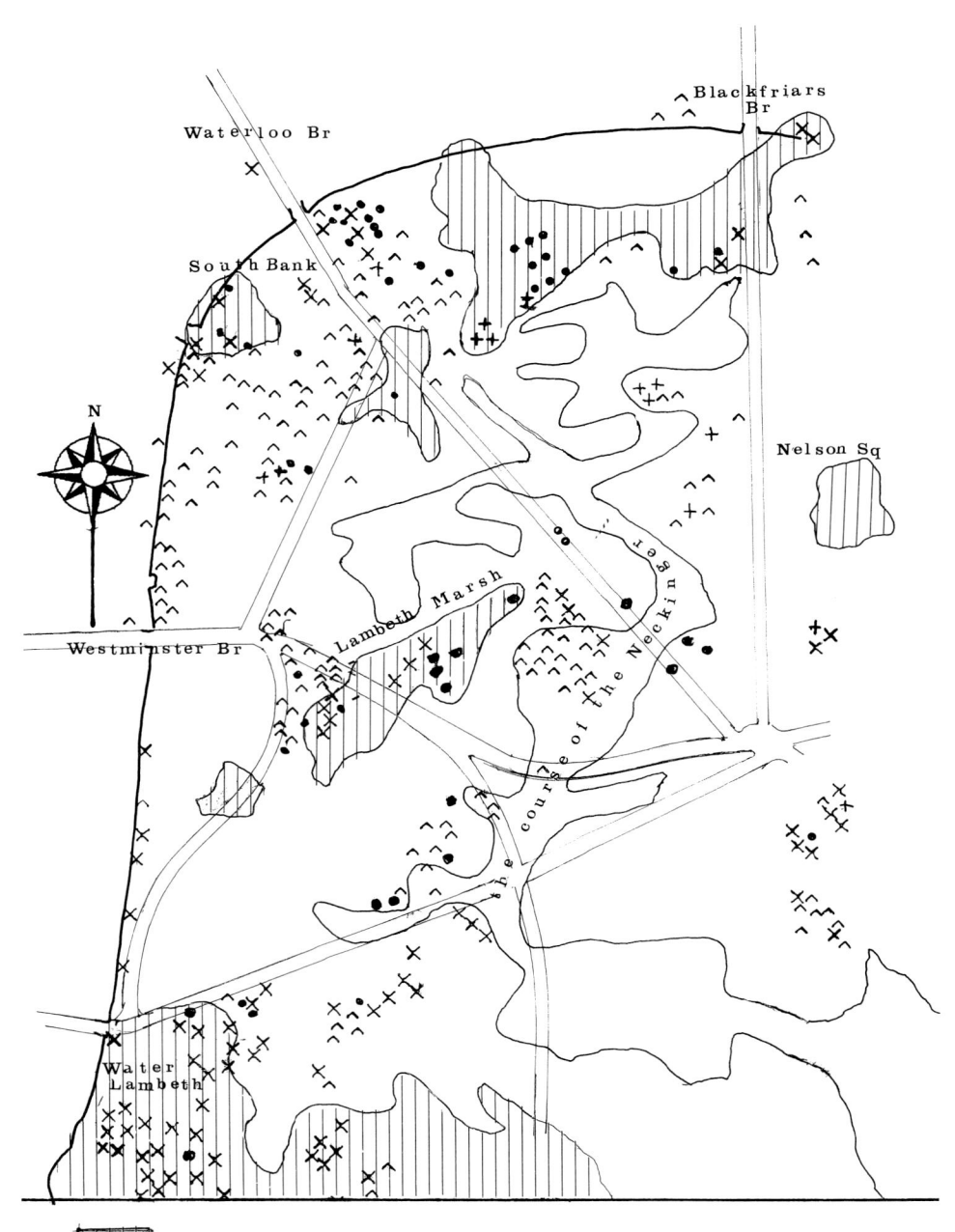

Ill. 23 Lambeth Marsh ground features

Another historical reference to water courses in the flood plain refers to a channel dug by Canute to bypass London Bridge when attacking London by boat in 1016. 'Canute's Trench' supposedly went from Rotherhithe through Newington [Elephant and Castle], to Vauxhall opposite Chelsea Creek.[4] Both Pepys and Defoe refer to its ditches at Kennington Common. Whether this is historically correct or not, the low-lying land would have made a canal quite possible, as the only piece of land to be dug would be a short length along Kennington Park Road to join the Neckinger with the Effra at the Oval.

Archaeological digs that have taken place along both banks of the Thames now confirm the written evidence of the changing shoreline and the rise and fall of the Thames water levels.[5] Receding floods deposit silt, thus raising the surrounding ground levels, and may alter the river bed, whilst constant river flows erode the bed and banks on the outside of curves but build it up on the inside. Lambeth Marsh on the inside of a curve of the Thames has varied little since neolithic times and has been inhabited by populations of various sizes ever since, with its shore slowly but naturally advancing into the Thames. The first revetments between the Marsh and the Thames were along Belvedere Road, and Lambeth Marsh island became, for the Romans, a stepping stone from London Bridge to the Westminster crossing. The sand-banks, also at Lambeth Palace and Nelson Square Blackfriars Road, had around them marshy areas made of rich and deep agricultural soil with a water table too high for building and draining. Milne's land-use map of London of 1800 shows how ploughed fields still existed here, the last remaining in central London.

When housing was built on the low areas between 1800 and 1830 it was all cheap and ill drained and very quickly became a centre of raging cholera epidemics. During four months of 1849 in just two streets, 544 died of cholera and 90 of diarrhoea and out of Lambeth's population of 139,000, mostly in Lambeth Marsh, the annual average recorded death rate was 1,690, more than 1:100. The Lambeth Vestry (the epitome of vested interests) were one of the last in London to implement Dr Snow's findings that connected foul drinking water with sewage as the cause of cholera epidemics. The deputation of 1849 squarely blamed the Commissioners of Sewers, and stated that £14,000 of sewer rates were collected but only £2,000 spent.[6]

It was a major advance in medical science that established the causes of these diseases, but a greater partnership of social and technical engineering had to occur before there were any practical results. Although water filtration became law with the Metropolitan Water Act of 1852, it was only when Bazalgette's brilliant and complete system for London's drains was operating that death rates began to drop. The southern outfall pumped up into the Thames first at Deptford and then later at Erith still efficiently serves the whole of South London and started to operate in 1862. Brick drains of diminishing size branched back from the main, deep below the watertable, ultimately connecting to every household with impervious salt glazed pipes that made fortunes for Doulton and other Lambeth potters.[7] There were even long arguments over the merits of porous pipes over impervious ones, vested interests saying that it was good for the ground that pipes be porous and leak as plants would grow better and pipes could be smaller.

RIVER TRANSPORT

From Roman times till the paving of roads in towns in the 1800s, heavy transport of goods in Britain took place by sea or by river; Britain was a maritime power with a merchant fleet that included coasters plying between all of Britain's ports and offloading to smaller boats to supply by river every major town in the land. By 1750 transport in the Thames was close to the limits that sail or oar power could sustain; over one hundred boat types plied the river and ferries crossed at hundred-yard intervals along the banks. But as early as 1650 river craft were so numerous that it was cheaper and easier for Pepys to cross the Thames to Southwark by boat than to pay the high toll over London Bridge a few yards away.

Hay markets were like petrol stations today, providing fuel for horse transport, hay at first arriving by cart over London Bridge from Kent and Surrey but, as London grew, able to come in large enough quantities only by boat. Coal, the other fuel used, had started to come from Newcastle as early as the 1560s, and the Lambeth Marsh river front had numerous coal wharfs. Pollution from burning coal is not therefore new to London; in 1661 John Evelyn complained bitterly that London 'should wrap her stately head in Clouds of Smoke and Sulphur, so full of stink and darkness' and he was glad when gardens flourished through the 'penury of Coales' at times of war.[8] Evelyn also knew and wrote against the culprits, who were the brewers, dyers, soap boilers and lime burners, in fact most of Lambeth Marsh's industries.

Other heavy goods arriving by boat included building materials such as timbers, stone, lime and sand. The earliest maps show the Lambeth Marsh shoreline with many timber yards and the 1731 windmill was a wind-powered saw-mill.[9] Building stone came into many wharfs till the 1930s and County Hall was built on the site of the LCC's own stone wharf. Large quantities of lime for mortar and wall plaster were used for building London, arriving by barge in the form of chalk from the Dartford quarries; the chalk was then burnt with Newcastle sea coal at lime kilns along the Lambeth waterfront to produce the lime. The spilled chalk of two hundred years ago is still to be seen on the shoreline.

However, the Thames will always have some basic technical difficulties as a transport river. Unlike Europe's other major rivers, it has a twice-daily tide, too strong when running with the river flow for boats to advance against, especially when their only power is oarsmen or wind. Even today with diesel engines, the fast flow makes tying up at a landing stage hazardous and fatal accidents still occur. Skill and organisation were necessary for the large volume of traffic that Canaletto's paintings and other records depict for us. The Waterman's and Lighterman's guilds were part of this control and even passenger fares were fixed and published (see ill. 24). By comparison the Thames today is almost unused.

Ill. 24 Standard ferry fares, W. Roades 1731

ROAD TRANSPORT

Many of the area's roads date back to the twelfth century or earlier and Lambeth Marsh road itself, being on higher ground, may have been the Roman road to the crossing at Westminster. The road 'Lambeth Marsh' [Upper and Lower Marsh] led to the Thames at the Stangate ferry, first mentioned in 1357; at its other end it went in a curve to St George's Fields [Webber Street], where it continued on to the Borough High Street. Another cart track across St George's Field was Lambeth Road to the horseferry at Lambeth Palace.

Lambeth Marsh was also linked by road with Lambeth Palace, having to skirt around the back of the Archbishop's gardens and the residence of the Bishops of Rochester [later Carlisle]. This medieval road ran a short length of Westminster Bridge Road into and then along Hercules Road to Lambeth Road and back to St Mary Lambeth. Carlisle House also had its twelfth-century way [Royal Street] to the Stangate ferry.

With all roads no more than dirt tracks around property, any water-filled ditches became a major hazard, and of course Lambeth Marsh was full of them. Lambeth Marsh road itself had five bridges crossing the ditches that flowed out to the Thames. Any bridge over a stream, however small, was of great value and often named, so on the Old Kent Road we have Lock Bridge and at every stream entering the Thames that had to pass under the river walk there was a named bridge: the Fleet Bridge, Strand Bridge, Cox's Bridge at Vauxhall and on Lambeth Marsh, Cuper's Bridge, the bridge over a sluice where the Neckinger entered the Thames [w3.46]. As time progressed, roads in towns were paved, generally with granite sets with a gulley along the middle. In 1800 only the new Georgian suburbs had side-walks or pavements to keep pedestrians above the filth of the road and these were rarely paved.

As the number of wheeled vehicles increased so the ruts and quagmires beyond the toll gates made the roads more and more unusable and there was a constant battle to keep them open: on many occasions St George's Fields became impassable.

WESTMINSTER BRIDGE [w4.21]

In London the demands on existing road and river transport were by 1740 so great that a new bridge between Putney and London Bridge became a necessity. London's busiest crossing point other than at London Bridge was from Stangate, the ferry of Lambeth Marsh, to Westminster and near the point that the Romans crossed with a ford to link with Watling Street [Edgware Road]. There were many vociferous arguments both in Parliament and among the public as to exactly where it should be, who should design it and how it should be paid for.[10] The ferrymen, fearing for their livelihoods, were against the bridge from the start, continuing throughout its construction to sabotage the work by cutting loose the stone barges and ramming the piers. In 1750 Westminster Bridge opened as the first to be built over the Thames for five hundred years; it heralded major changes in London's transport system, essential for the urban explosion that followed.

Much indecision at the outset of its building was caused by the technical problem that faced the Bridge Committee when they realised that the scouring

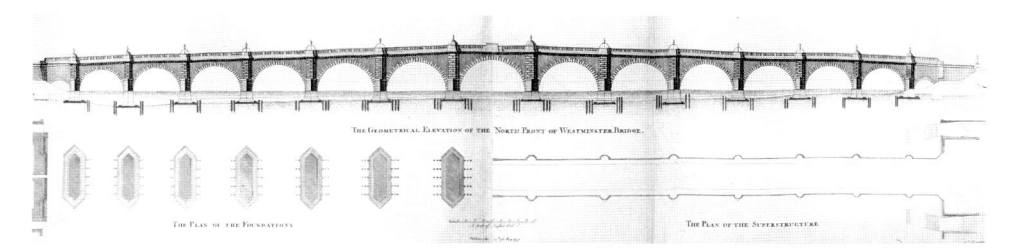

Ill. 25 Labelye's final design, Westminster Bridge

effect of the strong tides had to be overcome more effectively than it had ever been at the old London Bridge. No one they knew had experience in dealing with foundations in fast-flowing tidal rivers and without this experience they were loath to give the contract to Ripley, Comptroller of the Works and architect of the Customs House, or to Batty Langley, the well-known builder who had built much of Bloomsbury. The Earl of Pembroke, a bridge commissioner, encouraged Labelye, a young French-Swiss engineer with experience of tidal waters to submit his designs.[11] The Committee could not decide whether a light timber bridge would be better than a heavy but stronger stone one, so to make a start Labelye was commissioned on 10 May 1738 to commence the foundations only. After the successful execution of several piers and the decision to use a stone bridge, he was given the rest of the contract to complete to his own design.

Labelye, a competent craftsman, was one of the first of a new breed of truly professional people unheard of in Britain at the time. His proposals were highly innovative and decried by his English rivals, such as Batty Langley. The pier foundations were not piled but made by sinking wooden caissons into shallow dredged holes, whose bases then formed the foundations for building the piers in the dry. Many of the ideas and machines used on the bridge came from Holland and the use of caissons was an idea that had been used previously on a smaller scale on dykes. The caissons resulted in a very efficient and speedy building of the foundations, with only one almost disastrous mishap when a pier started sinking. Labelye rebuilt the necessary pier and arches with internal counter arches to reduce their weight, and triumphantly opened the bridge in 1750.

Labelye was also involved with the Lambeth Marsh approach road to the bridge and again used highly successful Dutch building techniques previously unknown in this country. The road was raised above the marsh on chalk foundations and culverts were built to allow field ditches to flow under the road. The road ran from the bridge across marshy fields called Sowters (shoemaker) Lands to the already existing road at Lambeth Marsh. At this new junction was placed Marshgate, the toll gate that is now the pedestrian crossing at the corner of the Red Lion, formerly Ye Flower Pot tavern.[12] The approach roads remained open to highwaymen for several years, with the lights vandalised and the bridge alcoves useful for secret liaisons.[13]

'The river is of sufficient expanse to be a grand object of itself: Westminster Bridge, with its fine arches, stretching across the water in splendid simplicity: and the edificial group of Westminster Hall, with the Abbey and its stately towers rising beyond it, form an union of the picturesque and magnificent . . . Westminster Bridge is among the finest structures of its kind in the world. It

The Island Village

Ill. 26 Rebuilding the collapsed pier 1750 by Canaletto

possesses a simple grandeur, that renders it a majestic feature of the Thames.'
                                            Ackermann's *Microcosm of London* 1808.

In spite of Ackermann's acclamation the bridge was actually too grand and heavy and continued to move on its foundations till eventually it was totally rebuilt, with its present iron arches designed by Thomas Page. Two years after it was opened to traffic, Queen Victoria opened the new bridge early in the morning to commemorate the very moment of her birth at 3.45 am on 24 May 1861.

BLACKFRIARS BRIDGE [w3.21]

In 1756, soon after the opening of the first Westminster Bridge, the City of London decided they needed an entry to their city from the south other than the dilapidated London Bridge and obtained an Act of Parliament to build a bridge at Blackfriars. The bridge was designed by Robert Mylne, who in 1780 built his own house on the Surrey side [site now under railway arches]. The bridge took an exceptionally long time to build owing to lack of funds; it was four years before the first pile was driven and the bridge was only partially completed when it was opened in 1766 to pedestrians with a temporary walkway on the Surrey end and to horses in 1768.[14] Further delays were due to the fact that no decisions had been made for the new roads that were needed. Many maps were published for the approach roads that had to connect with the Elephant and Castle, Borough High Street, Lambeth Road and the new Westminster Bridge.

In April 1769 a further Act was needed to enable the eighty-foot-wide road to be built to St George's Circus, to be the central spoke of Robert Mylne's grand plan radiating out to Lambeth Palace, Westminster Bridge, the Elephant and Castle and later Waterloo. The bridge itself opened to full traffic that same year, and with Mylne wasting no time in building the new approach road to the obelisk in the centre of St George's circus, the roads were completed early in 1771. Very quickly the roadside was developed with a mixture of housing and industry, and in 1786 the Albion Mills opened, using the newly invented

Ill. 27 Blackfriars bridge under construction by Edward Rooker

Watt's steam engine to grind flour [w3.20]. The millers viewed these new machines with fear and suspicion and when fire destroyed the building in 1791 it was suspected that Luddite arsonists were responsible. The road was originally called Great Surrey Street but in 1829 was renamed Blackfriars Road.

The roads actually built do make the required links but the geometry was not simple enough to create the grand Parisian vistas to Lambeth, Westminster, the Borough and later Waterloo that Robert Mylne and the Act had intended. In 1905 the obelisk was moved from the Circus to the corner of the Imperial War Museum grounds to smooth the flow of traffic, although with the present roundabout system it could well go back again. The bridge was replaced by the present iron bridge, begun in 1864 and opened in 1869.

'Returning, I came over Blackfriars Bridge, for the last time: on Monday or Tuesday it is to be closed and pulled down. Many a noble sunset have I seen from thence: and other very different sights too: for ten years ago the miry shore was crowded at low tide (it is not now) with female mudlarks, and many a time I have seen them, young women and matrons too, crawling out of the darkness between the barges, and wading up to their knee & far deeper, in black mud, even when it was thickly filmed over with ice.'
A. J. Munby, Saturday 4 June 1864.

Ill. 28 A woman mudlark at Blackfriars Bridge by Munby

The Island Village

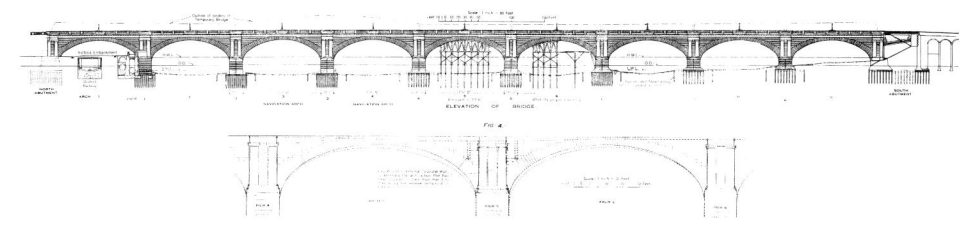

Ill. 29 Waterloo Bridge demolition drawings

WATERLOO BRIDGE [w3.32]

With the success of Parliament's Westminster Bridge and the City of London's bridge at Blackfriars, a private company, the Strand Bridge Company, felt that money was to be made with another bridge.[15] They obtained their enabling Act in 1809, several years before the battle of Waterloo, to build their bridge from the Strand to a point in Lambeth Marsh where Cuper's Gardens had once stood. John Rennie, who later lived at 18 Stamford Street, was appointed the designer and engineer and the first stone was laid in 1811. Only after the French wars in 1813 did the Duke of York push another Act through Parliament that bought off the shareholders and enacted that the name should be changed to Waterloo Bridge as a 'lasting record of the brilliant and decisive Victory achieved by His Majesty's Forces'. The bridge was opened by the Prince Regent in 1817, the second anniversary of the battle, with fireworks and entertainments, depicted by many painters including Constable.[16]

This bridge was never a financial success, being paid for by tolls whereas Westminster and Blackfriars were by then free. Not until the passing of the Metropolitan Toll Bridges Act of 1877 was it bought by the Metropolitan Board of Works for £474,200 and became free. The bridge stood longer than most of London's bridges, but after heated public debates as to whether such a fine stone bridge should be repaired or demolished it was finally closed to traffic in 1924. The present elegant reinforced concrete bridge, coming at the time of depression and war, was built with explosion chambers to allow for demolition if invasion were ever to occur. The bridge was finally opened formally in December 1945 though the new approach road, pedestrian underpasses and roundabout did not follow till 1968.

Westminster, Blackfriars and Waterloo Bridges defined the main roads that exist to this day and together they set off extensive building programmes that, by 1820, had covered the Marsh. The last of the new river crossings came in 1845 with the suspension footbridge to the Hungerford Market.

Ill. 30 Photograph of Hungerford Bridge 1850 by Roger Fenton

Ill. 31 Hungerford Bridge under construction 1844

HUNGERFORD BRIDGE [w3.40]

Hungerford Bridge, designed by Isambard Kingdom Brunel (1806-59) as a pedestrian suspension bridge and opened in 1845, led into a newly rebuilt Hungerford Market and thence at the same level to the Strand. It met the need of the thousands living in the Marsh who worked in the West End to cross the river cheaply. By the year 1853 three million were crossing annually, in spite of the arguments and riots about the tolls.[17]

In 1859 the London South Eastern Railway purchased the bridge with the market for the new Charing Cross station. The suspension bridge had to be demolished but the Brunel chains went to Clifton to complete his unfinished suspension bridge there, as a memorial to his death in 1859. The railway had by law to keep the pedestrian way in perpetuity and it is still used by large numbers of people going to and from the South Bank. The railway bridge required new tubular steel piers but was able to utilise Brunel's original brick piers, still in use today. These piers had the unusual feature of stairways inside them which led out on to small platforms on the pier and on to landing stages for pleasure steamers. The doorways to the stairs are still intact and visible in the piers.

Ill. 32 Hungerford Bridge chains being removed, Whistler 1861

THE RAILWAY [w3.6]

For the last 140 years Lambeth Marsh has been physically dominated by the railway and the station, effectively cutting Lambeth Marsh in two and dividing the old village along Upper and Lower Marsh from the waterfront land with a half-mile-thick bastion of raised brickwork. The isolation of the river strip of land caused by the railway created a planning disaster that extends from beyond Vauxhall to London Bridge. Very early in its existence the railway lobby acquired special legal powers, conferred on it by private bills, that gave it draconian powers of compulsory purchase and rights above the normal law, powers that British Rail still wields. In Lambeth Marsh the railway was not the easiest of lines to build as the lines and station had to be on a raised viaduct. Its construction meant the demolition of a large amount of densely built housing, much of it constructed only forty years earlier. However, the property was cheap with only one important landlord, the Archbishop of Canterbury; he was only too glad to sell off London's worst slums.

The first railways to South London came into London Bridge in 1836, followed in 1838 by the London South Western Railway (LSWR) coming from Woking Common to Nine Elms.[18] On 11 July 1848 the LSWR opened their line from Nine Elms on a viaduct through Vauxhall to Waterloo station. In 1864 the South Eastern Railway having converted the Hungerford pedestrian bridge, extended their London Bridge line to Charing Cross with a connecting branch to Waterloo over Waterloo Road [the existing pedestrian bridge to Waterloo East]. Waterloo station had at first only six tracks and four platforms but was increased in width in 1860, 1864, 1878 and 1910-22 to have twenty-one platforms, more platforms and more train movements than any other station in the world.

Without doubt the railway brought great benefits to London and to Britain, but for Lambeth Marsh, at least for the name, it was the end: the area lost any desirable residential qualities it may once have had. The railways never did build the grand hotel to be enjoyed at almost every other main-line London terminus and the only people living close by were railway workers or the poor. The sulphurous stench and solid black smut descending continuously through the air is something still remembered by those brought up before the 1960s.

Ill. 33 Building the first Waterloo Station, 1848

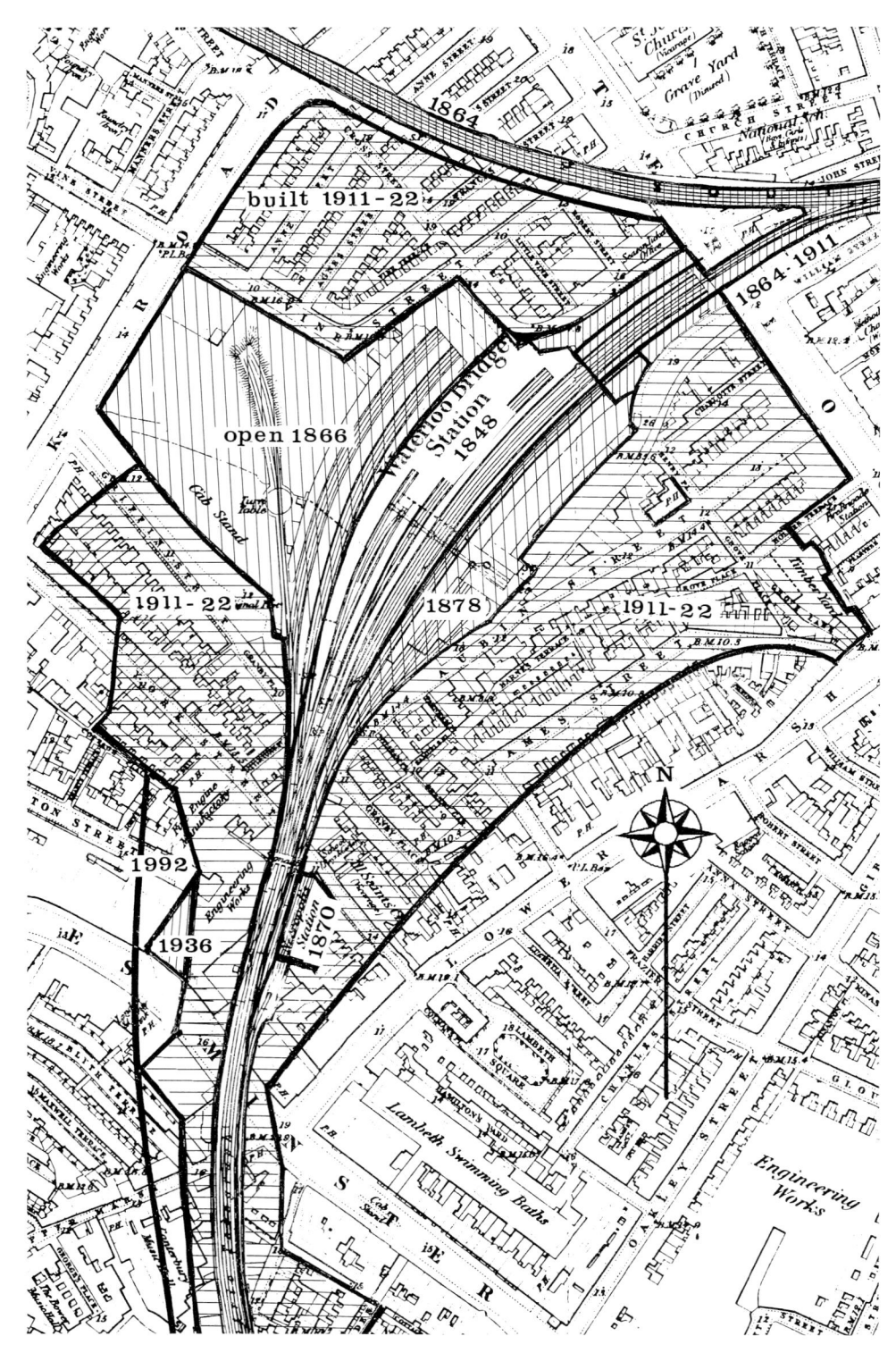

Ill. 34 Waterloo Station expansion, 1848-1991

The Island Village

In the nineteenth century the population of Lambeth Marsh had risen to thirty thousand or more and burying the dead had become a serious problem. The London Necropolis Railway, an independent private line running to the Necropolis Cemetery at Brookwood, Woking, provided the answer in 1870. The funeral cortege arrived through the arch at road level and the coffin was lifted to the platform, where rest rooms were provided. The wealthy could hire the whole train but normally as many as fifty a day from all classes used the regular service, the bereaved returning to London at the end of the ceremony.[19] The original building of 1870 was in Leake Street [w2.10] but when the station was enlarged in 1903 it was moved to Westminster Bridge Road, where the building still stands next to the post office [w2.19].

Between 1914 and 1940 Waterloo station thrived and expanded as part of the war machine of two world wars, an essential part of the supply route to Europe. The present station front and offices were completed in 1922 as a memorial to those employees who lost their lives in the first world war, and a grim reminder to the millions of others who saw their men for the last time leaving by train for cannon fodder. People in Lower Marsh can still remember the deserter shot in the back as he ran from his guards down Frazier Street, and the United Services Club (Union Jack Club) [now the tower block in Waterloo Road] must hold memories for many, of their last night on the way to and from the Front.

'Pile the bodies high at Austerlitz and Waterloo,
shovel them under and let me work-
I am the grass; I cover all.'
Grass   Edward Thomas, killed at Arras 1917

Since the Clean Air Acts and the end of steam trains in the 1960s, Lambeth Marsh is a cleaner, quieter place and has been able to rebuild a residential life of better quality, in spite of seemingly never ending railway development. Most recently, the latest work for the Channel Tunnel terminal is using more land and further blocking the river from the hinterland; while trains still belch diesel oil and the public address systems continue to shout over the Marsh into the night.

3

THE RISE AND FALL OF INDUSTRY

– River industries – tenter grounds – breweries –
– Beaufoy's wine and vinegar works – Carlisle House pottery –
– Coade stone – William Clowes & Sons –
– scrap metal merchants and William Roupell – ironworks –
– light industry – offices and the South Bank –

RIVER INDUSTRIES

Many of Lambeth Marsh's more interesting industries were set up between the sixteenth and eighteenth centuries when they expanded and broke loose from the restrictive practices of the Guilds of the City of London, that is, before the Industrial Revolution as we normally think of it. Early industry in Lambeth Marsh was indeed often the first to use, make or invent new machines. By the nineteenth century, however, industries were moving out again to the Midlands and the North as London turned into a commercial town. The industries described here do not include the 'leisure' industry of gardens, taverns and theatres, as these are the most important part of Lambeth Marsh's history and have their own chapter.

Industry in Lambeth Marsh was always based on transport up the Thames or on the plentiful supply of water in the marshes. Neolithic finds have shown that on the sand-bank of Lambeth Marsh men not only used flints but cut them here as well. The flints were readily obtained from Dartford and beyond where the chalk hills are cut by the Thames and where neolithic flint mines existed. The next chronological evidence of industry in the Marsh was the flat-bottomed Roman boat found under the foundations of County Hall during building operations in 1910 [w4.18].

The Thames frontage has, as far back as we know, moved very little. Belvedere Road and Upper Ground, previously called Narrow Wall, was a river wall that had on its river side a sandy foreshore, raised naturally above normal tide levels. This type of raised foreshore can still be seen along many French rivers such as the Seine or Loire, and on the South Bank at low tide its remnants are seen as a clean and natural sandy beach. The first river industry recorded used these fertile banks for osier (willow) beds on 'plantations' and in 1552 Robert Aylward was a tenant 'with one messuage . . . with wharf adjoining'.[20] Morgan's large-scale 1682 map, confirmed by many of the manors' records, shows the reclaimed land between Narrow Wall [Belvedere Road] and the Thames as a continuous line of barge houses, wharfs and docks all labelled with the tenants' names. However, twenty-five years earlier the river front is mapped by Wenceslas Hollar showing houses from London Bridge to Cuper's Bridge [Waterloo Bridge site] and with the Marsh much more built on. Could it be that in the twenty years of the Plague, the Fire and the Civil War the population of Lambeth Marsh decreased, buildings fell into disrepair and the land was used for the new water-based industries of cloth bleaching and brewing?

The Rise and Fall of Industry 55

'but the worst is I hear that the plague increases much at Lambeth, St Martin's and Westminster, and I fear it will all over the city.'

Pepys, 5 November 1665.

In 1690 the De Feuille map labels a continuous line of wood yards from Stangate [Westminster Bridge site] downstream to Cuper's Bridge [Waterloo Bridge site]. These yards imported the timber from around the coast, cut them into planks and seasoned them in large stacks; and we know that the windmill shown on Kip's view of 1710 was a wind-powered saw-mill [Royal Festival Hall site].

Boatyards and Barge Houses

Lambeth Marsh on the inside of the curve of the Thames and with a long, gently sloping beach was the perfect place for the building and keeping of London's barges and boats. The first known reference to them is to the King's Barge House at the time of Henry VIII, still recalled by Barge House Stairs [w3.24] next to the Oxo Tower.[21] This barge house straddled a branch of the Neckinger stream that flowed as the boundary between Paris Garden Manor and Prince's Meadow, part of Kennington Manor (see p. 73). By the seventeenth century barge houses had established themselves further upstream. Along Prince's Meadow [Barge House Stairs to Waterloo Bridge] were the barge houses of the Merchant Taylors, the Woodmongers and the Lord Mayor of London.[22] Between Stangate ferry and the Lambeth horseferry were the Royal Barge, and those of the city guilds of the Armourers, the Goldsmiths, the Grocers and the Barber Surgeons and also the Dukes of Richmond and Montagu [w4.24].

Canaletto's view of London from Lambeth Palace shows in detail the gilded Venetian-style barges and the boatyards where these and many other types of boats were built and repaired. Roberts and Searle's boatyards were building boats here for over a century from the 1750s, and many others have been depicted on paintings and engravings such as that of Lyon & Co. in 1831.[23]

On this same stretch of shore amongst the boatyards were warehouses and a few houses belonging to people working on the river. In one of these, John By (1779-1836) was brought up as a waterman to follow his father George By [w4.25].[24] John By went to Canada as an engineer, built the canal (1826-32) and founded Bytown, which later became Ottawa.

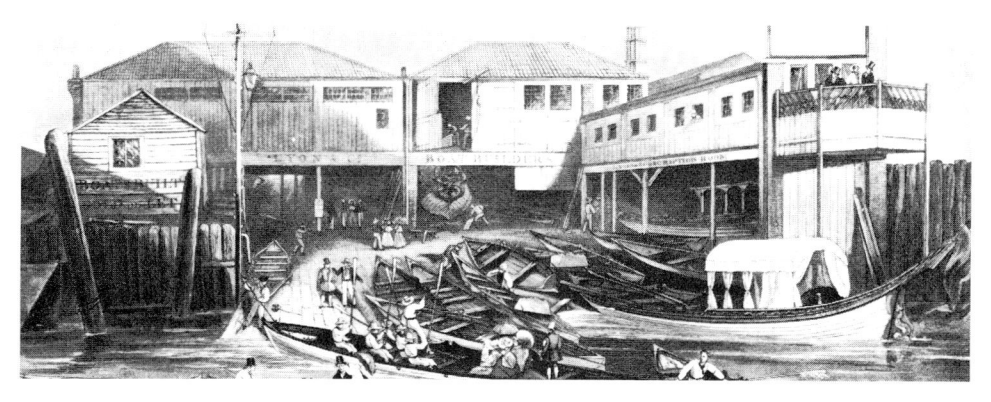

Ill. 35 Boatyards at Stangate

56 *The Rise and Fall of Industry*

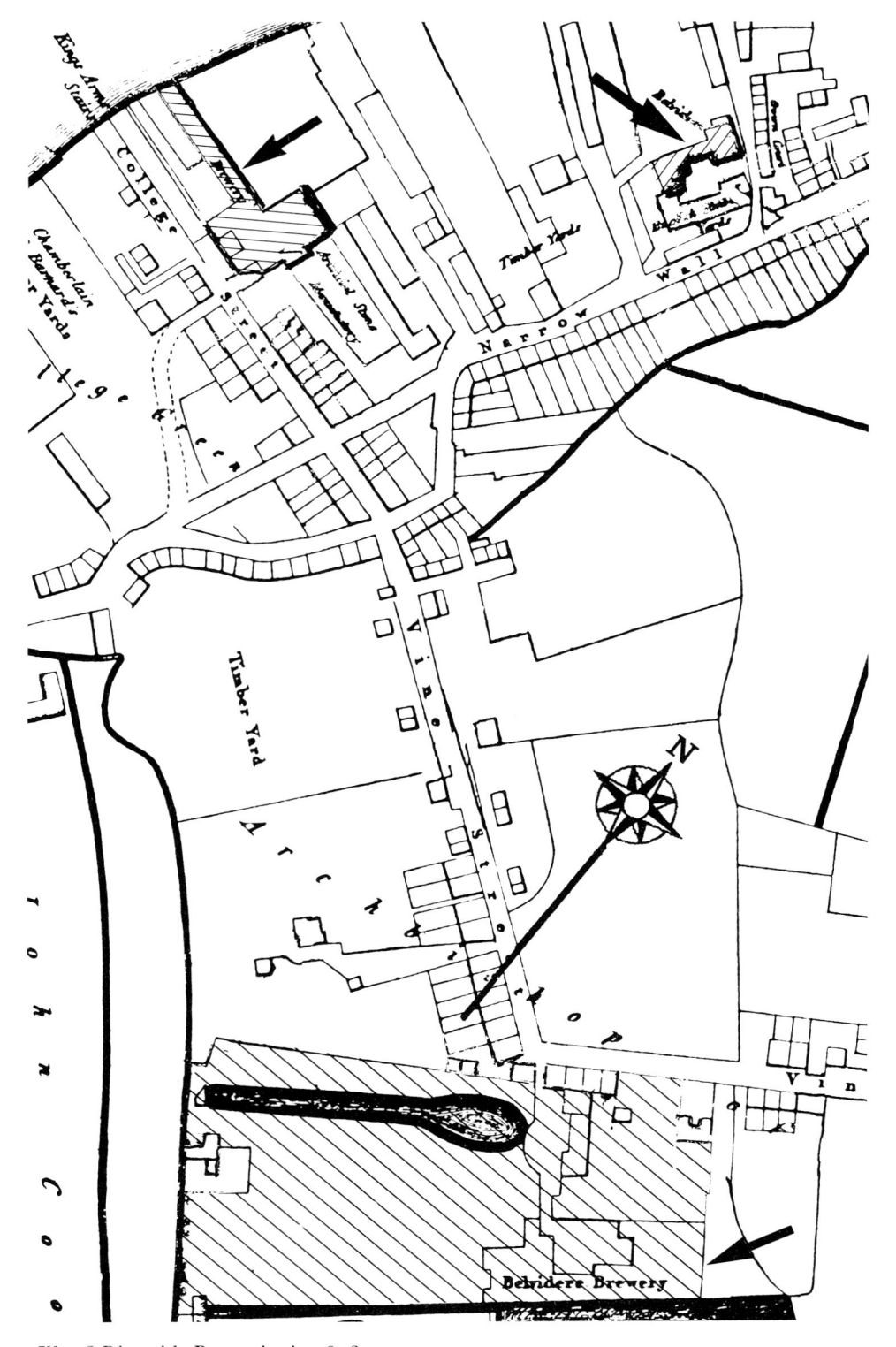

Ill. 36 Riverside Breweries in 1806

TENTER GROUNDS

Morgan's 1682 map shows large areas of ditches spaced at close intervals in long straight lengths. These were tenter grounds and they appear in this and other flat parts of South London, being last labelled in 1819 off Blackfriars Road. Tentering was a cloth-milling process that before the days of steam-powered presses had to be carried out in open ditches running with clean water. The cloth was unrolled to its full length into the ditch, soaked and then stretched out to dry in the open on wooden frames held there by hooks, the 'tenterhooks'. Lambeth Marsh was ideal for providing the two essentials for the industry: fresh, clean, running water for each milling and large areas of open flat ground for stretching and drying.

BREWERIES
See Index for a full list with locations.

Lambeth Marsh could also supply the large amounts of water required for brewing. The most famous brewery was the [Red] Lion Brewery, advertised by the red lion perched atop the waterside warehouse looking over to Westminster. The lion, renamed the South Bank Lion, was moved to Westminster Bridge in 1960 and is a remarkable example of Coade stone, another Lambeth Marsh industry (see p. 59). The brewery site [the Royal Festival Hall w3.39] was earlier the site of Belvedere House [Belvedere Gardens, see p. 85]. In 1853 the house plot became an addition to James Goding's existing brewery and was renamed the Lion Brewery. Horwood's 1799 and the 1806 Enclosure maps show a Belvidere Brewery in Vine Street [under Waterloo station w3.6] that later, in 1826, is located and described by Allen as Mrs Edward's Belvidere Brewery, supplied by pond and stream water.[25] This brewery was the part of 'the Seven Acres' that Goding leased in 1837.[26]

In the days of water-borne diseases such as cholera and typhus, alcohol was the safest drink that could be made from the plentiful supply of surface water in the Marsh. Later, as hygiene improved and drinking Thames water was not

Ill. 37 Horn Brewery and Windmill, The Cut 1804

permitted, the brewery drilled five artesian wells to provide pure clean water under pressure from the chalk layer beneath London's clay; they were in use till their destruction in the 1939-45 war.[27]

Many other breweries existed in the area, such as the Union Brewery in Frazier Street [w2.25] and the Horn Brewery in The Cut. The Horn Brewery, with its own windmill as a power source, had a taphouse that still exists as the Windmill pub [w2.48]. The windmill and brewery were operating in 1799 and the mill was still depicted by Barker on his panorama of 1857.

BEAUFOY'S WINE AND VINEGAR WORKS [w3.34]

In 1763, except for the Feathers run by Widow Evans, most of Cuper's Garden was derelict, when Mark Beaufoy (1718-82), a Quaker, acquired the lease of the remaining buildings for his wine and vinegar works.[28] The brewery flourished, and Mark Beaufoy built a row of cottages called Friends Row next door. However, he did have trouble with his lease from Kennington Manor, as they claimed he was responsible for the care of the property even though it was derelict when he took it over.[29] In 1810 John Hanbury Beaufoy built a new vinegar factory in South Lambeth Road, having by then dropped the manufacture of wine.[30] The Cuper's Garden site was left by Beaufoy to be taken by the New Strand Bridge company for the building of the bridge approach road [Waterloo Road].

CARLISLE HOUSE POTTERY [w4.35]

The Lambeth potters were mostly located between Lambeth Bridge and Vauxhall but one existed in Lambeth Marsh in Carlisle House [between Carlisle Lane and Hercules Road, under the railway] that produced pottery on and off between 1706 and 1741. In 1721 the lease between the Archbishop of Canterbury and Robert Henley stipulated that all salt glazing be done at night between

Ill. 38 Carlisle House site in 1840

The Rise and Fall of Industry 59

10 and 6 am and allowing only three firings in a three-month period.³¹ Salt glazing was a brilliantly simple way to waterproof pottery, requiring only the throwing of salt onto the pots in the kiln on a second firing, fusing it to the pot as a glaze. The only trouble with this process was that poisonous chlorine gas was given off and the Archbishop objected to that wafting over his premises too often.

COADE STONE [w4.20]

With a building boom under way in the latter part of the eighteenth century, economy and speed of building were achieved by using brick walls instead of stone or timber and by reducing the amount of external decoration, which needed to be easily and cheaply made. Mrs Coade's Artificial Stone, whose works and showroom were in Lambeth Marsh, produced the very product for this new Georgian style of architecture. Nearly every house in Georgian London had some Coade stone feature, whether it was a small keystone over the front door or, like Stratford Place off Oxford Street, almost the whole façade, with stone detailing around corners, window and doors, all in the same material. A range of off-the-shelf products filled catalogues and could be seen at the showrooms in Westminster Bridge Road.³² If these did not meet your needs then specials could be ordered to designs by either your own artist or that of the work's artists, or copies could be made from famous pieces of sculpture.

One key to Mrs Coade's success was that for the first time a mould was used in the method of production, keeping the price down by 'mass production'. The material, in use before the days of Portland cement (patent 1824) or its derivative concrete, was a twice-fired clay product that could be moulded into the most intricate or large forms. The first firing was used to make a grog, that was added to more clay to form a very stiff mixture and then put in the mould for a second firing. This process reduced the shrinkage to the finished article, shrinkage that normally prevents pottery articles from being large or intricate. Patent additives were also mixed in with the grog to give the product great strength and weatherability. The fact that two hundred years later, so many buildings still have the material unweathered on their face is testament enough for any artificial stone. The existing South Bank Lion [w4.20] and Imperial War Museum pediment crest are large examples of a purpose-made article of this material and because of their size were both reinforced with wire and made in several pieces. Most of this technical information was verified when the site

Ill. 39 Coade stone plaques demolished 1959, Blackfriars Road

Ill. 40 'Architecture' from Coade's catalogue

was excavated during the building of the 1951 Festival of Britain.[33] Found, with many other artifacts during excavation, was the mill-stone used for grinding the materials, now displayed at the lower drive-in to the Festival Hall by Hungerford Bridge [w3.39]. The factory was upstream next to Hungerford Bridge, now the car park.

Why Coade stone had died out by 1840 is difficult to understand. Some expertise was required to reproduce the correct proportions of additives in the mix, and this knowledge may have been lost. Or maybe it was because Portland cement was coming into use and the fashion for red pottery decorative features on red brick housing was replacing the stone and yellow brick of the Georgian period. By that date we also find that rising land prices of such a central area of London was pushing all industries to the Midlands, where the coal, clay or iron was dug.

WILLIAM CLOWES & SONS [w3.26]

The story of book printing in London is the story of William Clowes and Sons, the country's largest printing works for over a hundred years. The company records were meticulously kept and provide a source for many authors writing about the printing business, on labour conditions and on the trade union movement.[34] These important subjects have been well covered by other authors, who have shown vividly the appalling conditions under which men, women and children had to work in the Marsh from 1800 onwards.

William Clowes (1779-1847) opened his first printing shop at 20 Villiers Street at Charing Cross on 21 October 1803. He married into money and perhaps for this reason his business grew and he was able, within four years, to move three streets along to larger premises in Northumberland Court, where he employed twenty people. He started binding books on the premises, unheard of at the time, and lived over the shop with his wife Mary.

When Clowes started, printing was much the same as in Caxton's day, with everything done by hand; each letter a separate piece of lead and every piece of dampened paper hand-made and inserted by hand under the press. Printing required many side trades, such as paper making, binding, lead smelting, and of course ink making. It was in February 1824 that Charles Dickens was put to work at the age of twelve in a blacking factory in Hungerford Stairs, more than likely supplying the ink black for Clowes around the corner.

'The blacking warehouse ... was a crazy tumble-down old house ... its wainscotted rooms and its rotten floors and stair-case, and the old grey rats swarming down in the cellars at all times, and the dirt and decay of the place rise up visibly before me.'

David Copperfield.

William Clowes' continued success enabled him in 1824 to install the first steam-powered press for book printing in London. However, the press made so much noise that his landlord, the Duke of Northumberland, successfully sued him in June that year but had to compensate Clowes to get him to move. In 1825 Clowes crossed the river to Duke Street off Stamford Street in Lambeth Marsh [the Coin Street Housing site] where the works stayed for 120 years until bombed out. Before 1819 the site was leased by Applegarth and Cowper, partners and brothers-in-law who were famous for their innovative printing machinery and from whom Clowes acquired his plot. Augustus Applegarth lived at 239 Kennington Road.[35] The landlords for the site were Thomas and John Lett, timber merchants, the daughter of John Lett marrying into the Clowes family.

Earlier in 1815 Applegarth had patented the first curved stereotype plates for fixing to cylinder presses and by 1828 was producing patented presses that could print both sides at one thousand sheets an hour with seventy different models for printing books, newspapers, banknotes or any other printing requirement. Applegarth and Cowper machines were beautifully simple with minimum moving parts and so trouble-free that fifty years later Clowes was still using one. The eight-cylinder machine was one of several of their machines that were marvels of the 1851 Great Exhibition. To give some idea of the growth of the Clowes works in the mid nineteenth century here are just a few facts and figures:

1837   George Clowes installed paper machines enabling 5,000 copies to be printed in one go.
1840   600 people employed. 19 Applegarth Cowper machines, 23 hand presses and 5 hydraulic presses and a warehouse with 7,000 reams of paper.
1843   80,000 woodcut illustrations in stock and 2,500 tons of lead stereotype (curved plates) for 2,500 books of 320 pages each.
1862   568 employees, still the largest printer in Britain.

Not always the most innovative of printers, Clowes did have a reputation for caring for his workers. This meant that he was not always the first to make workers redundant when a faster machine was produced. Maybe he had learnt by experience: in 1848 hard times had almost closed the business when the *Penny Cyclopedia* failed, Charles Knight its publisher went bankrupt and William Clowes lost £40,000.[36] Yet examples of the Company's philanthropy include

Ill. 41 Clowes' type foundry 1842

such things as the sick fund for the employees, the Printers' Pension Corporation and Almshouses, and the financing in 1921 of the London School of Printing using the old Benevolent Society of St Patrick's school in Stamford Street. After the war the school became the Seamen's Mission School and the School of Printing moved to new premises at the Elephant and Castle. The story of the printers' unions is too long to tell here but, when Clowes moved to Lambeth, the First Trade Society of Compositors had already been operating for twenty years, successfully negotiating with employers and regularly using arbitration to reach agreement.[37] The compositors, bookbinders and other trades were artisans and considered by many in the labour movement as too well off and too well organised to be of much use to the poor caught in the poverty trap.[38]

William Clowes, the founder, died on 21 January 1847 and was buried at Norwood Cemetery in the family grave he had built for his wife. Her remains were moved from St Martins-in-the-Fields when Norwood Cemetery was first opened in 1837. The Cemetery still has William's grave (number 1616) with several others of his family around him.

SCRAP METAL MERCHANTS and WILLIAM ROUPELL

Like the shanty towns of modern South American cities, Lambeth Marsh was a fully integrated hive of industry. Waste tips were lived on by gangs of urchins recycling everything on the heap: coke or coal sieved from ash for reburning or, if too fine, ground down as blacking, the pure white ash being used for cement or mixing with builders' lime; bones were sold to the soap factories in Carlisle Lane and elsewhere, giving a stench of rotten meat to the whole area [w4.37]; rags or material went to make paper or were sold to clothe the poor; and even dogs' excrement ('pure') was collected for use in leather tanning in Southwark.[39]

Iron and brass were remelted and made into new articles; while the blacking and the lead trades sold their wares to Clowes the printer, with Stephens ink being made in the next street off Stamford Street. Lead smelters abounded in the area and gun shot was made by dropping molten lead from the top of a tower into a tank of water. Two such towers operated along the river side, a square shot tower (now the London Weekend Television studios [w3.29]) and a round Shot Tower, demolished only in 1962 when a tree was planted in its place between the Festival Hall and the Queen Elizabeth Hall [w3.36].

Families made fortunes in the scrap metal trade and the Roupell family was one of them. They say that family enterprises last just three generations, the first to establish the firm, the second to make the fortune and the third to dissipate it all. The Roupell's did just that.[40]

John Roupell (d. 1835, buried St John's Waterloo Road) was a scrap metal merchant and lived at 16 Cross Street [Meymott Street] where he married and had one child, Richard Palmer Roupell (1782-1861). John's works in Bear Lane Southwark prospered, and he began acquiring land. By 1818 he was developing his Roupell Street estate in Lambeth Marsh next to his old home as well as the estate of Roupell Park off Streatham Hill. In the 1820s John described himself as a 'gold refiner', the tops of the scrap metal business. However, he was a tyrant to his son Richard, who was too frightened to marry his beloved Sarah and had secret meetings with her every weekend for over twelve years. By 1837 when he was 55, Richard had four children born out of wedlock, John, William, Sarah and Emma, but not until 1838, after his mother's death, did he marry Sarah and have one more child, Richard.

The arrival of young Richard was to cause the family downfall since only the legitimate heir could inherit the family fortune. William, the second son, who by 1853 was helping run the business, was more educated and a clerk to an attorney, while the eldest son John had gone to sea. Richard the father was, like most fortune makers and his own father, tight with the money he gave his son William, but the fortune continued to grow with substantial estates in Kingston, Great Warley and Havering, together worth well over £100,000. In 1853 William committed his first forgery in a letter that supposedly handed the Roupell Park estate to himself, and with the letter raised money on the estate so that he could live in a grander style and enter politics. His father's death in 1856 presented William with a problem, as it was Richard, the legitimate son, who was left the Roupell Park estate. William then committed his next, more serious crime: he forged a new will.

While the falsehood was concealed, William's stature grew: in 1857 he was elected to Parliament, following a campaign that cost £6,000 and was questioned by a Parliamentary Committee. However, the petition against his election was even more dubious than the election itself and was thrown out. In 1860 he founded, and provided for, the 19th Corps of the Surrey Rifles Volunteers, but was by then spending money like water. 1862 saw his mortgages foreclosed and William absconded to Spain, although nobody missed him in Parliament as he had never made his maiden speech. On a visit later that year to England he was arrested and confessed to his forgeries. During his two trials his whole life story came out and he was sentenced to transportation for life. Twenty years later, however, between 1885 and 1890, he reappeared on the estates at Streatham and outlived his younger brother, the rightful heir, to die in 1909 at the ripe old age of 78.

IRONWORKS

Iron casting is a remarkably simple process, requiring a furnace and an earth floor for the sand-casting bed and any old scrap iron. The method of casting in sand moulds is so effective that many small pieces of ironmongery, such as bolts and hinges, can still use the master mould that was made over two hundred years ago. In 1838 Charles Collinge, makers of patent axle trees, sugar mills and engines, and hinges, manufactured at 64 Westminster Bridge Road [now where taxis enter Waterloo station] and, although long gone from the area, cast-iron door and gate hinges are still sold under their name, using the original patterns. Lambeth Marsh, a place for poor man's enterprises, had always had a surfeit of foundries and on the 1872 Ordnance Survey map at least twelve are shown. The map includes those engineering works that did their own casting, such as Applegarth's casting their printing machines, works casting brass and iron sanitary ware and a fire engine manufactury casting iron pumps [w4.6]. However, the following are the two best-known factories.

Maudslay Ironworks 1810-1900. [w4.60]

Henry Maudslay (1771-1831) opened his works in 1810 at the site of the present-day North Lambeth underground station and stretching back along Baylis Road almost to Frazier Street. He was most famous as a machine tool engineer who patented many machine tools for precision engineering, in particular the machine that could make accurate screw threads. In 1820 he combined with another famous engineer, Joshua Field (1757-1863), to become Maudslay Sons & Field. Their later machines were often large steam-powered machines for ships and boats that required heavy transport or railways to transport them. It was their engines that powered the *Great Western* steamship that in 1838 crossed the Atlantic, and both men were founder members of the Institute of Civil Engineers.[41]

The Dog and Pot Ironworks [w2.46]

The best-known small iron founders was J. W. Cunningham & Co. at 196 Blackfriars Road on the south west corner of The Cut crossing. The sign hanging over the showroom was a full size brass and wood dog feeding from an iron pot; this sign is to be seen in the Cuming Museum, Southwark, and on numerous coal holes in the area. Their premises grew to several works, in Union Street, Webber Street and others, and the firm was in business from the 1820s, when Dickens as a boy saw 'the golden dog licking a golden pot'. The premises were finally closed after being hit by the same bomb that destroyed The Ring in 1940.

LIGHT INDUSTRY

From about 1810 onwards directories were published giving the names and addresses of their subscribers, many of whom ran light industries selling their wares on the premises or with showrooms or shops nearby. During the nineteenth century their numbers in Lambeth Marsh steadily increased. Many famous names started in the Marsh with hat and shoemakers and clothiers in great numbers. Trussons was founded in 1866 as a menswear shop in Lower Marsh and now is in its fourth generation [w2.5], and Carter and Housten

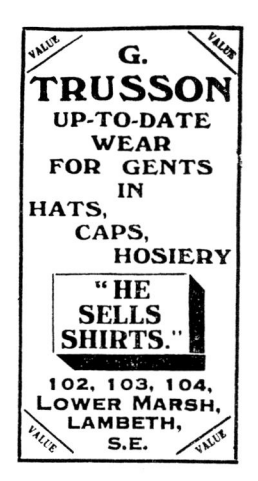

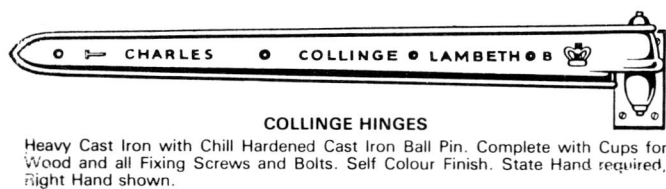

Ill. 42 Trusson and Collinge selling in 1992 after one hundred years

The Rise and Fall of Industry

in 1812 made corsets in Blackfriars Road. Mrs Carter expanded in 1814 with the shop in Stamford Street and later opened a fashion showroom in Regent Street with other branches around the south of England. Burton's and David Greig's had their headquarters in Waterloo Road. John Sainsbury was born in Oakley Street [Baylis Road] and Sainsbury's opened their second shop in Stamford Street; their headquarters still remaining in the vicinity. Small industries served the expanding road transport, with Lambeth Marsh having several coach builders and a wheelwright in Granby Place. The remains of a wheelwright's yard still exist in Tradescant Road, South Lambeth.[42] D.Napier & Son (1808-1958) had their engineering works in York Road starting as general engineers [w4.1]. A century later they were making cars and aeroplanes, and became famous for the Napier aero-engine.

'One of our principal amusements is to watch the gradual progress – the rise and fall – of particular shops ... They are never inhabited for more than two months consecutively, and, we verily believe, have witnessed every retail trade in the Directory. There is one, whose history is a sample of the rest, in whose fate we have taken especial interest, having had the pleasure of knowing it ever since it has been a shop ... It is on the Surrey side of the water – a little distance beyond the Marsh Gate.'

Sketches by Boz. 'Shops and Their Tenants. A Doomed Shop'.

A short length of those original shops still stands in Westminster Bridge Road, in exactly the same state, with their ups and downs still as Dickens described and with nothing changed [w2.20].

OFFICE WORKING AND THE SOUTH BANK

With the continuing success and failure of manufacturers in Lambeth Marsh into this century, each new venture became a cleaner and less heavy industry that reflected London's change to a commercial city. When the 1939-45 war came only a few industries remained along the river, such as Clowes, Bowaters and Eldorado's ice cream works, and even fewer survived the intensive destruction of that war. After the war and into a financial boom, the shipping trade required larger ships and the Tilbury docks were developed to take them, leaving no ships or barges coming to Lambeth Marsh.

As Lambeth Marsh industry declined it was replaced slowly from 1900 by offices. Initially offices were related to local industries which grew and spread

Ill. 43 Dog and Pot coal hole

nationwide but still needed head offices in London. The first large offices came when the LCC needed to expand from its first premises in New Spring Gardens, off the Mall. Already owning a stone wharf on Lambeth Marsh's river bank, it acquired more land there, including 'Pedlar's Acre', to build the County Hall that still stands [w4.17]. The design for the building was won in an architectural competition by Ralph Knott. The first block on the river front was opened in 1922 by George V. The building of the other blocks, that included those on York Road, Chicheley Street and the Island Block [York Road/Westminster Bridge Road], continued into the 1970s. The first-floor members' rooms are expensively finished with monolithic marble columns donated from Italy and with other marble from all over Europe, including Connemara in Ireland, Ashburton in Devon and Belgium and Spain.

In the inter-war years other offices were built in the Marsh but the next major change occurred as a result of the final destruction of industry by the 1939-45 war. In 1951 as a celebration of Britain's post-war rejuvenation, the Festival of Britain took place on the South Bank, and was built on the war-devastated industrial land newly acquired by the London County Council. The South Bank, one of the first designated Comprehensive Redevelopment Areas in the country, stretched from Westminster Bridge to Waterloo Bridge and was extended in the 1980s along the river to Blackfriars Bridge.[43] The development became one large building site that swallowed all of Lambeth Marsh on the river side of the railway.

The South Bank Comprehensive Redevelopment Area was to create for the nation an up-to-date centre of entertainment (described in detail on p. 115) and offices. The area would include concert halls, theatres, film theatre and art gallery that would also help to revitalise the local life of the Marsh down the Waterloo Road, Lower Marsh and The Cut. The South Bank buildings also included Britain's tallest office building of the day, the Shell tower of 1960, as well as the massive County Hall extensions. Further office development has continued on and off ever since and has now spread downstream to Blackfriars Bridge and beyond. The latest wave of South Bank offices have included several Fleet Street newspapers moving to within a few paces of the old site of the William Clowes printing works.

Ill. 44 Pedlar's Acre window in Tradescant Museum

4
LANDLORDS
– Kennington Manor – Lambeth Manor –
– Bishops of Rochester and Carlisle –
– Katherine, Howards and Culpepers –
– Paris Garden Manor and St George's Fields –

Lambeth Marsh was bordered to the east by Paris Garden Manor and St George's Fields [Imperial War Museum] and to the west and north by the Thames, but on its southern border to Water Lambeth it was ill defined (see ill. 45). The confusion to the south is mainly due to the fact that the two manors of Lambeth and Kennington have always themselves been very confused:

'Whether this town [Lambeth Marsh] is within the bounds of Kennington or Lambeth the jury is ignorant.'[44]

Thus in spite of its fourteenth-century name, Lambeth Marsh is best defined as a geographical area that has always managed to defy the bureaucratic mind and which has never been a single manor, vestry, ward, borough or parish. However, the confusion being only between the two, albeit powerful, manors of Lambeth and Kennington gave it an unexpected advantage. Lambeth Marsh appears to have been exempt from excessive exploitation, leaving the entrepreneurial spirit of the less wealthy to flourish. It became famous, or maybe infamous, for its bustling low life, it became London's industrial artery along the Thames, it had for a while London's largest street market, The Cut, and was, for five hundred years up to the present, an important entertainment centre for London and the nation.

KENNINGTON MANOR

'Within the Brixton Hundred in the holding of Teodoric the Goldsmith, who also held it before in the time of Edward the Confessor . . . it was then assessed for 5 hides, now for 1 hide and 3 virgate. The land is for 2 ploughs. In demesne there is one plough: and 4 villeins and 3 borders with 2 ploughs. There is 1 serf; and 4 acres of meadow. It was and is worth 3 pounds.'
Domesday quotation for Kennington Manor.

William de Fortibus, the Earl of Albemarle, then held Kennington Manor and on his death in 1260 it was probably conveyed to Richard de Bolebec. Richard's son, Hugh de Bolebec, had a daughter (married to Hugh Delavel) who sold it in 1276/7 to John de Warren, Earl of Surrey. John Plantagenet, the Earl's grandson also Earl of Warren and Surrey, granted the Manor to Edward II in 1316. The small amount of Lambeth Marsh property left for the Earls of Surrey and Warren (Dukes of Norfolk) is described below under the Howards, as these two families came together when Sir John Howard became the 1st (Howard) Duke of Norfolk in 1483.

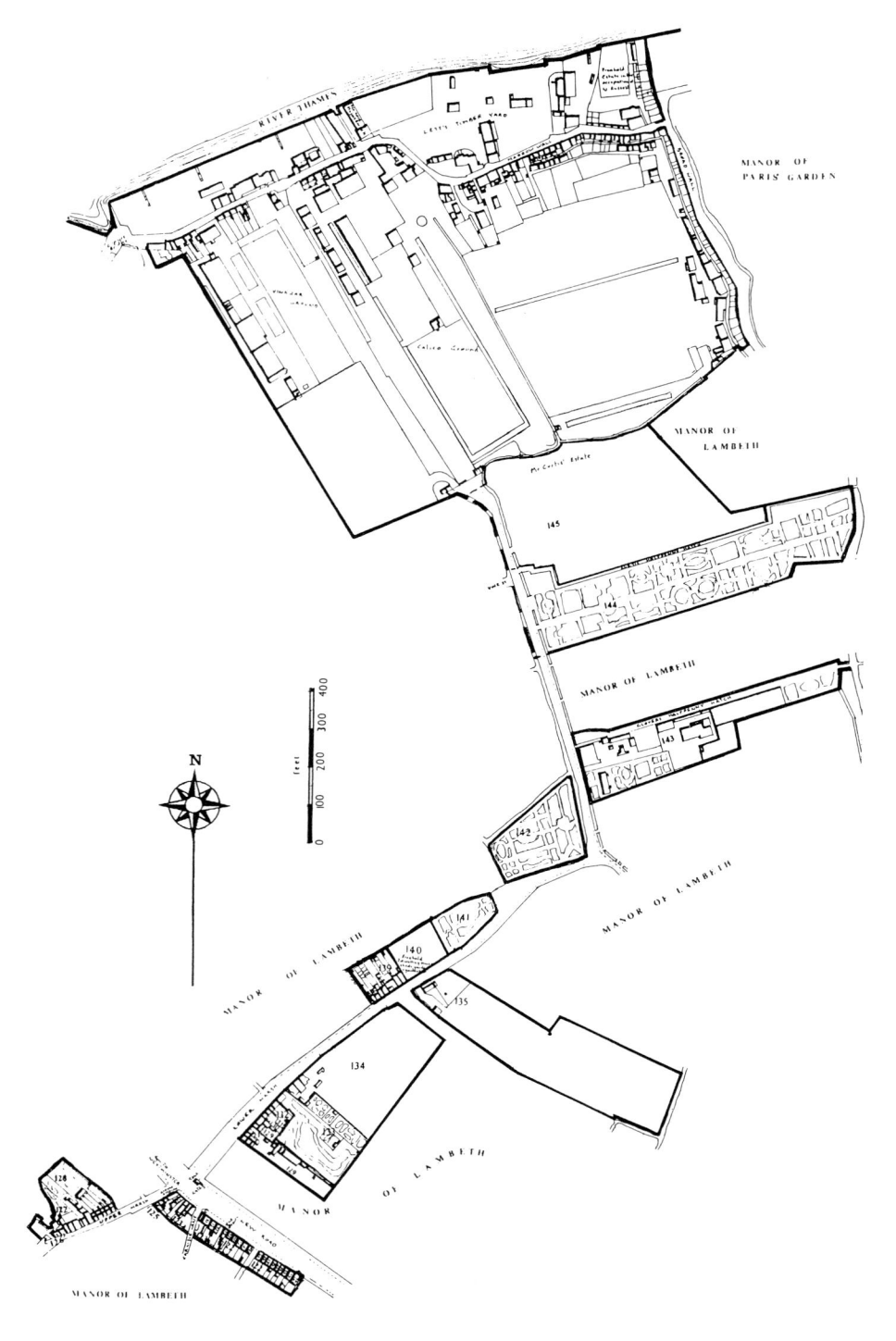

Ill. 45 Lambeth Marsh, Kennington Manor

In 1322 Kennington was granted to Hugh de Dispenser and when he was beheaded in 1326 it reverted to Edward II, worth £20. In 1327 he granted it to Elizabeth de Burgh, a relation. In 1337 she exchanged it with the King for land in Suffolk. Later in 1337, by a charter dated from Woodstock, Edward III granted the Manors of Kennington and Vauxhall with a meadow in Lambeth and Newington (again altering the boundaries) to Edward, Earl of Chester and Duke of Cornwall (the Black Prince), to be held by him and his heirs, heirs to the Kingdom, and not to be granted to any other. There being no son or heir it reverts to the Crown until such time as there is an heir apparent. Except for the Commonwealth period this grant has remained operative up to the present day, apart from sales and boundary changes.[45]

The Hodskinson and Middleton survey with maps of 1785-6 show the whole manor. This is a remarkable survey, drawn to a very large scale, dimensioned and with privies and wells drawn in back gardens and all trees over a certain girth recorded. The manor is in two parts, with Princes Meadow in the north between Blackfriars and Waterloo Bridges and the main manor at Kennington, joined by a string of pieces along Lambeth Marsh, and along the River at Water Lambeth [Albert Embankment]. The manor house at Kennington Cross was excavated and recorded in 1972.

In Lambeth Marsh, the survey indicates North Lambeth's oldest residence, number 17 Lower Marsh, a Queen Anne house of around 1804, now refaced but whose rear façades remain intact. All the maps and surveys up to and including the Enclosure Survey of 1806 clearly show how the area of Lambeth Marsh was broken into very small pieces of land belonging to only a few landlords.

LAMBETH MANOR

The first mention of Lambeth Manor is in the story of King Hardicanute dying while feasting at Lambhithe in 1042, and immediately at the feast the usurper Edward placed the crown on his own head. Edward the Confessor, crowned in 1042, gave the manor to his sister Goda, who first built a church in 1062 and still held it at Domesday 1086. Rufus confirmed the church and manor in the See of Rochester where it remained for a hundred years. In 1190 Glenville Bishop of Rochester gave 24 acres (not all the manor) to Baldwin just before Baldwin set off for the crusades. Baldwin laid out a house and chapel and without time to build was killed in the crusade in the same year, 1190. After many quarrels Hubert Walter became Archbishop of Canterbury, being opposed by the monks of Canterbury who did not like him so close to the King in London.

In 1197 Rochester granted the whole Manor of Lambeth to Canterbury, apart from land for the Bishop of Rochester's own house and a way to the river. This later became Carlisle House and Stangate Ferry (see p. 71). Archbishop Walter proceeded to build his first chapel but the monks in 1199 pleaded against it to the Pope and the chapel was demolished. In 1200 the Pope and monks finally agreed to let him build his own residence and other buildings at Lambeth. The first written evidence of archbishops living there was in 1207 with Archbishop Langton sending letters from Lambeth.

Up to the break-up of manors in the 1800s Lambeth was in the hands of the church, except in 1648 in Cromwell's time when hatred of the established

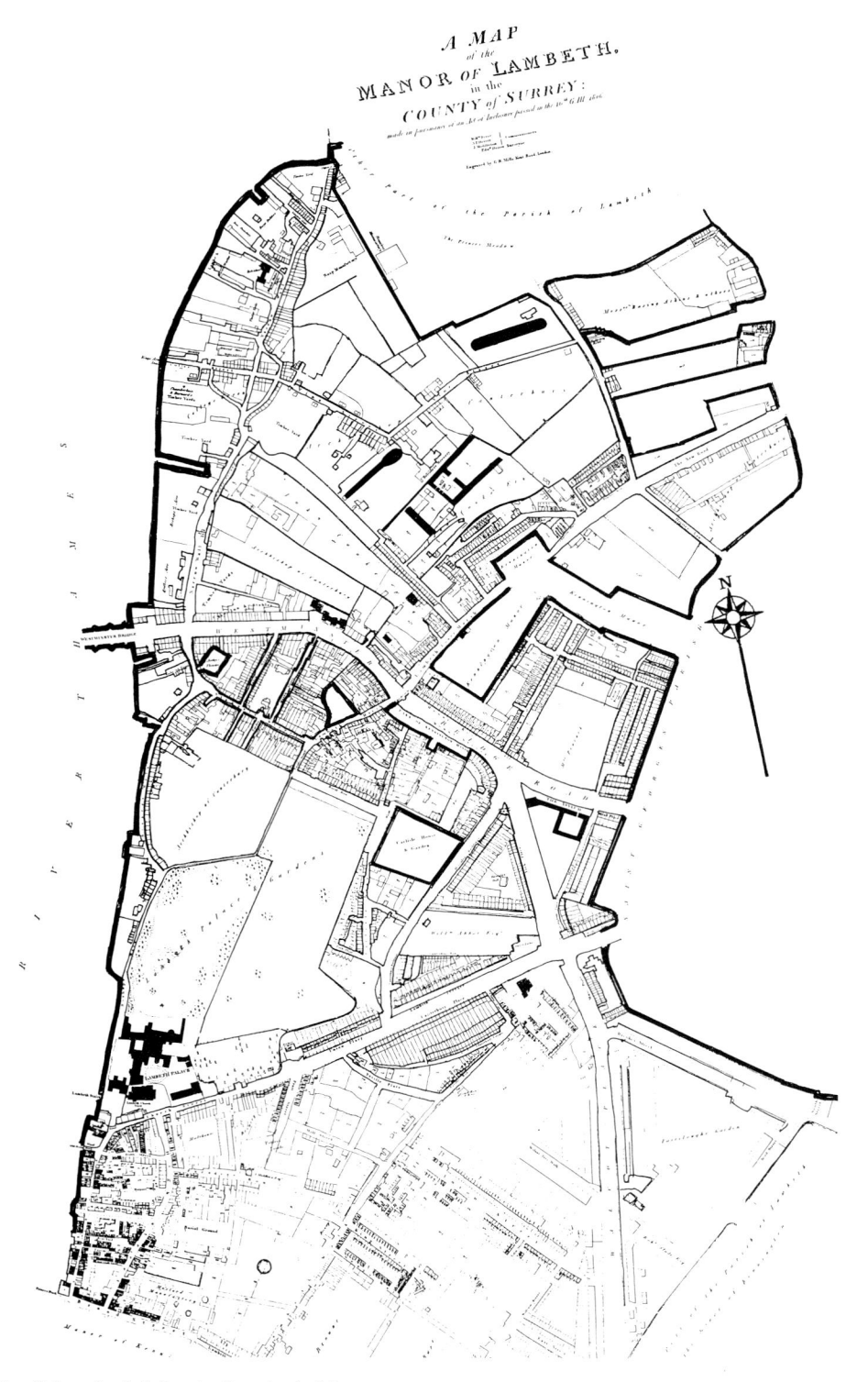

Ill. 46 Lambeth Marsh, Lambeth Manor

church was at its height. Sir John Wollaston and others, trustees for the sale of episcopal property in the Commonwealth, sold the manor of Lambeth for £7,073.0.8 to Thomas Scott of Marlow and Matthew Hardy of London, a draper. The sale consisted of '4 acres of ground, the 5-acre park with 2 fish ponds, Sowter's (shoemaker's) lands next to the park containing 14 acres, 5 closes of marsh ground lying between the Thames and Lambeth Marsh containing 28 acres, 5 acres of meadow ground lying in Lott Mead and commonly called the wild Marsh, and areas south of the manor in Northwood'. In an attempt to demolish the power of the church, it was intended to pull down the palace, including the barge houses whose materials were valued at £6,000, but the plan was never implemented.

Sancroft was made Archbishop of Canterbury in 1650 and Lambeth Palace was restored to the church.

LA PLACE, later Carlisle house [w4.35]

From 1197 the Bishops of Rochester had kept their plot of land with a right of way to their ferry from Stangate [w4.23] over to Westminster. Rochester House, the first of many on the plot, continued to be the London residence of the Bishop, who applied a toll on his ferry. Though it could not carry horses, the ferry was more convenient than its rival, the Archbishop's horseferry at Lambeth Palace, as it went direct to Westminster and was closer to London Bridge and the roads from Kent. In 1540 Henry VIII made Rochester exchange the land with the Bishop of Carlisle; the plot was renamed Carlisle House, a name that lasted till the land's demise when the railway came in 1848.

1197	First building by Bishop of Rochester.
1539	Second building by Bishop of Carlisle.
1647	Parliament sold it to Mathew Hardy.
1660	Reverted to See of Carlisle.
1690	Part a pottery.
1721	Pottery lease with Canterbury.
1723	Pottery Insurance.
1730	A tavern.
1739-1827	Carlisle Academy for Young Gentlemen.[46]
1827	Demolished and redeveloped.
1848	Railway demolished all except a row of houses in Hercules Road, standing 1990.

EARL OF SURREY AND WARREN AND KATHERINE HOWARD

As described earlier, the Plantagenet Earls of Surrey gave the manor of Kennington to the Duke of Cornwall, reducing their land in the area to just their house opposite St Mary Lambeth and a plot at Cuper's Gardens.[47] However, theirs was, and still is, the senior dukedom in the land, and in Henry VIII's day the 4th Duke of Norfolk was still a force to be reckoned with and soon embroiled Katherine Howard, his niece, in his power struggles. There is little to show today of her parents' two families or of Norfolk House: some monuments in St Mary Lambeth and a small alley off Lambeth Road called Norfolk Row [w4.30], the site of which was excavated in 1990 and the footings of the house found.

Katherine Howard was born in 1521 and both her parents, Joyce Culpeper and Lord Edmund Howard, had died by the time she was ten. She was brought up by her step-grandmother, the Dowager Duchess, Agnes Tilney, and on visits to London lived in Norfolk house in Lambeth opposite St Mary Lambeth (where Agnes and her aunt Elizabeth, the Countess of Wiltshire, Anne Boleyn's mother, were both buried).

The Howard family, which had the titles of Duke of Norfolk, and the Earl of Warren and Surrey and Arundel, was desperate to keep power, having previously failed the Tudors at Flodden Field and now again Henry VIII over his rows with the Catholic faith. Katherine's uncle Thomas, the 4th Duke, had sent another of his nieces, Anne Boleyn, to her execution in 1536 to help remain in favour with the King. By 1540 when Katherine was nineteen, the King was looking yet again for a girl who might bear him an heir, and the Duke was still looking for favours. With everyone at Court fearful for their heads because of the King's flights of fancy and tantrums, what else could people say when the King's eyes fell on Katherine but that she was a virgin? The Duke of Norfolk had anyway few scruples and was mostly concerned with his own fortunes and so encouraged the marriage of Katherine as Henry's fifth wife. However, within two years the enemies of Norfolk, the Seymours, knowing that life for young girls was never totally innocent, set out to prove that Katherine had lovers.

Like most rich households the Norfolks lived as an extended family with brothers, sisters, cousins, distant relatives, teachers and all, and on their trips to London would stay at Norfolk House. Children grew up quickly in those days, and at nineteen Katherine was a vivacious woman who gave mixed parties in the women's dormitories, verified by the several witnesses at her trial. There was nothing to hide in this and it was common in those days. The King himself was no different: for twenty years Henry had Anne Boleyn's sister Mary as his mistress and openly made their son the Duke of Richmond. It was easy, then, for Norfolk's enemies to find those who had no shame in admitting their liaisons with Katherine, especially as Katherine at the time was unmarried.[48]

Katherine herself was far too flattered by the high life of Court to realise the danger she put herself into, just by marrying Henry, but her open flirtation with Thomas Culpeper, a distant cousin at Court, is more difficult to understand. Maybe she thought she could handle Henry and that his love for her would win through, but she did not reckon on the scheming of her enemies, the Seymours. What none of the guilty youngsters thought possible was that Henry would execute them all. Katherine, Thomas Culpeper, her kinsman Francis Derham, her music master Henry Mannock [Manox] and her cousin's scheming wife Lady Rochford were all found guilty under the judgement of her uncle Thomas Howard and executed in 1542.

Katherine's mother Joyce was a Colepeper [Culpeper] of Preston Hall over the river Medway from Aylesford in Kent and was the co-heir of Sir Richard Culpeper. The Culpepers were extensive feudal landlords, with branches all over Kent and Sussex, some later famous at Leeds Castle and another branch with the 'Herbal' Nicholas Culpeper (1616-54). There are few other records of Joyce, but she must have been a remarkable woman to have given birth thirteen times. Joyce married twice, both times into the parish of St Mary Lambeth. First she married Ralph Leigh, the Lord of the Manor of Stockwell and Under Sheriff of London, by whom she had five children with two surviving, the future heirs to Stockwell Manor.[49] Following his death she married Sir Edmund Howard, brother of the Duke of Norfolk, and had eight more children (see Appendix p. 158).

Katherine (b. 1521) was the fourth of seven Howards who survived to adulthood. No wonder Henry VIII thought that Katherine might produce an heir for him. Joyce Culpeper, then, united two important Lambeth families, the Norfolks and the Leighs, and it was in 1522 that these two families together founded new north and south side chapels in St Mary Lambeth. When it was rebuilt in the 1850s both the Catholic family names were dropped from the chapels but they do still contain the memorials as indicated on the family tree.

PARIS GARDEN MANOR AND ST GEORGE'S FIELDS

The two adjoining areas to Lambeth Marsh are briefly described here as neither of their landlords wielded much power and with the coming of urbanisation in the nineteenth century the roads and property ownerships soon made the areas indistinguishable from the Lambeth Marsh and Southwark.

Paris Garden Manor [w2.43]

Paris Garden Manor was a small manor of a hundred acres on the Thames between Southwark and Lambeth Marsh.[50] Its boundary is still defined by roads that earlier ran along a well-defined water-filled boundary dyke. Starting at the Thames, upstream of the Oxo tower at Barge House Stairs the boundary passes along Hatfields to The Cut where it is broken for a short length, before continuing round its corner east along Boundary Row/Pocock Street till it meets Great Suffolk Street [formerly Gravel Lane]; here it turns north again to meet the river [near the Founders Arms]. The manor was first mentioned in 1113 and had a moated Manor House shown on early maps and engravings [now under the Blackfriars railway crossing Southwark Street]. The manor was first developed when William Angell sold it off in 1660 and the new parish church of Christ Church and houses were built. The first developments had poor foundations on undrained land and Christ Church Blackfriars Road, consecrated in 1671, had to be demolished in 1738. The second church was built between 1738 and 1741 with an elegant cupola bell tower and stood till bombed in 1941; the present church on the same site now hides amongst the mature churchyard trees, where the stone for the 1819 watch-house can still be seen. Blackfriars Road, built in 1769, cut the manor of Paris Garden in two, adding the area west of Blackfriars Road to Lambeth Marsh, in spirit if not legally.

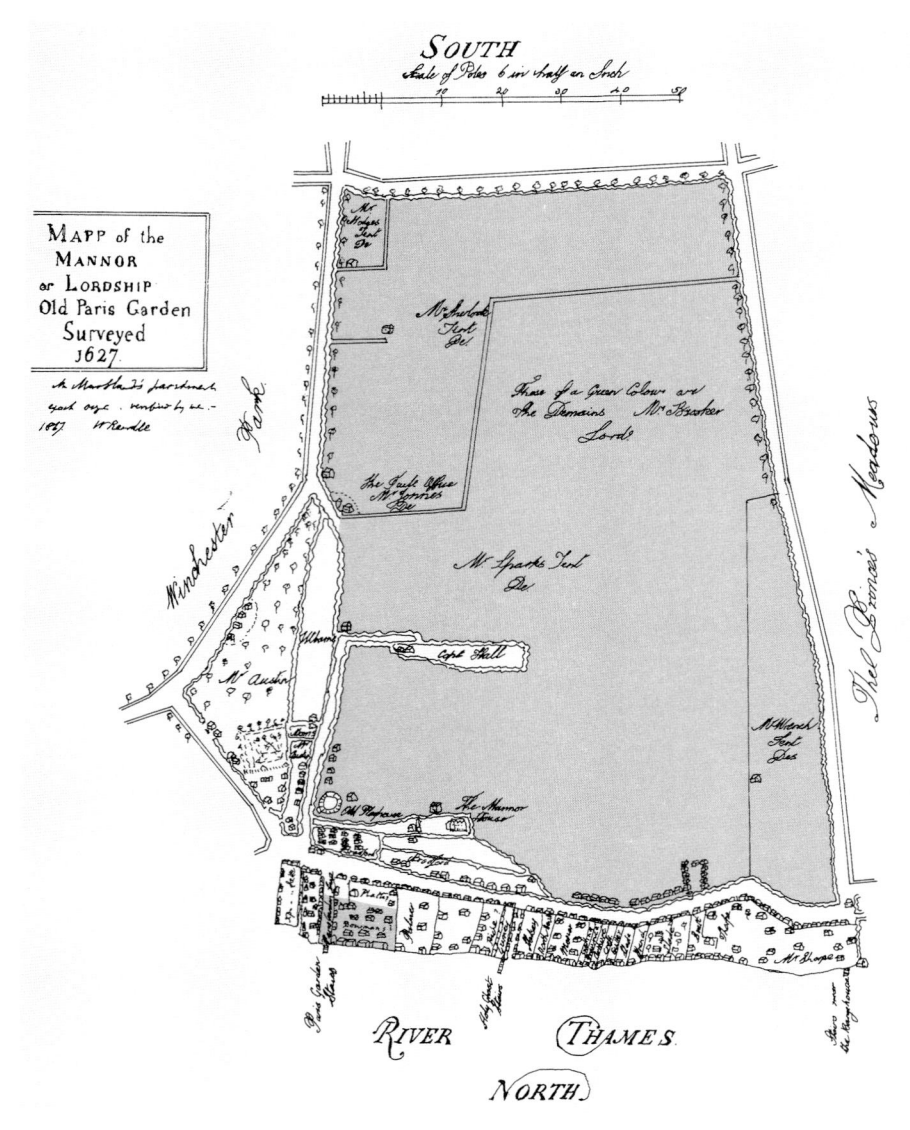

Ill. 47 Paris Garden Manor in 1566

St George's Fields [w2.32]

St George's Fields was about twenty acres to the east of Lambeth Marsh, between it and Borough High Street. Most of the area was claimed and administered by the Bridge House Estate. The Fields were not Common Land but were for centuries used as such, and in the 1780s the matter was taken to court. The Fields were ill drained and marshy, being even lower than Lambeth Marsh without any higher sand-banks. Up to the end of the eighteenth century the Bridge House estates succeeded in preventing building but never spent any money on drainage or on fencing the paths or roads. The Fields, seemingly an empty space, were often used by the maps' publishers to put their ornate label or map keys, making it even more difficult for historians to know

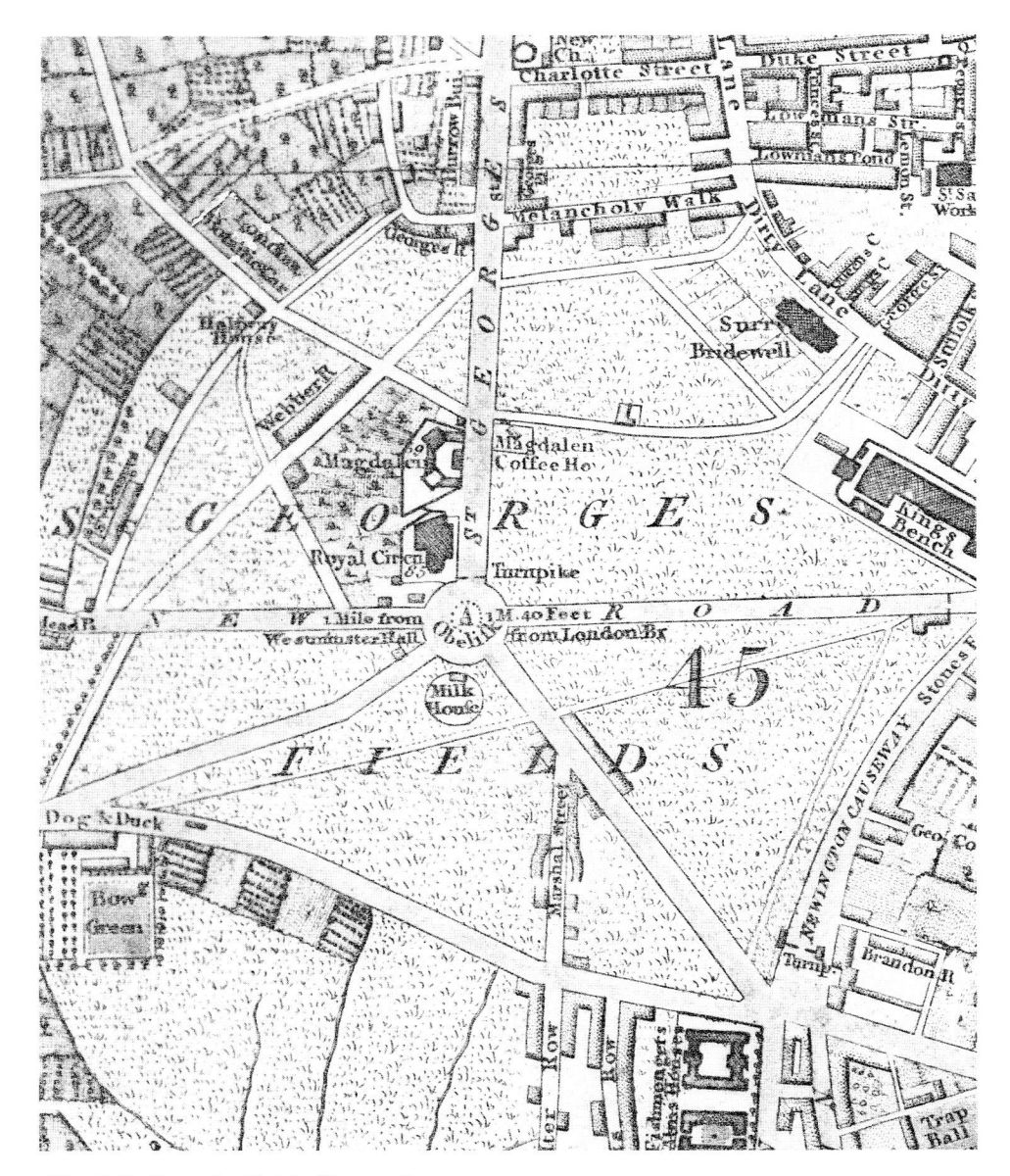

Ill. 48 St George's Fields, Cary 1787

what little went on there. With the pressure for new building created by the Westminster and Blackfriars Bridges, many tenants were building and subletting without permission. On plots bordering Lambeth Marsh speculators were able to play one landlord against another, referring to them as in the Fields when actually they were the Archbishop's or Duchy of Cornwall's. By 1800, after numerous new surveys by all the landlords the boundaries were better defined and the Fields became part of St George the Martyr, Southwark, with the border to Lambeth Marsh along the line of the old Neckinger stream. Described here as part of Lambeth Marsh are most of the buildings and the roads north of Brook Drive.

5
RURAL LIFE TILL 1820
– Introduction – Pepys pubs – gardens –
– Curtis's London Botanic Garden –
– James Sowerby – Gilbert White – Lambeth Marsh paintings –

INTRODUCTION

Until 1800 London was very much the same size as cathedral cities are now in the 1990s. Canterbury, Salisbury, Lincoln and Ely, each with a population of just five hundred thousand today, are like London used to be, with fields and rural living within easy walking of the centre. London then had its water meadows, here on the south side of the Thames at Lambeth Marsh, that provided a green undeveloped finger within view of St Paul's Cathedral. Many of the following stories show the importance of this green finger leading into the centre of London.

Pepys, living near the Tower of London [w1.22] and working in Whitehall, preferred the short direct route to work, cutting off the bend of the river by walking across the fields of Lambeth and avoiding the smelly, disease-ridden journey along the Strand and down Whitehall.

'and so was fain to walk to Lambeth on foot, but it was a very fine frosty walk, and great pleasure in it, but troublesome getting over the River for ice. I to the Duke of Albemarle.'

Pepys, 20 December 1665.

A rural setting with country tracks, some decaying weather-boarded cottages and farm buildings was an easy place for people to hide in, and according to Virtue, Inigo Jones, architect to Charles I, was supposed to have hidden his personal wealth in Lambeth Marsh. The story goes that being on the King's side in the Civil War he hid his wealth here in 1645. When his house in Scotland Yard was searched, little was found, and later when accused he paid only a small fine. What is known is that, when he died on 21 June 1652, his beneficiaries received £4,200, a great deal more than had earlier been accepted in court.[51]

The rural way of life continued into the eighteenth century with farms, country inns and milking parlours.

'Lactaria, the Inventress of the Lactarium in St George's Fields presents her best respects to the Public in general, thanks them for past favours and lives in hope that her milk and syllabubs will be recommended to persons in the country. Boarding school ladies and gentlemen that may come down for the holidays, ladies and gentlemen going to the Magdalen or the Asylum are welcome to leave anything in her care. The room is kept warm with a good fire. There is a conductor to render it a safe place in case of lightning and a garde-robe for ladies. She will accommodate no disorderly people. The well behaved who come to serve her, she is much obliged to, and begs such ladies as are fond of rural elegance will plead for Lactaria.'

Public Advertiser, 18 December 1773.

This milking parlour, supplying fresh milk from the cows in St George's Fields, by then an expensive luxury, is labelled on the 1787 Cary map as a circular building [w2.35]. This unusual circular feature carries on as a pond by 1819 and its footings can still be seen in a back garden in Gladstone Street [w2.35]; they could even be the remains of the fort that was one of a ring of forts built to protect London in the Civil War in 1641.

The manor records and maps as well as the three paintings (see p. 95) show how Lambeth Marsh remained the last of central London's ploughed fields and meadows. The whole of the south bank of the Thames east to Deptford was in the County of Surrey; the Surrey docks in Rotherhithe were in Surrey, whilst in 1785 Southwark was the capital and the largest town of the county. In the same way, the Old Kent Road was the old road *in* Kent, and why else is the Surrey Cricket ground at the Oval, other than that being the best place in the County for it?

Nicholas Hawksmoor the architect, Deputy Comptroller of the King's Works, was a tenant in Lambeth Marsh between 1702 and 1733 [w2.11] at the same plot as the Bell tavern, one of a row of large Queen Anne terraced houses of which number 17 Lower Marsh still stands.[52] Names of pubs and roads are often good indicators of history and rural pubs still existing in Lambeth Marsh are the Windmill in The Cut, the Three Stags, Kennington Road, and the Artichoke [the pub Streets]. Rural road names include Lower Marsh itself, Brook Drive, Pear Tree Walk and Belvedere Road. Further afield Great Suffolk Street is still labelled 'late Gravel Lane' and there is Manor Place off Walworth Road.

In the seventeenth and eighteenth centuries walking-out was a social activity in London, as it still is in small Mediterranean towns today. In the afternoon or evening all of London could be found promenading in the fashionable parks and gardens.[53] The south bank of the Thames, a short ferry crossing from the Cities of both Westminster and London, was well placed for this and other pleasurable activities. Out of reach of the taxes and laws of the two cities, entertainment was open to private enterprise and free to flourish (see Theatres, p. 102).

PEPYS' SOUTH LONDON PUBS

Pepys frequently went to the famous Vauxhall Gardens [w1.14], a mile up river from Lambeth Marsh, and his diaries give a vivid description of his many outings there that often degenerated into bawdy and licentious behaviour on the part of himself and his drinking friends.[54] However, other South London pubs, not actually in London at that time, have had little notice paid to them by historians. The following describes and locates five pubs Pepys visited south of the river.

1. The Halfway House – across the fields from Redriff to Deptford.

'so I home, and there found my wife and Besse gone over the water to Half-way house, and after them, thinking to have gone to Woolwich, but it was too late, so eat a cake and home, and thence by coach to have spoke with Tom Trice about a letter.'

Pepys, 16 April 1664.

The Rocque maps label a 'Halfway House' on the road between Redriff (Rotherhithe) and Deptford. The 1829 Cruchley map labels, in the same position, the 'Red Lion Halfway House' thus linking the two names. The roads on both these maps can be accurately found on the ground as roads still existing. The Red Lion [w1.17] still stands where the old maps place it but renamed in 1990 'Brady's'.

2. Half-the-Way [w2.52]

'Up, and being to go to wait on the Duke of Albemarle . . . and I being unwilling to go by water, it being bitter cold, walked it with my landlady's little boy Christopher to Lambeth, it being a very fine walk and calling at half the way and drank, and so to the Duke of Albemarle.'

Pepys, 27 November 1665.

A careful reading of the quotation reveals that the Rotherhithe 'Halfway House' is *not* being referred to here. Pepys walking to work with a lad from London Bridge to the Westminster Crossing at Stangate would not go five miles out of his way.

The 1787 Cary map of Lambeth labels a pub in the north-west corner of St George's Fields as the 'Halfway House'. Many other maps show a building here but the earlier ones do not label it. The pub's position is at the corner of Webber Street and Gray Street, exactly half-way from London Bridge to the Westminster crossing at Stangate, and named the 'Halfway House' till 1985. As part of the current widespread practice of disowning our heritage, the pub has been renamed the 'Stage Door' [w2.51]. The old path across St George's Fields is the present line of Webber Street and is shown as a dotted line as early as 1572 on the Stilliard map.

3. The King's Head [w2.42]

'Up, and after an hour or two's talk with my poor wife, who gives me more and more content every day than other, I abroad by coach to Westminster, and there met with Mrs Martin [Mrs Lane], and she and I over the water to Stangate, and after a walk in the fields to the King's Head, and there spent an hour or two with pleasure with her, and eat a tansy and so parted, and I to the New Exchange'.[55]

Pepys, 20 April 1666.

The Canterbury Arms was in the seventeenth century a tavern called the King's Head with its frontage on what is now Upper Marsh, and is the most likely candidate for Pepys' several visits to this tavern. However there is also an old tavern 'after a walk in the fields', on the boundary between Paris Garden Manor and St George's Fields [Blackfriars Bridge Road/Surrey Row] still called the 'Old Kings Head' pub.

4. The Old House in Lambeth Marsh [w2.12]

'and away to Westminster Hall, and there 'light of Mrs Lane, and plotted with her to go over to the old house in Lambeth Marsh, and there eat and drank, and had my pleasure of her twice, she being the strangest woman in talk of

Ill. 49 Bonner's House prior to demolition

love to her husband sometimes, and sometimes again she do not care for him, and yet willing enough to allow me a liberty of doing what I would with her. So spending 5s or 6s upon her, I could do what I would, and after an hour's stay and more, back again and set her ashore there again.'

Pepys, 25 July 1664.

There are several Victorian Histories that refer to Bonner's House as the 'Old House in Lambeth Marsh' and include engravings of it, but the 1806 Enclosure Survey labels it precisely at the Westminster Bridge Road end.[56] The site is now an office block, that before being bombed in the 1939-45 war, was a public swimming bath. Whether it was the only old house that Pepys could have referred to is another matter.

5. The Three Mariners

'I to Whitehall, and there with Captain Rolt and Ferrers we went to Lambeth to drink our morning draft, where at the Three Mariners, a place noted for their ale, we went and staid awhile very merry, and so away. And wanting a boat, we found Captain Bun going down the river, and so we went into his boat having a lady with him, and he landed them at Westminster and me at the Bridge.'

Pepys, 12 June 1661.

This pub is well documented from Norden's 1615 Survey and in consequent rentals on what was Fore Street. When the Albert Embankment was built land was actually given up to the river at this point, so the site for this pub is now below the high-water level in the river opposite where the present Salamanca Street hits the embankment road.

GARDENS

In an area where rents were low or even disputed, opening a garden to the public was yet another way for an individual to make an income. The Hodskinson and Middleton survey of 1785, drawn to a large scale, shows many large plots that contained no buildings but had decoratively laid out plant beds and were surrounded by water courses, the usual boundary around all the fields in the Marsh. On occasions these developed into open areas at the backs of taverns with attractive garden walks, drinking booths and fountains, that at Cuper's Garden grew into a full-scale entertainment centre with orchestra, fireworks and regular live entertainment. Lambeth Marsh also had garden nurseries and London's first Botanic Garden, which William Curtis opened to the public in 1779.

John Tradescant's Garden 1634-62 [W1.15]

Both John Tradescant the Elder (d. 1638) and John the Younger (1608-62) were buried in a tomb carved with their exploits, still to be seen at St Mary Lambeth [the Museum of Garden History and centre for the Tradescant Trust W4.27]. The two Tradescants became famous for their collection of curios, their garden and their many new plant introductions. The garden and two adjoining houses were leased as part of the Vauxhall Escheat (see location and list of tenants [W1.15]) with the larger house being that of his friend and patron Elias Ashmole and opened to the public with its first known catalogue published in 1634. Although out of the Marsh, the large house and gardens tie up with William Curtis's Botanic Garden via his friends Ben and Thomas White who lived in it a hundred years later (1787). Thomas White was Gilbert White's brother and like all good scientists was intently interested in the work of his colleagues (see Gilbert White and William Curtis's London Botanic Garden p. 88).

Both Samuel Pepys and John Evelyn wrote of John Tradescant, and the following quotations from Evelyn recall how Ashmole founded the Ashmolean Museum in Oxford using the Tradescant collection, called the Ark. (See Appendix p. 146 for all Evelyn's South London quotations.)

'and thence to John Tradescant's Museum, in which the chiefest rarities were, in my opinion, the ancient Roman, Indian and other nations armour, shields and weapons: some habits of curiously-coloured and wrought feathers, one from the Phoenix wing as tradition goes. Other innumerable things there were, printed in his catalogue by Mr Ashmole, to whom after the death of the widow they are bequeathed, and by him designed as a gift to Oxford.'

Evelyn, 17 September 1657.

'Went to see Mr Elias Ashmole's Library and curiosities at Lambeth. He has divers Mss, but most of them astrological, to study he is addicted, tho' I believe not learned, but very industrious, as his History of the Order of the Garter proves. He show'd me a toad included in amber. The prospect from a turret is very fine, it being near London, and yet not discovering any house about the country. The famous John Tradescant bequeathed his repository to this gentleman, who has given them to the University of Oxford, and erected a lecture on them, over the laboratory, in imitation of the Royal Society.'

Evelyn, 23 July 1678.

Rural Life till 1820 81

'I supp'd this night at Lambeth at my old friends, Mr Elias Ashmole's, with my Lady Clarendon, the Bishop of St Asaph, and were treated at a great feast.'

Evelyn, 9 July 1685.

Wenceslas Hollar, 1605-77 (See Appendix p. 148 for biography)

The above reference to Ashmole's History of the Order of the Garter makes a further connection to Lambeth Marsh. The Earls of Surrey (Dukes of Norfolk and Arundel, see p. 71) were the third most important landlords in Lambeth Marsh, who in addition to having Norfolk House opposite St Mary Lambeth also owned a derelict garden in Lambeth Marsh [under Waterloo roundabout]. After the Restoration the garden became Cuper's Garden (1691-1753, teas served till 1759, see p. 83).

Ill. 50 Tradescant's and Captain Bligh's tombs

Ill. 51 The Camberwell Beauty butterfly caught in 1793

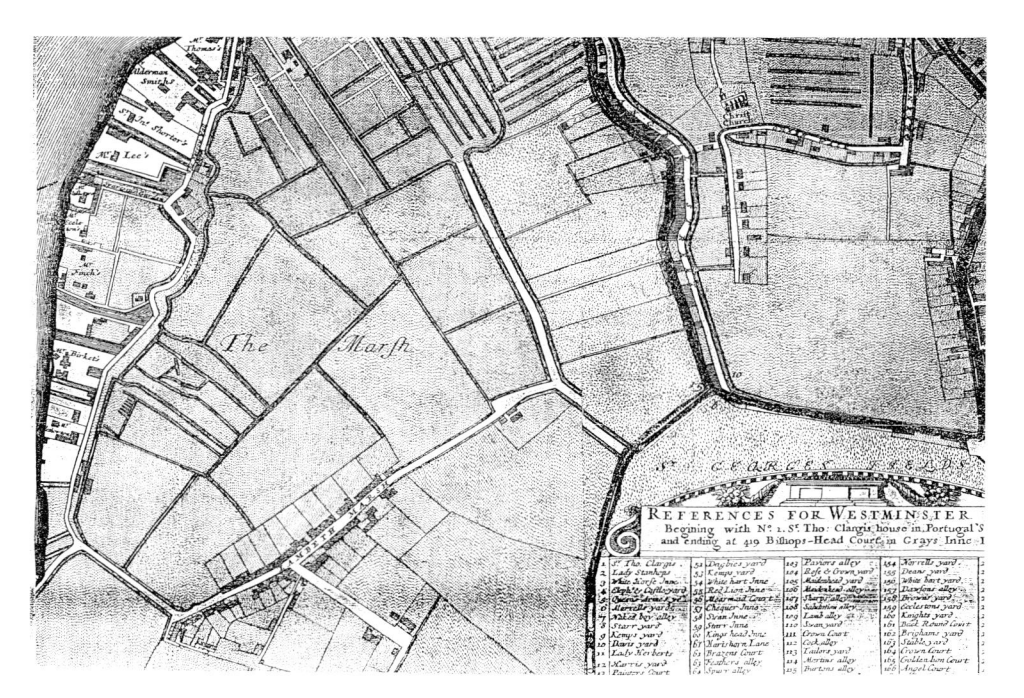

Ill. 52 Morgan's map 1782

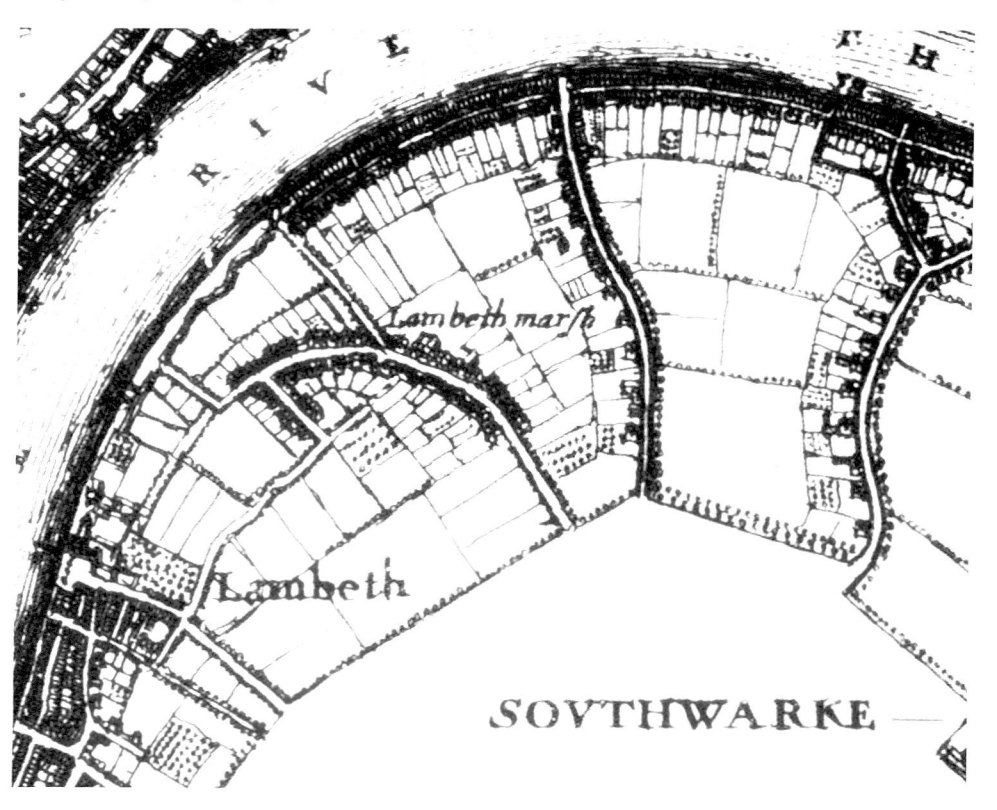

Ill. 53 Hollar's map before the Fire

Rural Life till 1820

In Ashmole's time Thomas Howard (d. 1646) lost the dukedom, and kept only the Earl of Surrey and Arundel title, generally being known as the Collector Earl.[57] He spent most of his life banished to the continent, sending the fruits of his collecting back to Arundel House in the Strand, which overflowed across the river to his garden in Lambeth Marsh. After the Earl's death the dukedom was restored to his grandson Henry and as described below many of the Earl's treasures joined the Tradescants' collection in the Ashmolean Museum at Oxford.

'When I saw these precious monuments miserably neglected and scattered up and down about the garden, and other parts of Arundel House, and how exceedingly the corrosive air of London impaired them, I procured him (Mr Henry Howard of Norfolk [in 1672 the 6th Duke]) to bestow them on the University of Oxford.'

Evelyn, 17 September 1667.

Whilst in Germany the Collector Earl discovered and employed the engraver Wenceslas Hollar (1607-77). Hollar was the engraver for Ashmole's History of the Order of the Garter and lived at one time in Larkhall village [Larkhall Rise, Stockwell], a short distance from Ashmole in South Lambeth Road.[58] Hollar must also have become familiar with Lambeth Marsh as two of his much published London views show it well, the first his panorama from the tower of Lambeth Palace and the second his view of London from Southwark. His famous maps of 'London before the Fire' were engraved in several versions. Lambeth Marsh was always labelled as separate from Lambeth. To achieve the incredible detail of showing individual houses, boundaries and paths, Hollar had to use a spyglass and eventually ruined his eyesight.

Hollar's and Morgan's maps, drawn just sixteen years apart, show features that still exist, three hundred years later, clearly demonstrating their accuracy; but when compared they do show significant differences. Morgan's map shows the short length of what is now Westminster Bridge Road leading to a right-angled bend at Hercules Road, a very strange way to build a road pattern, but Hollar's earlier map shows a road on the line of the present Baylis Road, making a much more explicable junction.

At the cab entrance to Waterloo station in Lambeth Marsh there still exists the wide pavement that Hollar shows as a road junction at the village centre. This road is also recorded in the 1670s as a way out of the back of Cuper's Garden to Lambeth Marsh and London Bridge.[59] However, the later Morgan map shows only a vestigial widening with no road junction and no buildings.

Hollar shows the east end of Lower Marsh in a slow curve that would now be under the playground [Waterloo/Baylis Road] and continuing under the Waterloo Road and the old David Greig building; the curved ends can still be seen in Lower Marsh and in Webber Street as bends in the roads.

Cuper's garden 1691-1759 [w3.34]

Boydel Cuper (also spelt Boyden and Cooper), claiming to be the gardener of the Earl of Arundel, opened his pleasure garden to the public sometime before 1691; the 1634 records quote Abraham Boydel Cuper, probably his father, as tenant of the Earl. Although the lease and copyhold changed through many hands, Cuper continued to build up a thriving entertainment centre on the site [under the Waterloo Bridge roundabout]. The gardens soon became known

Ill. 54 Hollar's engraving of insects

as Cupid's Garden, open through the six months of summer and using many of the Arundel marbles mentioned earlier by Evelyn as statues along the walks and arbour.[60] In 1738 Cuper died, leaving the business to his wife Elizabeth. Later that same year Ephraim Evans and his wife took over the running of the Gardens; they improved the entertainment there and built an orchestra or bandstand, shown on many engravings. In 1740 Ephraim died and his wife continued the business. On the river road [Belvedere Road] Widow Evans also had the Feathers pub that operated throughout the year and in 1741 the 'Fire Music' from Handel's work 'Atlanta' was performed complete with fireworks and fire pump. Watchmen were provided in the gardens and booths and for anyone leaving by the back way to Lambeth Marsh and on across St George's Fields to the City. Most transport in London in the days before bridges was by water, and customers normally arrived at Cuper's stairs where the stream at Cooper's bridge entered the Thames.

There is always a 'law and order' element in a community and in the seventeenth century these were the rich Dukes who owned London north of the river and who were envious of the low taxes in Surrey. In 1752 an Act was passed requiring a licence 'for regulating entertainment and punishing persons keeping a disorderly house' not only in Westminster and the City but for twenty miles around, and of course the Widow Evans' licence was refused. Not to be put off she reopened the Feathers and Garden the next year in 1753 as a tea garden and in 1755 revived her entertainments, advertising them as private subscription-only functions. The latter ploy does not appear to have worked, as it reverted to being a tea-house in 1756, and the last private concert took place in 1759. The Feathers tavern, however, continued and Thomas James was lessee in 1760.[61]

The site of Cuper's Garden remained derelict till 1769, when the lease was taken over by Mark Beaufoy (see p. 58). In 1816 Waterloo Bridge was opened and the Feathers tavern rebuilt at its side as an unusual multi-storey building,

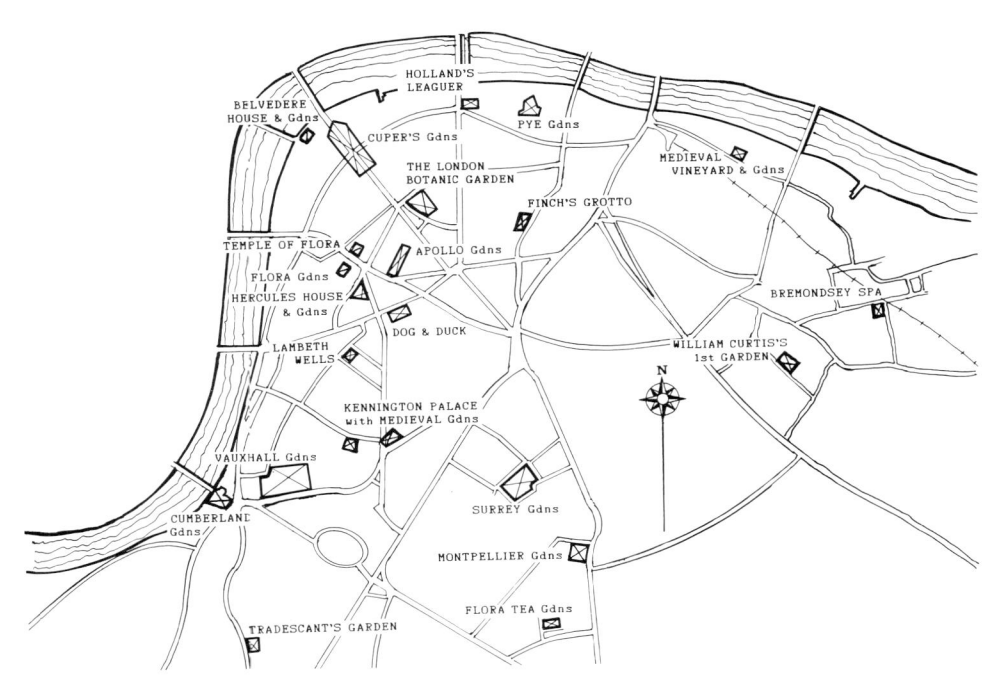

Ill. 55 Gardens open to the public

entered at the low level from Belvedere Road or from the upper Waterloo Bridge approach. This tavern, still remembered today by residents as a place for courting, remained here for 150 years till it was demolished in the 1950s to make way for a new approach road to the bridge.

Apollo Gardens [w2.26]

The Apollo Gardens, like all the plots in Lambeth Marsh, were surrounded by ditches filled with flowing river water and were located in the area now defined by the houses in Pearman Street. Walter Glagget opened the gardens in October 1788 with an entertainment in the concert hall, large enough for a fine-toned organ played by Jonathan Battishill, a band of seventy performers, a domed ceiling and an audience of nearly 1,300 people.

The gardens were continuously improved and in 1790 had elegant pavilions and alcoves. In 1792 new music by Messrs Haydn and Pleyel was performed and Glagget boasted of nobility and gentry that vaunted the 'Chastity and Dignity' of the place. By 1793 the magistrates suppressed yet another of Lambeth Marsh's entertainments and Glagget went bankrupt; the orchestra house was sold to Sydney Gardens in Bath. The site remained ruinous till built on between 1799 and 1806.

Flora Tea Gardens [w4.59]

The Flora Tea Gardens are known to have existed only for the years 1796-7 and were situated behind the houses in Westminster Bridge Road [behind the New Crown and Cushion], down a small lane called Mount Gardens shown on the 1799 Horwood map and referred to in Allen's history p. 335. The Gardens were open on weekdays and on Sundays till 11pm and admission was sixpence.

Temple of Flora [w2.21]

The Temple of Flora operated between 1789 and 1796 on the north side of Westminster Bridge Road in the terrace called Mount Row. Entertainments consisted of fireworks and waterworks and concerts, and the garden had painted seating boxes for eating and drinking in the open. In 1796 the proprietor, Mr Grist, was sent to the King's Bench Prison for keeping a disorderly house and the premises were closed, finally being built on by 1799.

Belvedere Gardens and House [w3.38]

In 1720 prints and records show that a Queen Anne house called Belvedere House was in the possession of Mr English (England) also being labelled by Stow in 1755 as Mr England's. Belvedere House was situated between Belvedere Road and the Thames [now the Festival Hall] and in 1757 Mr James Theobold had the house as a private residence. In 1781 an advertisement by Charles Boscom appeared opening the 'Belvedere' to the public with 'pleasant gardens and variety of fish-ponds', and accommodating guests with wine and eating and the 'choicest river fish which they might have the delight to see taken'; but this could have referred to the other Belvidere (see Brewery, p. 57). By 1785 the house had been taken over by the Lambeth Water Works and a portion by the Belvedere (timber) Wharf. Later the whole plot became the Lion Brewery.

Dog and Duck, 1642-1811 [w4.47]

The Dog and Duck was operating as a small inn by 1642 [Mary Harmsworth Park where Lambeth and Kennington Roads cross]. It was strategically placed out of reach of the Archbishop and the Duchy of Cornwall, over the boundary in St George's Fields on Lambeth Road, controlled rather negligently by the Bridge House estate. This important boundary was also the line of one branch of the Neckinger that entered the Thames at Cuper's Bridge and went inland up behind Brook Drive. Rocque maps show ponds on the brook at this point, no doubt used as duck ponds, where spaniels were used to catch ducks for their customers' dinner; the stone plaque from the tavern of a dog retrieving a duck can be seen in the Cuming Museum in Walworth Road.

Mineral water was first mentioned as being drunk here in 1695 and advertised in 1731. From 1754 till 1770 the wells were in good repute, recommended by Dr Johnson to Mrs Thrale and compared by the *St James's Chronicle* with Tunbridge, Cheltenham and Buxton. This suggests that in the eighteenth century the brook was providing passably clean and clear water through unpopulated rural fields, as all wells here were shallow, catching surface or river water. It was not until the nineteenth century, 1856 in fact, when the whole area was built on and all streams were sewers, that Dr Rendle had the premises closed. In 1770 Sampson used the premises as a circus to rival Astley's.[62]

The story of the Hedger family in the 1770s started with Mrs Elizabeth Hedger leasing the Dog and Duck and other properties in the Fields. The family were in business for the quick exploitation of the unused land and used the legal chaos surrounding the large bureaucratic absentee landlord, the Bridge House estate. The first confusion arose when the Court of Common Council tried in the 1780s to decide if the land was Common Land or not; if it was, the Fields could not be enclosed and built on. Hedger fought this saying that the leases were between him and the landlord and no one else; the court came

Rural Life till 1820

to no decision, letting the *fait accompli* continue. In 1788 George Dance the Younger (1741-1825) was brought in to survey the land for the Bridge House estate and further surveys were made in 1790, 1792, and 1794. The Dog and Duck was leased to Hedger with a licence but renewal of the licence was refused by the City Corporation, who also controlled the Bridge House estates; Hedger then had to appeal to the Surrey magistrates before getting his licence back.

Both parties broke their promises: in 1776 Hedger was promised a new lease but it was not signed till 1785. On the other hand all the leases were granted on the condition of no building but Hedger, by willingly paying the fine of £500, argued that building and sub-letting did not break the lease.[63] The lettings made him a fortune, and when the leases ended the Hedger family ensured that the day before repossession all the houses were demolished and the materials sold off.[64]

Richard North, Seedsman and other Nurseries

As would be expected in any rural area close to a city, Lambeth Marsh had its nurserymen, Richard North advertising as a seedsman and nurseryman in 1759 in Westminster Bridge Road and the Shield Nursery in 1787-97 on the plot now Surrey Lodge [w4.44]. Further out Samuel Curtis (1779-1860), who married William Curtis's daughter Sarah, set up in Walworth Road, and Samuel Driver of Drivers Jonas the estate agents had a nursery in 1766 in the Old Kent Road on the corner of East Street.[65]

The Folly [w3.46]

The Folly, a houseboat moored on the sand-bank at Cuper's Bridge, was used in Pepys' day as a dance hall and entertainment centre.[66] The Folly continued into the 1780s, when it was painted by Paul Sandby in a river painting, but shortly afterwards was closed as a disorderly house.[67]

Lambeth Wells and Chapman's Gardens [w1.13]

Lambeth Wells in Lambeth Walk was first recorded as open to the public in 1697. There were two wells in the rear gardens and the water was sent to St Thomas's Hospital, then situated in the Borough. By 1740 Lambeth Wells had reverted to use as a tavern and a meeting hall for concerts, dancing and lectures and no longer sold the water, even though Stow still labelled it with the name in 1755. By 1786 the gardens along Lambeth Walk had been built over but the Fountain tavern continued, last mentioned in 1829 [now Sheltered Housing between Fitzalan and Lollard Streets]. The rear part of the gardens continued as Chapman's Garden, shown on Cary's 1787 map.

Ill. 56 The Dog and Duck sign

Ill. 57 The Folly

Finch's Grotto [w1.6]

Finch's Grotto was on the border between Paris Garden Manor and Southwark [the Fire Brigade in Southwark Bridge Road, past the Goldsmith's Arms pub to Great Suffolk Street, and with Grotto Court off it]. The Grotto opened in 1760 and in 1764 issued tokens. In addition to the usual drinking, dancing and tavern food, Finch's became famous for its music, an organ by Pike of Bloomsbury being installed in the garden. Concerts with many notable singers took place every summer evening till 1770, when Finch died. Williams took over that year and continued with the concerts:

'Mr Smith to sing Russell's Triumph in the character of a Midshipman. After which will be played a Grand Transparent Painting of Fountains with serpents jetting water.'

After making a loss in 1773 the Grotto was demolished and it reverted to being a tavern. This was later rebuilt as the Goldsmith's Arms, a Victorian pub that still stands.

> 'Here herbs did grow
> and flowers sweet
> but now is called
> Saint George's Street.'
>
> Christopher Logue *London in verse*.

Holland's Leaguer [w3.18]

This was the old moated manor house of Paris Garden Manor [now just east of the Blackfriars Road] and was noted as a stew (brothel) in the days of Charles I, supposedly run by a Mr Holland.[68]

'This may be termed a foul dene then a faire Garden ... the rotten bawdy, the swearing Drunkard, and the bloody Butcher, have their rendezvous here.'
London and the Countrey Carbonadoed 1632.

By 1662 the property had been sold by William Angell to Hugh Jermyne and was used along with adjacent tenter grounds for milling cloth. Angell was responsible for the earliest speculative development on the low ground of this manor next to Lambeth Marsh. By 1671 Christ Church had been built, the first new church between St Mary Lambeth and St Saviour, Southwark.

CURTIS'S LONDON BOTANIC GARDEN

William Curtis (1746-99) remains to this day one of the country's most famous early botanists. After serving his apprenticeship as an apothecary in Bishopsgate [a plaque to his name], Curtis soon decided that he was more interested in the growing of plants than in medicine. To this end he took a small plot of land in Bermondsey, off Willow Walk [w1.19], where he is remembered by the naming of roads in the housing estate. After a short while this plot was considered not suitable and he moved to Lambeth Marsh. Curtis opened the London Botanic Garden to the public in 1779, complete with prospectus, garden plan, and plant catalogue naming all the species.[69] By the time he left, ten years later, it contained six thousand different plant species, all labelled to the Linnaean system of which he was the first systematic user in this country.

Ill. 58 *Curtis's London Botanic Garden by Sowerby*

In 1787 William Curtis started one of the world's greatest works, *The Botanical Magazine*, that was continuously issued under that title until April 1984 [unfortunately then changed to *The Kew Magazine*]. This magazine with its beautiful hand-coloured prints has described newly-found plant species for almost two hundred years. Initially of course these were most often English wild species. With his friends the Whites, mentioned on p. 94, he was interested not only in plants, but in all forms of the natural world he saw around him and wrote about butterflies and moths and other insects.

In 1985 London had a scourge of the Brown Tail moth, whose caterpillar covered trees by the millions and produced skin rashes if touched; in 1782 Curtis observed the same phenomena, but in those days people really believed they caused the plague or other diseases. Curtis was the first naturalist to study the insect and to publish a tract on it to allay people's fears. Although the caterpillar looks so destructive, in fact it rarely kills the tree and turns into a small beautiful pure white moth with a brown tail.

Curtis was not a good businessman, always borrowing from his brother Thomas, who also published his books, and although his many achievements have gone down in history they were never money-spinners. After only ten years, the open ditches that earlier flowed freely into the Thames were becoming stagnant as the back flooding of the tide became more and more frequent.[70] The ploughed fields and meadows so close to London were also being built on, so that the ditches, a healthy form of drainage in a sparsely populated area, were now open sewers that, together with the ever increasing air pollution, did nothing for the wild bog plants, or Curtis's own health. In addition he was a victim of planning blight; there was talk of the New Cut road being built, and this would block his ditches to the Thames even if it did not go over his land (The Cut was shown dotted on Cary's 1787 map). All these factors led Curtis to leave Lambeth in 1789 and set up a new garden off the Fulham Road not far from the Chelsea Physic Garden, where he was Demonstrator. Battersea Parish Church has a modern memorial window to his name that records his death in 1799 aged 53 years.

THE BOTANIC GARDENS SITE [w2.51]

The site of the botanic gardens is behind the Old Vic, bounded by Webber Street [formerly Higlers Lane], the north edge of Mitre Road, the eastern edge of the recreation ground and to the south the back boundary between Gray Street and Ufford Street.[71] The present cottage-style Victorian houses in Ufford Street are one of Octavia Hill's estates and in medieval times the site was said to have been a lazar-house (leper house).[72]

Two written descriptions of the garden exist. William Curtis's own garden catalogue describes it as 'situated very near the Magdalen Hospital, St George's Fields, in the road from the said Hospital to Westminster Turnpike, through Lambeth Marsh village'. The second description is by James Edwards: 'on the left are the Blue Houses; and at about 100 yards distance are some gardens, belonging to Mr William Curtis'. Stockdale's 1797 map shows the blue houses and the garden such that by walking from Lambeth Marsh towards the Borough the Blue Houses and garden would be passed on the left.[73]

Rural Life till 1820

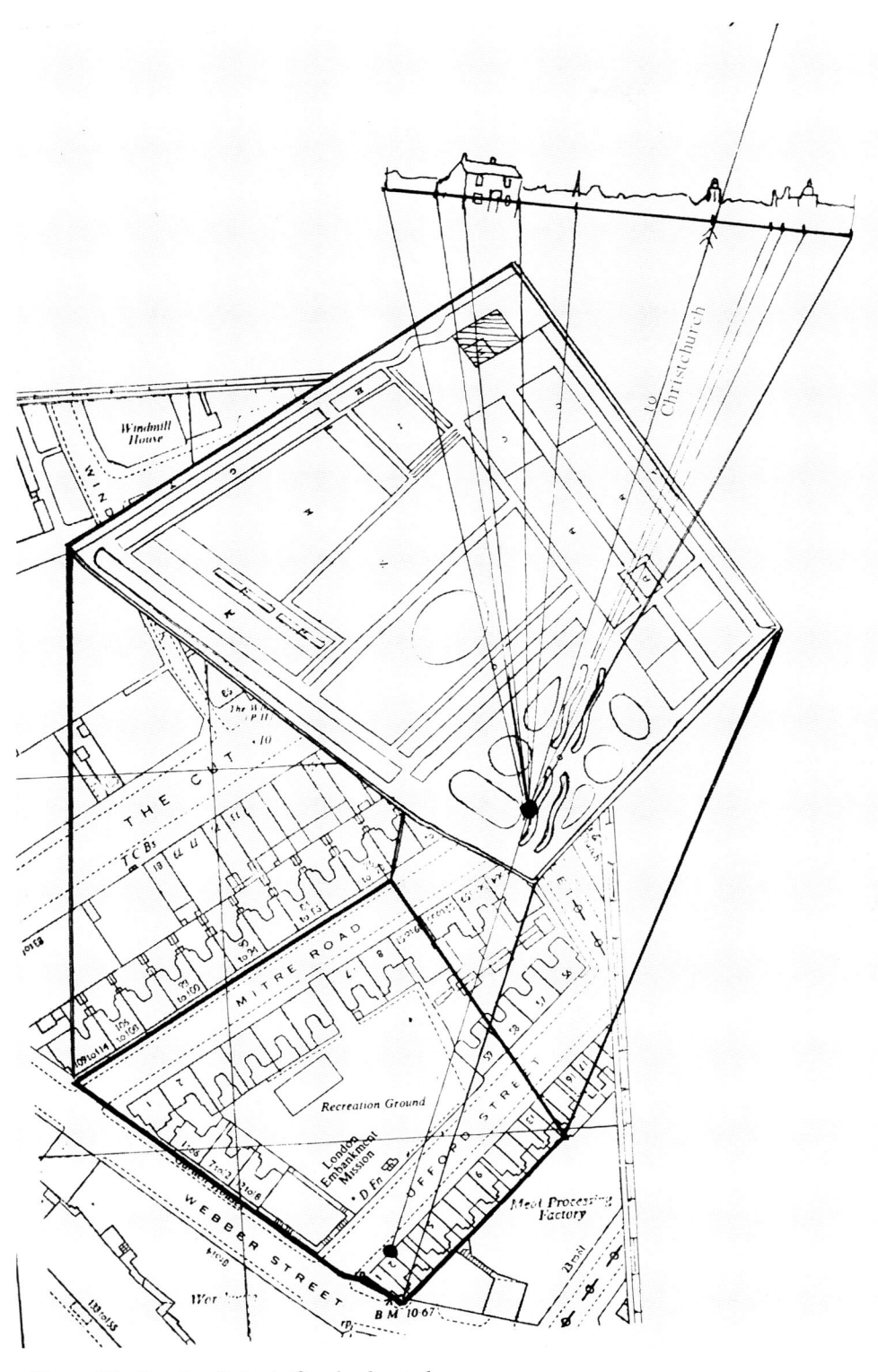

Ill. 59 The London Botanic Garden located

James Sowerby, the botanic illustrator, painted the watercolour illustrated here with its view of the garden and in the background St Paul's, St Bride Fleet Street, St Martin Ludgate and Christ Church Blackfriars Road.[74] The positions of these churches if projected on a map show that the painter's view (standing in the garden) falls exactly on the Webber Street site. The painting's detail of the garden with the pond on the left and the timbered house coincides with Curtis's plant layout, which also labels the museum room in the house.

The size of the plot is known from the fact that in 1771 one acre was taken.[75] When a projection is made on a large-scale Ordnance Survey map and the garden plan overlaid, the boundaries fit so exactly that a kink in the back wall boundary of the Ufford Street houses finishes exactly on the garden corner where the water-filled ditches formed a T-junction.

Cary's map of 1786 and Stockdale's of 1796 specifically label the London Botanic Garden at the Webber Street site. William Hagley issued a halfpenny token at 'ye Restoration in St George's Fields' at the time of Charles II and in 1714 there was a new cockpit in the grounds. In 1733 its water, lately discovered', was known for curing humours. Maps label the site Spring Garden in 1731 and Restoration Garden in 1755.[76]

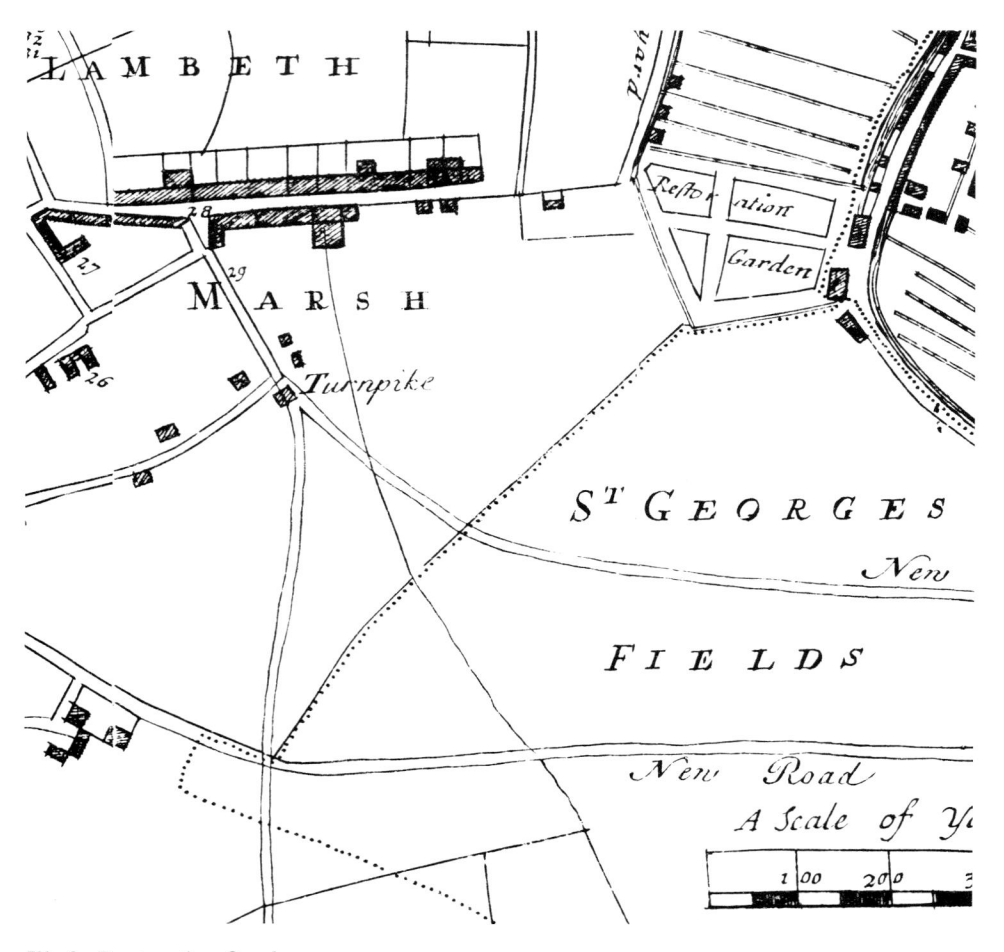

Ill. 60 Restoration Garden 1755

JAMES SOWERBY 1757-1822

Sowerby started his career apprenticed to Richard Wright, a marine painter, for whom he painted portraits and silhouettes. Later, when employed by William Curtis he painted his only known water-colour landscape, the painting of Curtis's garden mentioned above, but, more importantly, became famous for his botanic paintings. He then lived at No. 2 Meads Place [w4.56]. William Curtis used Sowerby from the start of the *Botanical Magazine* in 1787, as illustrator, which built Sowerby's reputation as a botanic illustrator. Later Sowerby set up on his own and produced the plates for the *English Botany* and other works on natural history. His sons, born in Lambeth, helped to found the Royal Botanical Society. Sowerby was buried in the Burial Ground in Lambeth High Street [now an open space and playground].

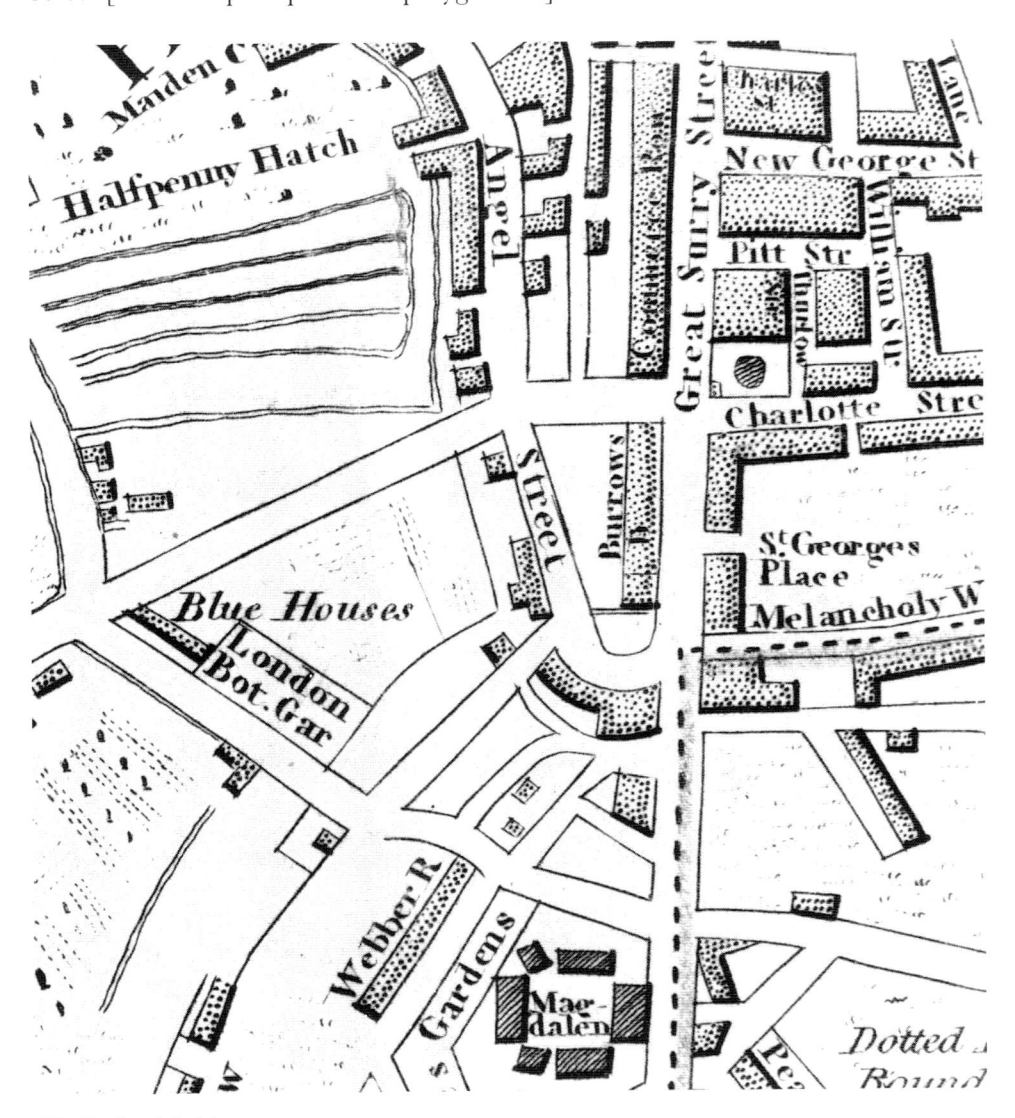

Ill. 61 Stockdale's map 1797

GILBERT WHITE
(See also Appendix p. 149 for quotations and [w1.15] for the Vauxhall Escheat tenancies.

Descriptions exist of Lambeth Marsh as part of rural Surrey, many of them by famous eighteenth-century naturalists such as James Edwards or recorded in the specialist journals of that period. The Camberwell Beauty (Nymphalis antiopa), a rare migrant butterfly from Norway that requires willows and plenty of water for survival, was recorded in *The Auralian*: 'the first two were taken about the middle of August, 1748, Cool Arbour Lane near Camberwell; the last in St George's Fields, near Newington Butts, the beginning of last month'. The Dale Collection has a specimen caught in Camberwell in 1793.[77]

Britain's most famous naturalist, Gilbert White (1746-99), had two brothers, Thomas and Benjamin, living in Lambeth. Ben White, the wealthiest member of the family, was a bookseller in Fleet Street. He leased a farm for Thomas in South Lambeth Road, Vauxhall, where he and his family also stayed when his Fleet street premises were being rebuilt. Gilbert White's *Journal* records frequent visits to the Lambeth countryside while London was always carefully mentioned separately. His journal tells of hay-making, big dinner parties and specifically of the taking of barometer and temperature readings in Curtis's Lambeth Marsh Botanic Gardens.

Ben White's tenancy of the farm was part of the Vauxhall Escheat (see [w1.15] for location and tenants) in South Lambeth Road whose large house had been the residence of Tradescant and Ashmole a hundred years earlier. This house, not demolished till 1879, is illustrated in several prints and its boundary wall still stands [in Stamford Buildings]. Thomas White was friend and patron to Curtis, as is acknowledged in the introduction to the *Botanic Garden Catalogue*:

'To the generosity and public spirit of the honourable Daines Barrington and Thomas White Esq., his principal patrons in this undertaking, the garden to a great degree owes its existence.'

Gilbert White refers in his *Journal* (full quotations and references see Appendix p. 149) to Curtis's botanic gardens as follows:

1780 June 23-9 [S. Lambeth]
June 27. Swallows feed their young on the ground in Mr Curtis's botanic garden in George's Fields.

1789 Sept 12. Sent 12 plants of Ophrys spiralis to Mr Curtis of Lambeth Marsh.

1790 June 22. My Bro. Thomas's thermometer in Blackfriars Road against an eastern wall in the afternoon was 89.

1792 Mar 15. The thermometer at George's Fields Surrey 82.

Rural Life till 1820

LAMBETH MARSH PAINTINGS

In addition to Sowerby's painting described above p. 92, two more important paintings depict the start of Lambeth Marsh's change from rural village to metropolis.

1. 'Lambeth Marsh' by Paul Sandby, c. 1770, is in the possession of London Borough of Lambeth Archive Department.

2. 'A View from a Gentleman's Seat in the Lambeth Marsh' signed and dated William Capon 1804, and in the possession of the Greater London Record Office.

All the paintings were painted in the field as almost photographic representations of the view seen by the painters located at the following grid references:

Painting by Sowerby	TQ 3144.0 7976.5	[w2.51]
Painting by Sandby	TQ 3104.8 7964.8	[w2.7]
Painting by Capon	TQ 3096.8 7963.5	[w4.7]

'LAMBETH MARSH' BY PAUL SANDBY

Paul Sandby (1730-1809), born in Nottingham, became President of the Institute of Painters in 1765, and helped to found the Royal Academy in 1768. He never became a fashionable artist but did acquire a name as a master of technique. He advanced the technique of aquatint by introducing the spirit-ground process that quickly became universal, and developed the use of watercolours. Sandby taught the King's children and many of the future watercolour masters of the nineteenth century. His prints and paintings were always full of the rigours of life, never romanticised; his famous print the 'Rare Mackerel' shows a ragged hussy shrieking her wares, with even the cat looking frightened. Gainsborough referred to him as 'the only man of genius' who had painted 'real views from Nature in this country'. Thus we would expect his small painting of Lambeth Marsh to be painted on the spot as an accurate view of what he saw.

On the left of the painting is a row of houses, and on the right one house just coming into view, followed by a fenced field and then a single group of buildings with outhouses to the rear. From maps there is only one place in Lower Marsh where this arrangement occurs: this position is located today at the pub 'Streets' looking north-east to the city. The pub depicted, clearly the predecessor of 'Streets', was in 1982 called the Artichoke. The shadows on the painting confirm that the view is looking with the sun due south, thus making the time of day around noon.

The 1785 Hodskinson and Middleton survey map has two features that correlate accurately with the painting. These maps are drawn to a large scale and show details such as privies, wells and tree positions. The painting's isolated house with outbuildings to the rear are clearly drawn on the map. The house appearing on the right of the painting is not only shown on the map but appears from its accurate dimensions to be still standing as a sushi bar.

Ill. 62 *Painting of Lambeth Marsh by Paul Sandby 1770*

Rural Life till 1820

Ill. 63 A View from a Gentleman's seat in Lambeth Marsh by William Capon 1804

In the distant skyline the painting shows three features which are too tall for anything this side of the river. The one with a swirl on top is clearly the Monument and the tall spire to its right is on the sight line for St Margaret Pattens, a church still standing in Rood Street. The double feature at the end of the road is two of the four tall pinnacles on the corners of St Michael Cornhill, in the City.

The precise position of Sandby's viewpoint [w2.7] is found by projecting the features on an Ordnance Survey map, and the angle of vision for the painting is exactly forty-five degrees, something only likely to have been achieved by the use of a drawing frame to assist the perspective drawing. His eye level is also well above the people dancing, suggesting that Sandby was sitting on an high seat, another aid used by painters in those days.

'A VIEW FROM A GENTLEMAN'S SEAT IN LAMBETH MARSH'
signed and dated, William Capon 1804

William Capon RA (1757-1827) was well known for his detailed views of the ruins of Whitehall and Westminster Palaces and prided himself on the accuracy of his drawings, although some did not consider this an asset: Sheridan, also of the Royal Academy, called him 'Pompous Billy'. However, this would suggest that the painting may be an accurate representation of a view in 1804.

There are four large-scale maps whose details help to locate the viewpoint of the painting: three editions of Horwood, 1799, 1806 and 1819, and the Enclosure Survey of the Manor of Lambeth, 1806. By projecting the 63 features that can be seen on this amazingly detailed painting on to an Ordnance Survey map, the viewpoint can be located. The painter was viewing from the attic window of the large house on plot 1173 on the Enclosure Survey, now at the taxi entrance to Waterloo station as it is bridged by the railway at Westminster Bridge Road [w4.7].

Fore and middle distance features from left to right
A. The square Shot Tower on the waterfront [now London Weekend Television].
B. The vent on the top of Beaufoy's Wine and Vinegar Factory, previously Cuper's Gardens.
C. Houses in front of Belvidere Brewery (later spelt Belvedere).
D. A large Queen Anne style brick-built house.
E. The lane where crinolined women are walking is today Leake Street, the road passing under Waterloo station to York Road. Note that the lane rises to the right on to Lower Marsh, the high ground above the flood plain.
F. What looks like a tower but is the end wall of a house being built with scaffold poles stored at its side.
G. The Horn Brewery in The Cut with the windmill that powered the brewery and that had its tap-house on the site of the present Windmill pub.
H. A row of houses in Granby Place, an existing alley now much shortened at the side of 'Streets', the pub in Lower Marsh.

Rural Life till 1820

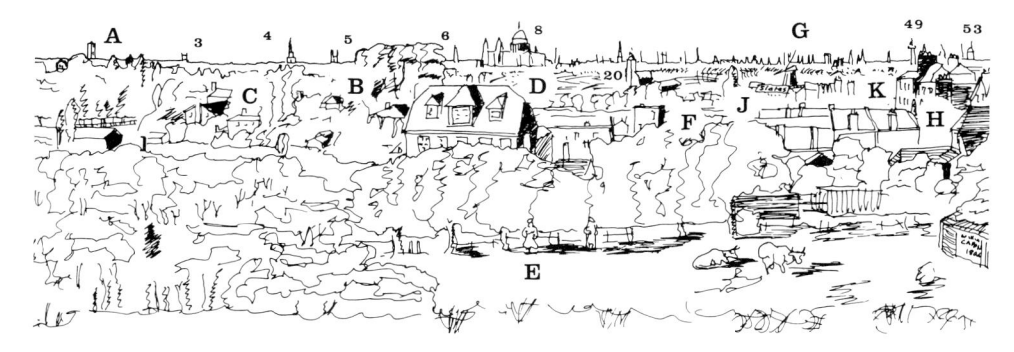

Ill. 64 Features of the view from a Gentleman's seat

J. A note on the painting shows a roof that says 'slates' to remind the painter that this roof, unlike all the others, had this new London building material, rather than the tiles that were traditionally used.
K. The backs of tall houses in Lambeth Marsh that were older, and of which many still stand.

Skyline features
* indicates that the feature no longer exists (1992).

1. Square Shot Tower, South Bank*
2. Temple Inn Church
3. St Andrew's, Holborn
4. St Bride's, Fleet Street [w1.3]
5. St Sepulchre
6. Christ Church, Newgate Street
7. St Andrew the Wardrobe
8. St Paul's Cathedral, cross on dome [w1.2]
9. St Vedas, Foster Lane*
10. St Alphage, London Wall*
11. St Mary, Aldermanbury
12. St Leonard, Shoreditch
13. St Benet, Paul's Wharf
14. St Matthew, Friday Street*
15. St Mary Magdalen, Old Fish Street*
16. St Lawrence Jewry
17. St Nicholas, Cole Abbey
18. St Margaret Somerset
19. St Mary-le-Bow, Cheapside
20. Christ Church, Blackfriars Road
21. St Stephen, Coleman Street
22. St Mary Aldermary
23. St Margaret, Lothbury
24. St Michael, Queenhythe*
25. All Hallows, London Wall

26. Dutch Church, rebuilt*
27. St James, Garlickhithe
28. Mansion House with attic storey
29. St Stephen Walbrook
30. St Peter-le-Poor, Broad Street*
31. St Botolph, Bishopsgate
32. St Michael, Paternoster
33. St Benet Fink, Threadneedle Street*
34. St Mary, Woolnoth
35. Christ Church, Spitalfields
36. St Swithun, Canon Street*
37. St Michael, Cornhill [w1.25]
38. St Mary Abchurch
39. St Peter, Cornhill
40. St Edmund the King
41. St Mary Axe*
42. All Hallows, Lombard Street*
43. All Hallows, Upper Thames Street*
44. St Clement, Eastcheap
45. St Benet, Gracechurch Street*
46. St James, Dukes Place*
47. St Michael, Crooked Lane*
48. St Botolph, Aldgate
49. The Monument [w1.24]
50. St Margaret Patten, Rood Lane [w1.23]
51. St Magnus the Martyr
52. Trinity Minories* (spire in doubt)
53. St Dunstan-in-the-East

The following are further observations about some of the above features.

Although small, the dome and lantern of the Temple Inn Church can be seen.

The tower of St Andrew the Wardrobe lines up precisely with the western edge of St Paul's Cathedral, giving a good projection line.

The spire of St Vedas, Foster Lane, is visible above the chancel of St Paul's.

St Leonard's, Shoreditch, two or three miles away with its very tall spire (192 feet), is shown on the same line as St Benet, Paul's Wharf, giving another very accurate sight line.

The Mansion House is pictured with its extra attic storey which was demolished shortly after.

Some features appear so close together on the picture that a change of the viewpoint of only two or three feet would change their relative positions. In spite of that the viewpoint works correctly for every single feature; not possible for a painter to have depicted correctly from memory or by guessing at a later date.

6
THE CHANGE TO URBAN LIVING

– Introduction – places of entertainment –
– plays and players –
– from charity to elected representatives –
– women at work –
– institutions – places of worship –

INTRODUCTION

We have seen how the eighteenth-century naturalists watched the erosion of their beloved countryside occurring in front of their eyes in Lambeth Marsh with houses and institutions erected along the new roads. Some of these houses which still stand along Lambeth Road and Kennington Road, had large back gardens and servants quarters in the attic floor, with the servants' separate kitchen and living area in the basements. These houses were occupied by the increasing numbers of middle-class professionals and self-made businessmen or shop keepers. Many of those living here were famous. One such was Vice Admiral William Bligh (1754-1817), who between 1794 and 1814 lived in Lambeth Road [plaque at w4.51], where he brought up his family of five daughters. He was much liked in the neighbourhood as a benign old sea dog, maybe too benign ever to have been an effective naval captain. In 1812 his wife died and he moved away with his unmarried daughters to Sydenham, where he died in 1817. He was buried in the churchyard of St Mary Lambeth and the Coade stone memorial is still to be seen, commemorating also the death of his beloved wife, two infant sons and a grandson [w4.28].

Lambeth Marsh and The Cut were written about on many occasions throughout the nineteenth century, by Dickens and Booth with their moral values and by Mayhew with his statistical fervour. However, it took a Londoner of Italian stock, George Augustus Sala (1828-95), recommended by Dickens himself, to catch the specific essence of the Marsh, so different from the rest of London.

'There is nobody about us whom we can use . . . more advantageously than this young man . . . suggest to him . . . the New Cut.'

Dickens to W. H. Wills, 27 October 1851.

and again later:

'Waterloo Bridge . . . would be a fine subject for Sala, in another article. If the Waterloo Bridge people would give us a little information, . . . see whether it will do for me, before you lay Sala on.'

7 October 1852.

Here is a small extract of Sala's description from *Twice Round the Clock* in 1858:

'I wish that I had a more savory locality to take you to than the New Cut. I acknowledge frankly that I don't like it . . . It is not picturesque, it isn't quaint, it isn't curious. It has not even the questionable merit of being old. It is simply

Low. It is sordid, squalid, and, the truth must out, disreputable . . . It is horrible, dreadful, we know, to have such a place: but then, consider – the population of London is fast advancing towards three millions, and wicked people must live somewhere – under a strictly constitutional government. There is a despot, now, over the water, who would make very short work of the New Cut. He would see at a glance the capacities of the place: in the twinkling of a decree the rotten tenements would be doomed to destruction; houses and shops like palaces would line the thoroughfare; trees would be planted along the pavement; and the Boulevard de Lambeth would be one of the stateliest avenues in the metropolis. But Britons never will be slaves, and we must submit to thorns (known as vested interests) in the constitutional rose, and pay somewhat dear for our liberty as well as for our whistle.'

Material progress did not cease but it was the Victorian concern for eliminating the causes of poverty that actually had the greatest effect on the life described by Sala. Although the technology for main drainage, clean piped water, and medicine existed, it was not until the vestries were replaced by more democratically elected Metropolitan Borough Councils and in 1888 by the London County Council that improvements really affected the people.

PLACES OF ENTERTAINMENT

Lambeth Marsh has been a place for London's entertainment throughout its history. When it was still countryside it was a pleasure to walk across fields, to visit laid-out pleasure gardens and to end the afternoon in a country tavern with live entertainment. As building developments destroyed the rural setting, so there grew a demand for all-the-year-round activities. To meet this demand Lambeth Marsh's entertainment moved indoors and became more imaginative, with music, theatre and dancing. When by 1820 the ploughed fields, cows and gardens had gone, continuity was not lost, as establishments such as Astley's, The Canterbury, the Bower Saloon, Lambeth Wells and the Dog and Duck had already adapted to the new urban setting.[78]

Unique for London, Lambeth Marsh seemed to encourage enterprise where anyone with a flare for entertaining could find premises with few strings attached by the landlords, who were not interested in developing the land or in imposing restrictions. Over the river in the City of Westminster it was different: there the land was carved up amongst the Lords or Dukes of Bedford, Grosvenor, Gloucester, Albemarle, Portland, Westminster, and so on, who were always eager to make a property fortune of their own. In the theatre business north of the river, the King's patents to Killigrew and Davenant gave them and their heirs a duopoly for licensing theatres that lasted from 1622 to 1843 and effectively stifled the small entrepreneur. However, none of these powers was able to exploit the land over the bridge, 'transpontine' in Lambeth Marsh, although frequent attempts were made to do so by rewriting the licensing laws.

Many instances of prosecutions occurred, described later, against proprietors for breaking licensing laws, for keeping disorderly houses and for showing cuts from Shakespeare that were 'liable to corrupt'. Luckily for London's artistic freedom, here in the Marsh anything went, without censorship and often without licence. The arguments for and against censorship and artistic and moral 'values' has now raged for centuries, with the 'nannies' who know best ranged against the 'freedom fighters'. Sala had this to say:

'But when I find shrewd police-inspectors and astute stipendiary magistrates moralising over the dreadful effects of cheap theatres, attended as they are by the 'youth of both sexes', I deem them foemen worthy of my steel . . . Come with me, and sit on the course deal benches . . . and listen to the . . . mouthing and ranting and splitting the ears of the groundlings. But in what description of pieces? In dramas, I declare and maintain, in which . . . cowardice and falsehood are hissed, and bravery and integrity vehemently applauded; in which, were we to sift away the bad grammar, and the extravagant action, we should find the dictates of the purest and highest morality. These poor people . . . have not been to the university of Cambridge . . . they can't afford to purchase a 'Shilling handbook of etiquette'. Which is best . . . that they should lie in wait in doorways and blind alleys to rob and murder, or they should pay their threepence for admission into the gallery of the 'Vic' . . . If we want genteel improprieties, sparkling immoral repartees, decorously scandalous intrigues . . . we must cross the bridges and visit the high priced theatres of the West-end.'

Following the Napoleonic wars and with the opening of the first Waterloo Bridge (1817) the next flurry of entertainment building occurred and many taverns became music-halls, entertaining the tens of thousands of ordinary people teeming the streets at night. Mayhew tells how 'Three times a week is an average attendance at theatres and dances by the more prosperous costermongers . . . "Love and murder suit us best, sir; . . . Flash songs are liked, sailor's songs, and patriotic songs . . . A song to take hold of us must have a good chorus".'

Into the 1900s and the Edwardian era, popular entertainment was more sophisticated and the world of fashion came to Waterloo Road. London's nightspot, the 'Surreyside', is well captured in the painting of photographic detail

Ill. 65 Sala's interior of the Coburg tavern

by W. H. Lambert in the London Museum, called 'Popularity'; it was painted between 1901 and 1903. Lambert, whose stage name was Lydia Dreams, fills the foreground with most of the popular stage characters of the day including: Albert Chevalier, Jenny Hill, Arthur Rigby, Marie Lloyd, Vesta Victoria, Little Tich, Alec Hurley, Fannie Leslie, Dan Leno, Eugene Stratton and George Roby.

The theatrical activity in the area extended not just to performances but to the professionals' whole lives. Poor actors lived in the slums, whilst those with a name lived in the middle-class areas along Kennington Road or Lambeth Road or further out at the Oval or Stockwell. Many in The Cut still recall the now famous actors who started in digs in Lower Marsh. Theatrical agents staying in London would put up at the York Hotel, a gin palace that stood on the corner of York Road and Waterloo Road, with its back to the railway arches, until finally demolished in 1960. Every afternoon hundreds of out-of-work extras, stage hands and 'resting' actors would crowd the corner waiting to be hired that evening for any walk-on or scene-shifting job on the Surreyside, or with luck in the West-End.[79] Even today actors have little security, but before the coming of the Variety Artistes Federation in 1906 a contract was unheard of. Many of the halls thrived in Lambeth Marsh for over a century to be replaced by the cinema, and after the 1939-45 war by a new intellectual generation of theatres and concert halls on the South Bank. Popular entertainment was taken over by television and the popular music scene.

Between 1865 and 1950 very little new building for entertainment took place and it required a post-war building boom following the blitz to revitalise the Surreyside entertainment. The South Bank Comprehensive Redevelopment brought the Marsh up to date in the entertainment business with a glittering modern array of concert halls, theatres and a film theatre that added new life to the Waterloo Road, Lower Marsh and The Cut. The South Bank now includes the Royal Festival Hall, two Queen Elizabeth Halls, the National Theatre's three theatres, the National Film theatre, the Museum of the Moving Image and the Hayward Gallery as well as new eating and shopping venues at Gabriel's Wharf and under railway arches. In The Cut the Old Vic is augmented by the Young Vic and the Upstream theatre and serviced by a large number of eating and drinking places.

Old Vic Theatre [w2.53]

The Royal Coburg was opened in 1818. Its original foundation stone is still visible in Webber Street:

THIS FIRST STONE
OF THE ROYAL COBURG THEATRE
WAS LAID ON THE
14th DAY OF SEPTEMBER IN THE YEAR 1816
BY HIS SERENE HIGHNESS
THE PRINCE OF SAXE COBURG
AND HER ROYAL HIGHNESS
THE PRINCESS CHARLOTTE OF WALES
BY THEIR SERENE AND ROYAL HIGHNESS'S
PROXY
ALDERMAN GOODBEHERE

Ill. 66 View in the New Cut

'Here they amuse themselves with theatrical converse, arising out of their last half-price visit to the Victoria Gallery, admire the terrific combat, which is nightly encored, and expatiate on the inimitable manner in which Bill Thompson can 'come the double monkey', or go through the mysterious involutions of the sailor's hornpipe.'

Sketches by Boz, The Streets – Night.

(half-price means half-time, enabling you to pay for half the show.)

'The authorities of the Victoria Theatre have preserved, I am glad to say, a wholesome reverence for the Strong Beer Act, and it is, I believe, a clause in the Magna Charta [sic] of management, that the performance on Saturday evenings shall invariably terminate within a few minutes of midnight, in order to afford the audience due and sufficient time to pour out their final libations at the shrine of Beer, before the law compels the licensed victuallers to close.'

'There are many gradations of rank among the frequenters of the Victoria Theatre. Many of the occupants of the boxes sat last night in the pit, and will to-morrow in the gallery, according to the fluctuations of their finances; nay, spirited denizens of the New Cut will not infrequently, say on a Monday evening, when the week's wages have not been irremediably dipped into, pay their half-crown like men, and occupy seats in the private box next the stage. And the same equality and fraternity are manifest when the audience pour forth at half-price to take their beer. There may be a few cheap dandies, indeed – Cornwall Road exquisites and Elephant-and-Castle bucks – who prefer to do the 'grand' in the saloon attached to the theatre; there may be some dozens of couples sweethearting, who are content to consume oranges, ginger beer and

Abernathy biscuits within the walls of the house; but the great pressure outwards, and the great gulf stream of this human ocean flow towards a gigantic 'public' opposite the Victoria, and which continually drives a roaring trade.'

Sala in *Twice Round the Clock*, 1858.

How glad the abstainers, charity and the chapels were when the Coffee Hall Music Company bought the theatre in 1880 and Emma Cons cleaned up the act at the Old Vic, renaming it the Royal Victoria Tea and Coffee House. The theatre was made 'dry', 'blood and thunder' Shakespeare was banned and the auditorium was used for the blend of coffee with moral and educational lectures that later became Morley College (see p. 121). Morality made no more money and the theatre had to reopen with some variety shows, but still without much financial success. It was only when Samuel Morley paid for the lease on the condition that it remain a temperance house that finances were secured. Emma Cons, so active in charity work, also set up the 'South London Dwellings Company' and built Surrey Buildings in 1879. Here she and Lilian Baylis, her niece, lived in a square of two-storey cottages and shops in what today would be called a Housing co-operative. The lavatories were in one block, one per tenant with their own key, and the wash-house and drying ground were on the roof. The present new Surrey Lodge on the same site now provides student accommodation [Lambeth Road/Kennington Road w4.43].

It was not until after Emma Cons' death in 1912, when Lilian Baylis (1874-1937) took over the Old Vic, that Shakespeare was considered educational and allowed to be performed; if it was always played straight through, it could fill the theatre without a riot every night. For the first time one of the theatres not a 'King's theatre' had made the grade to international standards, producing full-length plays. Meanwhile the other music-halls continued as popular entertainments, becoming cinemas when these in their turn became the new centres of mass entertainment.

Young Vic [w2.48]

The Young Vic was inaugurated in 1946 as a theatre workshop of the Old Vic. In 1970 the present building was built and the Young Vic was launched by Frank Dunlop as an independent theatre company that quickly acquired an international reputation. The auditorium constructed in The Cut as a theatre in the round was able to use existing old shops for the entrance and actors' areas. It is still unusual in London for such a young company to have its own permanent home and to have kept its reputation through more than one generation of actors and directors. The theatre has continued to maintain drama workshops and local youth theatre groups and in 1988 founded a new Young Vic Youth Theatre.

Astley's 1769-1893. [w4.15]

'There is no place which recalls so strongly our recollections of childhood as Astley's.'

and:
'We defy anyone who has been to Astley's two or three times, and is consequently capable of appreciating the perseverance with which precisely the same jokes are repeated night after night, and season after season, not to be amused with

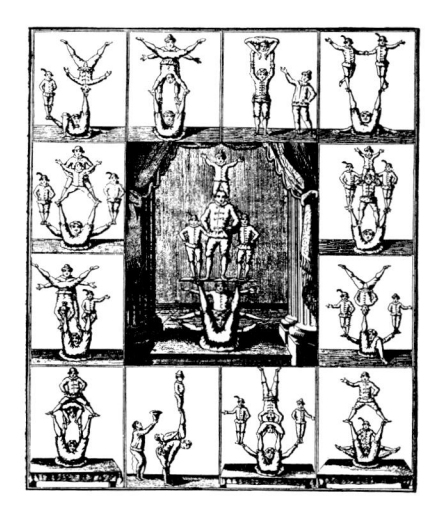

Ill. 67 Signor Calpi's Acts in 1771   *Ill. 68 Astley's Westminster Bridge Road entrance*

one part of the performances at least – we mean the scenes in the circle. For oneself, we know that when the hoop, composed of jets of gas, is let down, the curtain drawn up for the convenience of the half-price on their ejectment from the ring, the orange-peel cleared away, and the sawdust shaken, with mathematical precision, into a complete circle we feel as much enlivened as the youngest child present; and actually join in the laugh which follows the clown's shrill shout of 'Here we are!' just for old acquaintance sake.'

Charles Dickens, *Sketches by Boz*, 'Astley's'.

A letter by John Reynolds, future poet and friend of Keats, writing when sixteen in 1810 from his school home in Lambeth Green:

'You ought to be in London now to see the Blood Red Knight at Astley's Royal Amphitheatre, the last scene a Battle upon real horses in Armour, I and my Father expended two shillings upon him the other night 'Half Price' – much pleased – Blue light'.[80]

Sergeant Major Philip Astley (1742-1814), late of the 15th Light Dragoons, took a field in the Halfpenny Hatch [Roupell Street] in 1768 and charged a shilling for spectators to watch him do dare-devil horse riding around the ring. The following year he leased a plot in Westminster Bridge Road [the new St Thomas's nurses home], where it remained for the next 130 years.[81] In 1779 a permanent and partially roofed building was erected called the Amphitheatre Riding House, where equestrian feats, conjuring and fireworks were shown; by 1783 Astley had obtained a licence for stage shows in opposition to the Surrey Theatre at the Obelisk. In 1794 and 1804 the theatre was burnt to the ground and immediately rebuilt.[82] Various proprietors under different house names ran the entertainment over the years, creating a tradition as the first indoor circus in the country. Astley was successful enough to be able to lease a triangle of land [bounded by Hercules Road, Kennington Road and Cosser Street] which he developed with a terrace of houses around the edge and the Hercules tavern. Hercules Hall [w4.58] where he lived was in the centre of the triangle. The

Ill. 69 Hercules and the flesh eating horses of Diomedes

Ill. 70 Ticket for Sanger's Circus

name Hercules referred to his strong man act of 'the twelve trials of Hercules', where the eighth trial was to capture the flesh-eating horses of Diomedes.

Proprietors succeeding Philip Astley (Hercules) were: John Astley (son) 1795, Andrew Ducrow 1804, William Batty 1843, William Cooke 1853, George Sanger in 1871.

Other house names were: Astley's Amphitheatre 1771, Amphitheatre Riding House 1779, Royal Grove 1780, Royal Saloon 1794, Davis's Amphitheatre 1817, The Theatre Royal Westminster 1863, Sanger's Amphitheatre in 1871.

In March 1893 Sanger was obliged to close the Amphitheatre for being a disorderly house, under pressure from the LCC's tightened licensing laws and his landlords, the Ecclesiastical Commissioners.

Canterbury Arms 1780-1945 [w4.11]

The Canterbury Arms was the most important of all the London music-halls but before the days of the music-hall it had been a tavern [in Upper Marsh], first mentioned in 1780 and also shown on the 1806 Enclosure Survey. The tavern, like many public houses today, expanded its premises by adding halls at the rear, becoming so large that by 1900 it filled most of the triangle behind the shop fronts, bounded by Upper Marsh, Carlisle Lane and Royal Street.[83] However, Charles Dickens describes it in the 1830s before the railway came, at Marsh Gate, just outside The Canterbury's entrance [w2.15]:

'The more musical portion of the play-going community betake themselves to some harmonic meeting ... In a lofty room of spacious dimensions are seated some eighty or hundred guests knocking little pewter measures on the tables, and hammering away, with the handles of their knives, as if they were so many trunk-makers. They are applauding a glee ..., and it is quite impossible to witness unmoved the impressive solemnity with which he pours forth his soul in 'My 'art's in the 'ighlands' or 'The brave old Hoak'. 'Pray give your orders, gen'l'm'n – pray give your order', – says the pale-faced man with the red head; and demands for 'goes' of gin and 'goes' of brandy, and pints of stout, and cigars of peculiar mildness, are vociferously made from all parts of the room ... Scenes like these are continued until three or four o'clock in the morning ... we make our bow, and drop the curtain.'

Sketches by Boz, 'The Streets at Night; A Cave of Harmony'.

In 1850, the year after the railway went over the site, Charles Morton and his brother-in-law Frederick Stanley took the premises and although not the first, it became famous as the 'mother of music-hall'. They rebuilt the hall, made use of the railway arches for exhibitions, bars and arbours and made no charge

Change to Urban Living 109

Ill. 71 The Canterbury in the 1870's

for entry as more than enough money was made on the drinks. Over the years all forms of side shows were tried, with art shows and an aquarium that still has three tank bases visible at the entrance in Westminster Bridge Road. Every time the railway line was widened, five times in all, The Canterbury was able to rebuild its premises. In 1852 a new entrance was built [behind a hoarding, Westminster Bridge Road w4.10], leading through a labyrinth of tunnels painted as arbours with gilt and greenery [visible inside the arches], to the ever grander Hall. In 1867 William Holland took over from Morton on his retirement, later followed by Villiers in 1876. Villiers specialised more in ballet and art shows, renaming the theatre the 'Royal Academy over the Water'. His theatre was patronised, as were most theatres of that date, by the Prince of Wales, later Edward VII and became part of the fashion for slumming it in the poor areas. Thus The Canterbury Arms continued to prosper into the twentieth century and now made entry charges, till it was finally extinguished by a bomb in 1945.

The Bower Saloon [w4.13]

The Bower Saloon was earlier a tavern called the Duke's Arms and was situated in Upper Marsh at its junction with Stangate and first recorded in 1697/8. In the 1806 Enclosure Survey it is labelled the Duke's Arms and drawn with extensions to its rear but around that time is shown on an engraving with drinking booths and fountains and labelled the Bower Saloon. In 1838 the Bower Saloon was a music-hall that became in its heyday in variety the famous 'Twopenny gallery, Four-penny Pit'. The Bower Saloon was the original 'Little Theatre in Stangate' in Tom Robertson's play called *Caste*. The Bower's greatest theatrical fame was that Henrietta Hodson, later married to Henry Labouchere MP, started here before becoming lessee and leading actress at the Queen's Theatre. The Bower Saloon closed in 1879.

The South London Palace of Varieties [w1.9]

Situated in London Road [on Ontario Street] towards the Elephant, the 'Sarf', as it was affectionately called, was a favourite music-hall that took over the site of the first Roman Catholic chapel in the area that had been built in 1840. The music-hall opened on 30 December 1860, built and decorated to look like a Roman villa and with the original black-faced comedian, E. W. Mackney, in the opening bill. It burnt down and was rebuilt in 1869, when ballet became a feature of the performances. Like many other theatres in the area, it ran continuously till closed for ever by bombing in 1940.

Surrey Music-Hall [w1.8]

The Surrey music-hall was in Southwark Bridge Road, outside Lambeth Marsh. It started as a tavern called the Grapes and in 1840 became the Surrey Music-Hall, at one time owned by Mr Fair. In 1878 it was demolished and replaced by the Winchester pub, that still exists.

Gatti's [w4.8]

Gatti's Palace of Varieties was better known as Gatti's-in-the-Road to distinguish it from Gatti's-in-the-Strand [the Adelphi]. Built in 1855 the theatre was between Westminster Bridge Road and Addington Street [the County Hall Island Block]. Harry Lauder made his debut here. By 1937 it had declined and cinema performances were shown between the live performances. Gatti's was bombed in the 1939-45 war and finally demolished in 1950.

The Ring, 1910-1942, the Surrey Chapel, 1782-1881 [w2.45]

This octagonal building had a long and varied history starting as the Surrey Chapel. Rowland Hill (1744-1833) was brought up by wealthy parents, attending Eton as a scholar and with a reputation as a good speaker and a witty tongue. His questioning approach to authority made it difficult for him to obtain

Ill. 72 The Ring in the 1920's

Change to Urban Living

Orders with the Church of England but he did so in 1773. His brilliant manner in the pulpit always drew crowds and he spent most of his time preaching at the invitation of dissenters at wayside pulpits around the country. In 1782 with the financial help of his brother, Sir Richard Hill, Rowland leased the plot on the north-east corner of the junction of Blackfriars Road and The Cut to build the Surrey Chapel. He lived around the corner at 45 Charlotte Street [Union Street]. Surrey Chapel was built to Rowland Hill's wishes as an octagonal building with an interior gallery on all sides and with cast-iron columns and roof, to give the best vision for all the congregation, '. . . for it prevented the devil hiding in any of the corners'.[84]

Ill. 73 The Ring's destruction in 1942

Rowland Hill was much liked by his followers, who gave generously to the collections, and his amiability contributed greatly to the success of his Sunday School. His reputation was such that his church grew to become the Congregational Church and he numbered William Wilberforce and Sheridan amongst his listeners (Walford in his history of London devotes seven pages to his story). As his memorial, Christ Church in Westminster Bridge Road was built, using some of his acquired trust fund money. On occasions the Surrey Chapel was used for purposes other than preaching: in 1829 for example it was used by Sloman as a variety theatre, and Dan Leno's parents appeared there as duettists and dancers. The congregation moved from the chapel in 1876. Later in the century the premises were closed because of their use for cockfighting and the building was left largely unused for the next twenty years.

In 1910 Bella Burge (Bella of Blackfriars) and her ex-champion husband Dick Burge acquired the lease of the premises as an ideal building for a boxing ring.[85] Bella (1877-1969) was born Bella Orchard and was brought up in the theatrical world, making her debut at the age of ten at the Pavilion Theatre, Leytonstone. In her teens Bella became a companion to Marie Lloyd, a friendship that lasted throughout their lives. As in other music-halls, many acts at Gatti's included bouts of boxing and it was here that Bella first met Dick Burge the prize fighter. Dick Burge, born in 1865, married Bella on 26 October 1901 at Brixton Registry office. Within a year her world collapsed when he was indicted on charges concerning the biggest bank fraud then known: £169,000 being the huge sum involved. He was sentenced to ten years, but his sentence was remitted and he went free in 1909. It was after his release and his retirement from active boxing that the couple took a lease on the now disused Surrey Chapel and opened it on 14 May 1910 as The Ring.

The Ring, the first indoor ring for those with little money, played to packed houses of three thousand people. After some years of watching the matches as the only woman in the audience and following the unwritten rule that boxing was a male-only event, Bella took matters into her own hands. In 1914 she brought all her famous actress friends to a show and sat them at the ringside, and from then on women have always formed a large portion of any boxing audience.

Dick Burge died in 1918 and Bella continued to run The Ring on her own, personally breaking up the fights in the gallery and suspending trouble makers as the occasion warranted. Through the twenties and thirties the audiences diminished and between boxing bouts variety shows were performed: in 1937 Robert Atkins performed Shakespeare's *Henry V* to help Bella along. By 1939 and the war, Bella was losing money, spending her savings on paying the boxers and pawning her jewellery. The V2 bomb in 1942 was the end to a building that had lasted since 1782 and had for so long been packed with people from The Cut and the Marsh.

Surrey Theatre 1782-1934 [w2.39]

The Surrey theatre was, like The Ring, to be used for many forms of entertainment over the 150 years of its existence. Located in Blackfriars Road just before St George's Circus, the theatre opened in 1782 as the Royal Circus and Equestrian Philharmonic Society and labelled on Cary's 1787 map. Opposite the theatre were still the open St George's Fields and in the 1780s open-air shows were often performed there. On 29 June 1785 in front of a large crowd

Change to Urban Living

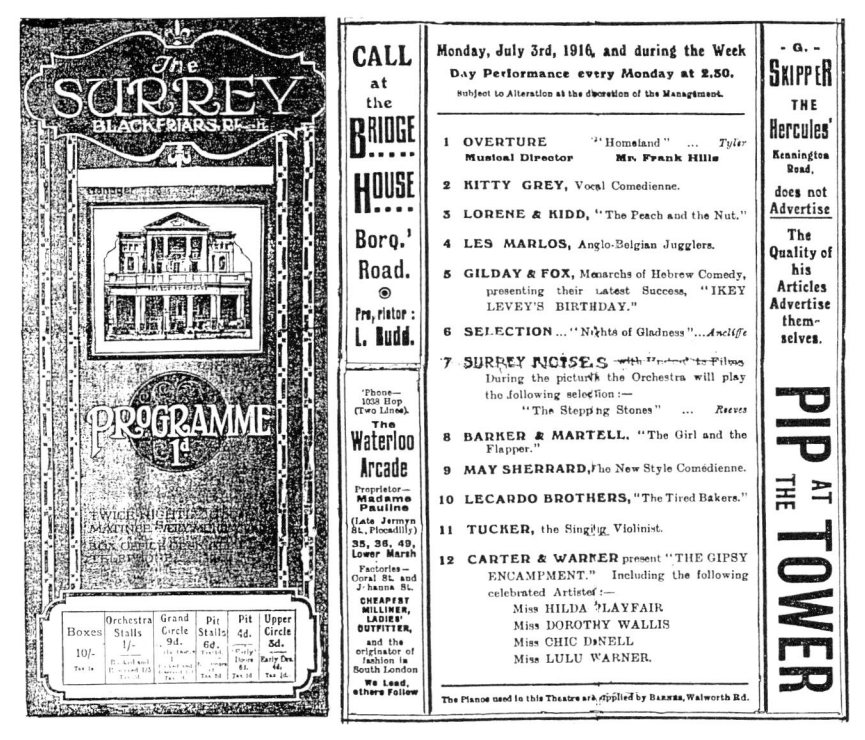

Ill. 74 A 1916 programme of Surrey Theatre

Lunardi sent up his hot air balloon with Mrs Sage, a well-known beauty, and George Biggin as passengers.[86]

In 1803 the Circus was burnt to the ground but was rebuilt the following year. In 1809 Elliston converted it to a theatre and by including ballet somewhere in the performance of every play was able to avoid the Patent Act and the West-End monopoly. The main events that followed in the theatre's history are:

- 1814 Returned to being a circus.
- 1816 Named the Surrey by Dibden.
- 1823 Dibden failed and it was taken for the second time successfully by Elliston till his death.
- 1831 Taken by Osbaldiston and followed by Davidge, Dick Shepherd and Creswick. Finally George Conquest took it till his death in 1901 and from thence the music-hall declined.
- 1920 The theatre became a cinema, with people in 1992 still able to recall evenings there.
- 1934 The cinema was demolished to make way for an extension of the next-door Royal Ophthalmic Hospital.

Frazier's and other Penny Gaffs [w2.6]

Penny or sometimes tuppeny gaffs were derelict halls or disused buildings where out-of-work mummers and actors performed, strutted or bellowed grossly garbled versions of Shakespeare and blood and thunder melodramas. Dickens described them in *Sketches by Boz*, chapter XIII 'Private Theatres' and they

Ill. 75 *Amateur theatre by Cruickshank*

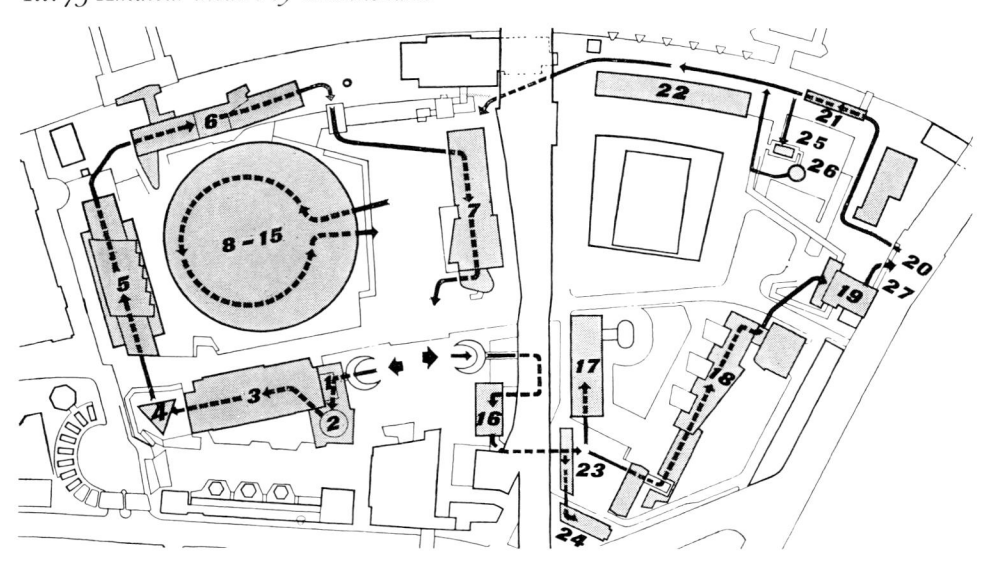

Ill. 76 *The Festival of Britain*

were illustrated by Cruikshank. We know that many existed around the Marsh and The Cut. Mayhew refers to one in his description of 'London's street markets on a Saturday Night' which also enables us to identify how the present Frazier Street acquired its name:

'or else you hear the sounds of music from Frazier's Circus, on the other side of the road, and the man outside the door of the penny concert, beseeching you to 'Be in time – be in time!' as Mr Somebody is just about to sing his favourite song of the 'Knife Grinder'. Such, indeed, is the riot, the struggle, and the scramble for a living, that the confusion and uproar of the New-cut on Saturday night have a bewildering and saddening effect upon the thoughtful mind'.[87]

When describing 'the penny gaff clowns', Mayhew gives the clown's statement as follows:

'I'm a clown at penny gaffs and the cheap theatres, for some of the gaffs are twopence or threepence – that's as high as they run. The Rotunda in the Blackfriars Road is the largest in London, and that will hold one thousand comfortably seated, and they give two in one evening, at one penny, twopence, and threepence'.[88]

Earlier the Rotunda had been the Surrey Institution (see details p. 135).

The Royal Festival Hall [w3.38]

The Royal Festival Hall was built by the London County Council, as the world's most up-to-date concert hall for the Festival of Britain in 1951 and as the exhibition's only permanent feature. The concert hall holds a seated audience of 3,300 people such that everyone is equally comfortable and hears the same high standard of acoustics wherever they sit. None of the sounds from the adjacent railway can be heard in the auditorium, and the generous foyers enable shops, bars and exhibitions to be open on several levels. When the Greater London Council was abolished in 1986 the Royal Festival Hall came under the control of the South Bank Board Ltd.

National Film Theatre, 1952, and Museum of the Moving Image, 1988 [w3.45]

The National Film Theatre was set up by the British Film Institute in 1952 following the success of the Telecinema during the Festival of Britain. The auditorium presented three-dimensional films to the public long before any other and in addition was able to present full screen performances from projected television. The Telecinema, originally on the site now occupied by the downstream Shell building was forced to move to No. 1, Abutment Arch, Waterloo Bridge when the latter was built in 1957. It was at the same time renamed the National Film Theatre. The space under the arches became its permanent home with the NFT2 and restaurant added on the river walk in 1968. The National Film Theatre, financially independent from the very beginning, succeeded within its original temporary confines till 1988, when it created a new venture, the Museum of the Moving Image (MOMI) under more of the bridge arches. MOMI displays the history and development of moving images and very aptly demonstrates to visitors how the art of the stage-set designer can create illusions of space.

The buildings, if that is what they can be called, make full use of the bridges that form their envelope; still to be seen hidden in a projection room is one pier of Rennie's first Waterloo Bridge whilst the present concrete bridge forms the ceiling to many parts of the complex. Like other successes in the Marsh before them, the National Film Theatre and MOMI are financially obligated to no one.

Hayward Gallery and Queen Elizabeth Hall, 1968 [w3.35]

The Queen Elizabeth Hall and Hayward Gallery were completed in 1968 by the LCC as part of the South Bank Redevelopment Area. The entrances to these buildings are placed at the upper walkway level with easier access off Waterloo Bridge but leaving a concrete jungle for skateboarders and for the ill-devised surface car parking at the level of the river walk.

National Theatre, 1976 [w3.31]

The National Theatre opened in 1976 after nearly fifty years campaigning and many false starts, with the first foundation stone laid in 1952 by Queen Elizabeth II at the side of the Festival Hall. The present building, Britain's first national theatre, was designed by Denys Lasdun with three integrated theatres, the Olivier, the Lyttleton and the Cottesloe, and with bars, restaurants and shared green rooms and actors' facilities. The art of make-believe on stage has been altered little by the dramatic technical changes that have transformed the nineteenth-century penny gaff into the twentieth-century electronic-controlled set; there never will be a substitute for the brilliant actor.

Television studios and the electronic age

Forms of entertainment continue to change and today we have television with its film studios, television theatres, 'venues' and everything else that goes with the mass media industry. These new forms reduce the numbers of people going out for entertainment, as they can be entertained in their living rooms via the airwaves. Even with these dramatic changes Lambeth Marsh still manages to hold centre stage. The cheap premises there, often old warehouses or redundant factories or offices, make ideal recording studios or live music venues and the millions who watch the news with London Weekend Television [w3.30] see the background view of London from Lambeth Marsh, close to the spot where Cuper's Gardens stood. 'Soaps' are frequently shot in the streets of Lambeth Marsh giving those in the know or with friends working in them the backstage pleasure of recognising their home ground on the screen.

PLAYS AND PLAYERS

It is not the intention of this history to recall the numerous famous actors or their performances. Lambeth Marsh is so well documented by theatrical biographies that it is necessary to tell of only few forgotten aspects of the actor's life; just a reminder of the thousands who spent their lives giving a little cheer in grim times past and whose only claim to fame was twenty minutes behind the footlights. Others more qualified have written of the famous, although there are those '... who would look rather shame-faced (though I cannot see why they should be ashamed) were they reminded, now, of their achievements in

BLUE BEARD   MUTINEERS (*Casco Bay*)   IMP AND DEMON   MEG MERRILIES

Ill. 77 Cut-out characters from toy theatres

the service of transpontine melodrama at the Coburg . . .'.[89] It is good to recall that even at the peak of his career the clown Joe Grimaldi (1779-1837) was one of the few who remembered his past and would come to contemplate in the little overgrown orchard garden in Stangate Street where he was brought up by his Italian immigrant parents.

Toy Theatres

The entertainment business has always advertised its wares with printed handbills, helped along by newspaper criticism. Handbills, often full of flowery words, puns and hyperbole, were printed in very large quantities and became a major market for the printing business, frequently printed in the Marsh itself. In the nineteenth century printing became so cheap that another whole industry grew up, that of the toy theatre. It is difficult for us in days of photography and electronic communications to conceive of the time when all printed pictures were hand-drawn. How could a handbill express the excitement of a firework display from the backs of circling horses or the cut and thrust of Ivanhoe duelling with Sir Brian de Bois Guilbert? From 1811 onwards there were specialist printers in this market, such as William West (1783-1854), Skelts, Hodgson and Co. and B. Pollock. The important thing about toy theatres was not the intricacy of the cardboard theatres themselves but the accuracy of the paper cutouts of the characters that slotted into their holders. With every new character staged, the printers would produce for sale a complete cast, the video cassette of its day. Important actors were not just drawn from memory, but were seen on stage by the artist on the first night, or at a rehearsal or preview. The artist raced back with his sketches to the printers where blocks were made, printed and sold to the public before those of any rival.[90]

The following are a few of the complete sets of shows published by just one firm, W. West, that were performed at Surreyside theatres between the years 1811 and 1818.[91]

5.8.1811	Surrey theatre	Lady of the Lake.
11.9.1811	Astley's	Tyrant Saracen and Noble Moor.
17.4.1812	,,	Old Beelzebub, or Harlequin Taffy in Ireland.
6.5.1812	Surrey	Valentine and Orson.
4.7.1812	,,	Harlequin Colossus.
23.9.1812	Astley's	The Blood Red Knight, or the Fatal Bridge, seen by John Reynolds (see p. 126).
7.4.1819	Coburg	The Forty Thieves (R. B. Sheridan and Colman Junior).

Chevalier D'Eon de Beaumont, 1728-1810

Another certain draw for a cheap laugh was a joke at someone else's expense. In early days this could be animals performing as people, or people as animals; any unusual animal or person, small, deformed or diseased, was exploited by the theatre manager. So Lambeth Marsh was also a melting pot of humanity, where unusual people or strangers from foreign lands could be seen. It was here that a North American Chief from Canada buried his wife in St John's church on their visit to negotiate his country away to Queen Victoria. The funeral was followed by a large cortege of actors, with whom he was staying in the Marsh.

However, Man's inhumanity to Man did lessen over the years; reform laws did in the end control the worst excesses. By 1900 when the Prince of Wales was spending much of his time with actors, they were very much more respected, and their names and skills were talked of in society. In 1800 things were different. The French were enemies and when a woman spy came from France to live in Westminster Bridge Road and gave public fencing performances, people stared. Walford, in *Old and New London* sums up the attitudes of the day well:

'Another eccentric resident in the Westminster Bridge Road, in former times, was Chevalier D'Eon, concerning whom there was so much doubt raised as to whether he was a man or a woman. Angelo, in his 'reminiscences', tells us that he used to see the Chevalier D'Eon here. *He lived a few doors beyond Astley's Theatre. He always dressed in black silk, and looked like a woman worn out with age and care.*'

The story of Chevalier D'Eon comes best from a Frenchman twenty years after his death, when people had become a little more sympathetic and is told by Antonia White in *The Memoirs of Chevalier D'Eon* from the original by Frederic Gaillardet of 1836.[92] The book's introduction corrects the few embellishments of Gaillardet, who was one of the first to treat a transvestite with sympathy rather than as a freak.

The story unfolds like a romantic novel full of intrigue and adventure, authenticated with letters from the archives of his family and the French National Archives; a spy story to match any *Tale of Two Cities* or *Three Musketeers*. All details are confirmed by the memoirs with the exception of two rather blatant fabrications that were used by Gaillardet to explain D'Eon's transvestitism. Firstly he invented a woman who was to be D'Eon's lifelong mistress and who nursed him into his old age, Nadejda Stein, whereas the evidence shows that his companion in old age was a Mrs Marie Cole, the widow of his friend, a marine engineer. The second, even more unfounded implication, was that D'Eon was the father of George IV, simply because D'Eon was a friend of Charlotte in Germany before her marriage, a friendship which lasted throughout their lives, and because the dates and meetings were right to make it possible.

These two twists of Gaillardet suggest that D'Eon was a normal heterosexual who was pushed by circumstances into having to renounce manhood and to wear women's clothes. However, most of the other evidence shows that from childhood he liked dressing as a girl and that after the Revolution when he was no longer obliged to wear women's clothes he did so freely till his death. Records support Walford's account in that he did live from 1796 to 1804 at number 33 Westminster Bridge Road [w4.9] with his housemaid Mrs Cole but

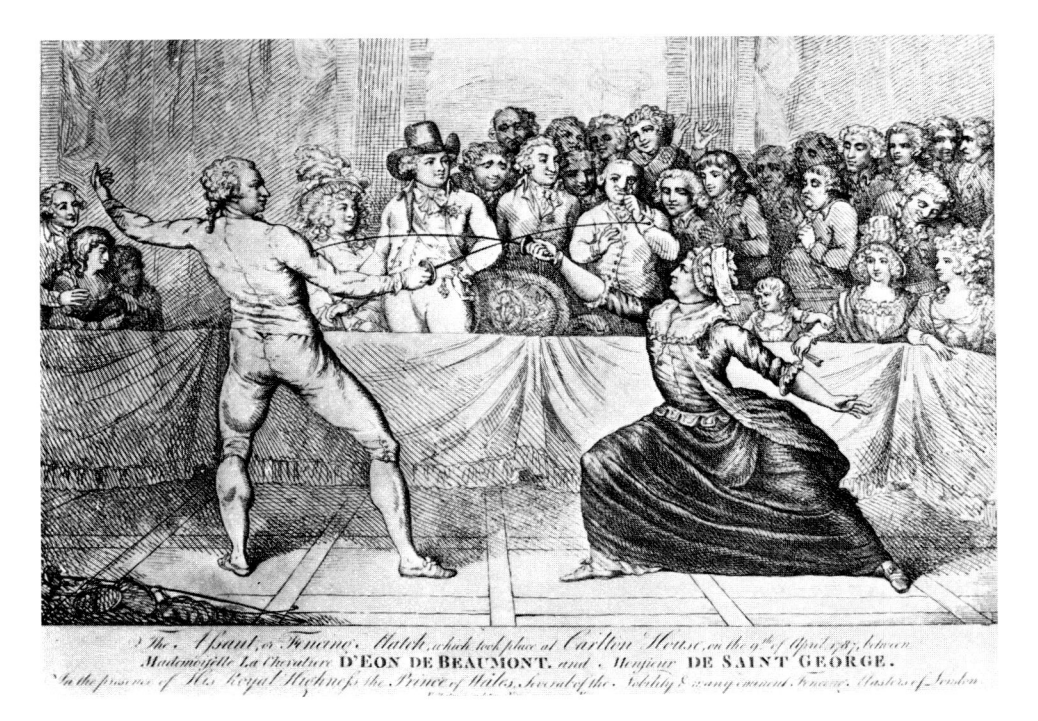

Ill. 78 Chevalier D'Eon's dual at Carlton House

with little money, being bailed out of the debtor's prison by her in 1804. On his release they moved to 26 Milman Street [Soho] where he lived until his death in 1810.

FROM CHARITY TO ELECTED REPRESENTATIVES

The first documented welfare operating in the area was given by monasteries that provided teaching and rudimentary care of the sick within their walls and who were financed by tithes or charity. St Thomas's at Southwark, first mentioned in 1212, was the nearest to the Marsh, as Lambeth Palace was never any more than a residence for the Bishops or Archbishops. As time passed St Mary, the parish church, administered the welfare and although, for Lambeth Marsh the manor was also the Archbishop's, this made no difference to the squabbles that frequently occurred between the church and the Lords of the Manor. As recently as 1979 the Church wanted to demolish the historic parish church of St Mary Lambeth, it mercifully being saved by the Tradescant Trust [w4.28]. Thus help from the Lord of the Manor was very much dependent on the benefaction of the man himself, and a few Archbishops, such as Tenison and Temple, did start local charity schools.

By the eighteenth century Lambeth Marsh, so close to the twin Cities of London and Westminster, was becoming part of a larger London. The building of the bridges suddenly opened up the Marsh to the expansion of the City that was forcing charity hospitals, prisons and asylums to move. Lambeth Marsh and the neighbouring St George's Fields, both still green, were ripe for development. Then as now, people had not learnt that the mere fact of building in the country destroys it; and so it was that, with the reformers' ideal of a rural life for the needy of London, Bethlem Hospital, the King's Bench Prison, the New Bridewell and the Magdalen Hospital were all interspersed in the Fields. It took the next hundred years to put to rights the mess that these institutions created when placed amongst the exploding population of Lambeth Marsh. Not until the administration system was changed, till parish charity was replaced, till raising revenue was changed by law and with elected councils, not until then did standards of living begin to rise again. The Guardian for the Poor (1834), the Metropolitan Board of Works (1856) and the School Boards (1870) amalgamated in 1888 to form the London County Council that in 1965 became the Greater London Council.

Democracy and the elected control of welfare was developed throughout the nineteenth century as an improvement on the failure of the church and parish charity systems. 'Victorian values' were not only those of the free market economy but included the reform and labour movements that set up local democracy as we know it today, slowly but successfully raising the standards of health, education and every other aspect of metropolitan life. Victorian Britain evolved a system of elected representatives in the two tiers of county and borough councils, a local democratic government paid for by local taxes and envied throughout the world. In Britain, so far at any rate, this system devolves power to the largest possible number of people, including minorities and immigrants.

Local councils continued to develop into the twentieth century, reaching the peak of their influence following the 1939-45 war, writing and enforcing their own bye-laws and acquiring massive compulsorily purchased land holdings. The London County Council, now with a greater population than many nations, became the major landlord in Lambeth Marsh, carrying out extensive rehousing and office schemes and eliminating private slums. With the loss of population to the outer areas of the London County Council, reinforced by the new large-scale office and road building, the visual character of the Marsh was changed beyond recognition and any remaining village feeling was crushed. The post-war boom came to an end in the 1970s and, none too soon, people came to understand the failings of comprehensive redevelopment areas. Recognising the social destruction of the post-war era, the Coin Street Action Group, and in turn the Coin Street Community Builders, made a start in the 1980s on rebuilding more of the Marsh for residential and amenity purposes and to renew the depleted village.

WOMEN AT WORK

Many stories of women in Lambeth Marsh have already been recalled. Sometimes as with Joyce Culpeper these were previously unsung, but frequently, as in the case of Widow Evans, the two Eleanor Coades or the milkmaid and woman mudlarks photographed by Munby, their work is well documented. The work of four women not previously mentioned now follows:

Annie Besant, 1847-1933

A brief life of Annie Besant is told here despite her tenuous connection with Lambeth Marsh. Her grandmother lived in Stockwell, her brother-in-law Walter Besant wrote the Histories of London and South London and her own work brought her many times to the industries here. Annie Wood married Frank Besant in 1867 but after six years the marriage ended in disaster when she was assaulted by him. She then brought up her daughter as a single parent whilst Walter Besant, a kinder man, paid for her son's education. Annie Besant's notoriety first came when she went to prison for having written a penny tract on the facts of life. At the much-publicised trial in 1877 she took her own defence and passionately maintained that women should know about their own bodies and that the only way they could learn would be to read about them. Annie went on for the rest of her life continuously fighting the iniquities of a male-dominated, hypocritically moral and bigoted society.

This campaign for women led her to meet and work for socialism. Three aspects of her socialist campaign stand out, Bloody Sunday 13 November 1887, the Bryant and May match girl strike and the Tower Hamlets School Board. After being at the front of the Bloody Sunday march she and her new paper *The Link* were frantic with activity, appearing for the defence of prisoners, supplying bail and caring for the discharged, and continuing to expose the conditions of sweated labour. When in the same year 1400 match girls went on strike, Annie and Edith Simcox were the Matchmakers' delegates to the International Trades' Union Congress in London.

During her life her achievements for women were underestimated because she was always so vehemently against any type of organised religion, always in search of religion's answer to poverty. It was this trait of hers, even before her campaigns started, that caused her marriage to collapse. For the vicar's wife to lose her faith and refuse communion was too much for her husband Frank. They rowed, he hit her and she walked out, never to return. She went from one hotly contested belief to another, from socialism to the Fabian Society and Bernard Shaw's personal friendship, to Theosophy where she was in charge of the 'Esoteric Section' of the Society at her own home in St John's Wood and on to India, where in 1913 she founded a Hindu College at Benares. During the 1914-18 war she became an Indian Nationalist and in 1917 was interned, only to be elected the first woman President of the Indian National Congress at the age of seventy. She loved to be called the 'Mother of India' and died aged 86 at Adyar, the Theosophists' headquarters near Madras.[93]

Emma Cons and Morley College [w4.55]

Morley College, started by Emma Cons in the Old Vic (see the Old Vic. p. 104), was reopened by the Prince of Wales in Westminster Bridge Road in 1924. It took over empty property which five years earlier had been the Britannia Club for Soldiers and Sailors. The building had been substantially rebuilt by the Yorkshire Society School in 1885 from the earlier 1812 house on the site.

The Prince of Wales Hall was added to the rear of the old house to allow for the rapid expansion in student numbers that took place over the next few years. In the academic year 1923-4, the last at the Old Vic, there were 1,520 students and in 1926-27 numbers had risen to 2,171. The student numbers continued to rise and new extensions at the rear kept pace with their needs. In

Ill. 79 Morley College 1992

1940 most of the building was bombed beyond repair but took till 1956-8 before it was rebuilt with the help of government grants.

Teaching at the college, from Emma Cons' day to today, has emphasised the arts and humanities rather than career crafts and skills. Following Gustav Holst's appointment as director of music in 1906 the college has always maintained many orchestras and choral groups.[94]

Charlotte Sharman, 1832-1929

In 1867 Charlotte Sharman founded a school for orphans, situated between West Square and the Lambeth Road [primary school site w2.36]. The school, founded with ten children, opened in her father's house where she lived, with the principle of giving a kind and loving education to orphaned girls.[95] Within four years the school had grown into four houses and in 1875 Samuel Morley presided while the Duchess of Sutherland laid the foundation stone to the purpose-built home. At the same time Charlotte's success was such that homes were also opened at Gravesend, Tunbridge Wells and Hastings, and in the year of her death she saw the removal of the West Square Home to new premises in Newlands Park.

Charlotte was a great Christian and believed in divine providence, telling of one incident when drains had to be laid on order of the Sanitary Commissioners and were to cost £50; when the workmen dug the ground an existing drain was found thus saving the cost, for Charlotte an Act of God. Charlotte was kindly, intelligent, sharp-witted and humorous, with an interest in all the concerns of this world till the day she died at 97. From their first day at school all children were treated as responsible individuals, and wherever possible she let them organise the running of their own lives; she kept a suggestion box, always acted on, to ensure the smooth running of the place.

Octavia Hill, 1838-1912

Octavia Hill, best known for her work with the National Trust, had earlier in her life instigated and designed many cottage housing estates. Her first housing scheme still stands in Sudrey Street off Southwark Bridge Road [w1.7], and nearby in the small open space off Redcross Way is a plaque recalling her work with Red Cross Hall and Cottages, that were opened in 1888 and still stand between Ayres Street and Redcross Way [w1.5]. Lambeth Marsh has the Ufford Street housing to her design, built in 1901 behind the Old Vic, and her largest London scheme of eight hundred cottages is off the Walworth Road. Under Octavia Hill's persuasion the Lambeth Vestry purchased the land necessary to form the present Vauxhall Park and she attended the opening in 1890 by the Prince of Wales.[96]

For further reading about women in Lambeth Marsh within living memory the following books are detailed in the bibliography:
The Battle of Waterloo Road by Forbes-Robertson
A Sense of Adventure by Dolly Davey
Growing Up in Lambeth by Mary Chamberlain.

INSTITUTIONS

See Index for the complete lists of locations of hospitals, prisons, schools, places of worship and other institutions.

The County Gaol (Surrey County Gaol)

For many years the County Gaol was rented out and hardly used, the Surrey Quarter Sessions in Borough High Street sending their prisoners to the Marshalsea. In 1650 it was referred to as the House of Correction. In 1773 a new County Gaol and House of Correction was built in St George's Fields [north side of Webber Street at its junction with Great Suffolk Street]. The Cary map of 1787 labels it Surrey 'Bridewell', Bridewell being a name given to Quarter Sessions gaols not necessarily at the original Blackfriars 'Bridewell'. The gaol stayed here only a short while till 1791, when it was moved back again to a site behind the Sessions House in Harper Road.

Christ Church Workhouse [w2.47]

The Christ Church Workhouse was built sometime before 1787, on the border of the parish with Lambeth Marsh, the old border between Paris Garden Manor and Lambeth [Southwark College in The Cut]. In 1862 it became known as St Saviours Workhouse, in 1872 the St Saviours Union Workhouse and in 1937 Christ Church Institute.

Lambeth Workhouse, later Hospital [w1.12]

Situated on the south side of Brook Drive, out of Lambeth Marsh, this hospital was at one time the Lambeth Workhouse where Charlie Chaplin's mother was an inmate, but is now demolished except for the preserved Master's House.

Bethlem Hospital [w4.54]

Bethlem Hospital, colloquially referred to as Bedlam, was the successor to the medieval hospital in the Priory of St Mary of Bethlehem in Bishopsgate and first referred to in 1329. In 1676 Bethlem was moved by the City to Moorfields. As London grew and the care of the mad became more sympathetic it was necessary to move again to more open green fields. In 1815 the new hospital was opened in St George's Fields on the previous site of the Dog and Duck Tavern, the 122 patients conveyed there in hackney carriages. Of the hospital and its several large wings only the central portion with its grand portico is still standing. The large coat of arms in the pediment is made in Coade stone and the building was designed by James Lewis, who won the commission in a competition. The building provided separate wings for the sexes and a special block for insane criminals, who were paid for by the government. In 1835 Sydney Smirke was asked to make considerable enlargements to the building including more wings and the single-story lodge on Lambeth Road that still stands.

As the nineteenth century advanced more county asylums were built and the Bethlem catered less and less for the criminal or poor. Many patients could afford their keep and under Dr Hood amenities improved. By 1869 Bethlem had built a convalescent home at Witley for patients on their way to recovery and in 1926 the governors decided to build new premises at Monks Orchard in Addington. In 1930 the London County Council bought the property, demolished the side wings to form the Mary Harmsworth Park and leased the remaining central wing to house the Imperial War Museum.

Ill. 80 Bethlem Hospital portico and Coade stone crest of 1815

Change to Urban Living

Ill. 81 Bethlem Hospital in the 1870's

Private Madhouse, Lambeth Marsh

An unlocated private madhouse existed in Lambeth Marsh between 1746 and 1763 when it was closed for three year's debt. (Dorothy Owen. *A Catalogue of Lambeth Manuscripts 889 to 901 : Carte Antique et Miscellanee*, p. 171.)

Ill. 82 Freemasons' School for Girls

Freemasons' School for Girls [w2.29]

The Royal Freemasons' School for Girls opened in Westminster Bridge Road [side of Dodson Street] on a site in a temporary building rented from James Hedger in 1788 in another of his dubious transactions. Before their permanent school on the same site, to house a hundred girls, could be built there were protracted negotiations for a new lease with the ground landlord, the City Corporation. Wallis's 1797 map is the first showing the new school. The children, daughters of masons of at least three years' standing, were taken between five and ten years old. Every effort was made 'to impress strongly on their minds a due sense of subordination, in true humility and obedience to their superiors'. No child who had smallpox or any defect or infirmity was admitted. The girls left and were apprenticed at fifteen. In 1852 the school moved to Wandsworth.

The Parochial Boys' School and George Reynolds headmaster [w4.41]

George Reynolds became headmaster to the Boys' School on Lambeth Green in 1806 as well as part-time teacher to the girls in the Female Asylum. Lambeth Green was an open patch of ground [Carlisle Lane as it turns into Hercules Road w4.39] within a road pattern that predates the railway. The school was an old charity founded by Richard Lawrence on the front of the Green, and under George Reynolds' direction had grown by 1809 to school 400 boys. Reynolds' life as headmaster is well documented in letters sent between 1808 and 1816 to the family of J. M. Dovaston, old friends near Shrewsbury (Richardson, J. *Letters from Lambeth*, Boydell Press, 1981).

Reynolds had five children, Jane b. 1791, John Hamilton 1794-1852, Marianne b. 1797, Eliza Beckford b. 1799 and Charlotte b. 1802, but it was John, the future poet, and his mother Charlotte who wrote most of the letters. John became a lifelong friend of Thomas Hood and Keats, reviewing Keats' poems in *The Champion* in 1817 and introducing Keats to many of his future circle; in turn he was treated by Keats 'as a brother'. In 1822 John Reynolds wrote the opera *Gil Blas* with his future brother-in-law Tom Hood, and it was shown at the English Opera House. However, as a writer he seems to have dried up when he lost both his children and life went sour for him. He went bankrupt, became an unknown County Court Clerk in Newport, Isle of Wight, and died of drink.

George Reynolds (1765-1835) was a dedicated schoolmaster, already teaching by the age of twenty-five, at which age he married Charlotte Cox of Wandsworth. George Reynolds himself was a charity boy, but his wife had a little more money, being connected with Sir Richard Cox, Chancellor to Ireland. From their letters it is clear that this was a happy and affectionate marriage, with Charlotte and her society connections encouraging her son John to be a poet. William Blake (1757-1827), the painter and author of the 'Lambeth Books' (a name sometimes given to the works written here), lived in Hercules Road between 1793 and 1800 [plaque on wall of flats, w4.38] and his friend John Flaxman (1755-1826) the sculptor lived in Stangate.

George Reynolds was an advocate of the Bell system of education, and in 1807 Dr Andrew Bell was sponsored by Lord Radstock who persuaded the Archbishop of Canterbury to establish the system in the Charity School. Robert Southey tells of how '... Dr Bell's labours were well seconded in every respect. With the master of the school, Mr Reynolds, he was particularly pleased, and used to allude to him as a memorable exception to the general run of schoolmasters.' Soon after, the system was introduced in the Female Asylum, where Reynolds also taught.

The following quotations from Reynolds' letters relate how in 1808 a new school and schoolhouse were built.

'We are in our fresh habitation [temporary], situated opposite the Asylum late the Williams's Auction Room which makes an excellent schoolroom [empty petrol station 1992 opposite North Lambeth station].'

21 April, Mrs Charlotte Reynolds.

'We hope to be out of here by Michaelmas as our building goes on very well ... the Elevation of the building here roughly sketched.' (see ill. 84).

9 June, George Reynolds.

'The end of next week or the beginning of the following we move to our comfortable new House where we hope to see you soon ... I will just tell you in what manner I am writing. Jane is reading the book I laid down when I began this letter – the consequence is that she every now & then breaks forth into such noisy laughter that I am in doubt whether she may not be a little beside herself – Eliza & Charlotte are in full speed after the Cat with a ball & Marianne tormented with a vile cold with a perpetual sneezing ... the day has been unusually wet, I scarce ever saw so heavy a rain – but yet there are many People walking about, & a few Gigs – this afternoon we saw three people neatly canted into the Mud out of one of these ill contriv'd carriages.'

11 September, Mrs Charlotte Reynolds.

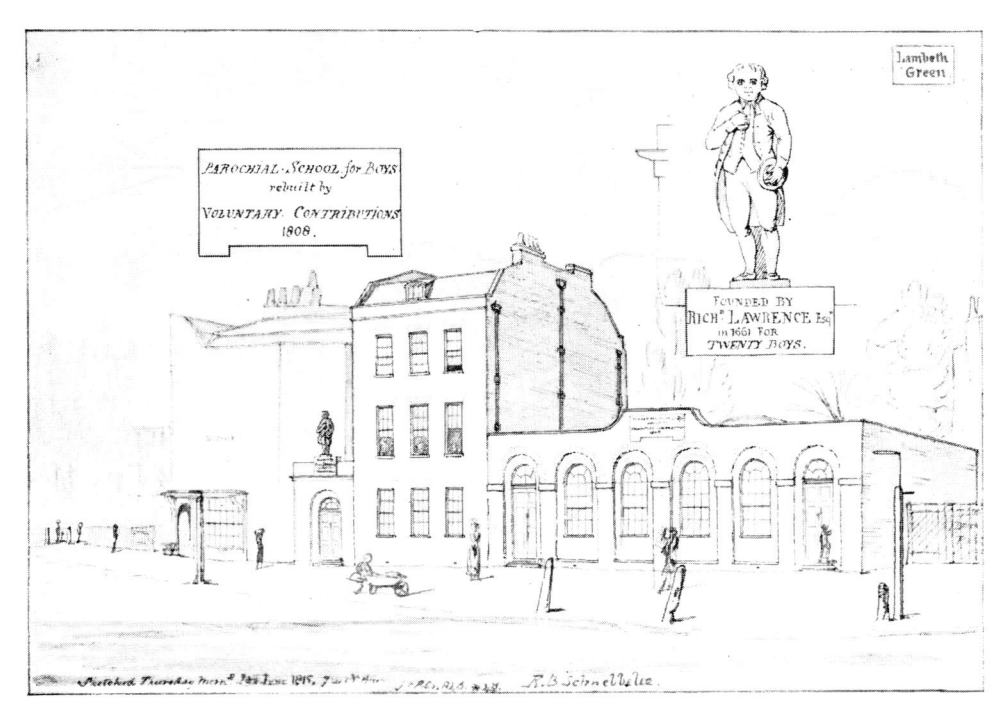

Ill. 83 Charity School for Boys, drawing by R. B. Schnebbelie

Ill. 84 George Reynold's drawing of his new school

Over the Charity School entrance was placed the life-sized Coade stone statue of a boy purchased from Mrs Coade's works in 1785. The statue remained displayed externally at each new location as the school expanded or moved and today resides indoors at the Archbishop Ramsey School in Wyndham Road, Camberwell, still in pristine condition. At the same time a Coade stone girl was purchased for the Female Asylum but the statue appears to have been lost from its hiding place since the second world war.

Change to Urban Living

Ill. 85 Coade stone statue of Charity Boy

Ill. 86 A Magdalen Girl in 1766

The Magdalen Hospital [w2.41]

The Magdalen Hospital was founded by Robert Dingley, Jonas Hanway and others in 1758 for the reception and training of penitent prostitutes.[97] It was so successful that in 1772 it was able to move from Prescott Street to new expanded premises in St George's Fields on the west side of the Blackfriars Bridge Road, the first building on the newly made road (see ill. 87). The success of the institution may have had something to do with the fact that services in the Chapel were open to the public, with the girls arrayed in the box pews for all to see. In the early eighteenth century large contributions were made through collections at the services and their honest use was put to question with the case of Dr William Dodd, who was hanged for forgery in 1777.

Ill. 87 The Magdalen Hospital in St George's Fields

Dodd's fall from grace began over the matter of the living of St George's Hanover Square. The wife of the Lord Chancellor received a letter offering her £3,000 if Dodd were appointed to the living. The letter was brought to the notice of the King, from whence the handwriting was traced to a lawyer's clerk who admitted that it was at Mrs Dodd's dictation. George IV instantly dismissed Dodd as his Chaplain.

By then Dodd's habits were extravagant and he was '... so deeply in debt that he descended so low as to become the editor of a newspaper'. However, he always drew large crowds and this publicity made his sermons at the Magdalen a top social attraction. In 1777 he went too far by forging the signature of the Earl of Chesterfield, an old pupil of his, for the sum of £4,200 on a bond of £700 per annum on the Earl's life. On Thursday 6 February 1777 he was arrested and he returned in full the sum of £4,200 that he had received. He was tried at the Old Bailey, found guilty and hanged for it. Some people felt that the sentence was unduly harsh, but the way in which he had deceived people throughout his life was held against him.

In 1868 the Magdalen moved to cheaper premises in Streatham and raised much-needed money by selling its old site to the Peabody Trust, who built there one of their first housing schemes, still in use. The Magdalen continues to work as a charity for young girls in trouble, a need no different from when it started; indeed it is perhaps worse today because of drug-taking and the decline of state assistance.

Lambeth Asylum for Girls [w4.57]

'Carefully instructed in the principles of religion: in reading, writing, needlework, and household business, they are trained to habits of industry and regularity, by which means there is a supply of diligent and sober domestics for the use of that public, which, by its contributions, has so nobly acquired a right to their services.'

Ackermann's *Microcosm of London* 1808.

The Lambeth Asylum for Girls (House of Refuge or Female Orphan Society) was founded in 1758, another institution placed in green fields before the industrial revolution. Although the girls in the Asylum frequently had their lives saved, they were treated as chattels and kept only as long as they were potential money earners; if they were found unfit for domestic service, often because of physical disability, they were sent wholesale into manufacturing as apprentices.[98]

The Asylum stayed on the site [Christ Church, Westminster Bridge Road] till 1866, when it moved to Beddington Park. In 1939 it evacuated to Cornwall, returning in 1943 to High Wycombe and later back to Beddington, closing finally in the mid-1960s.

The building, of which Ackermann made several engravings, also contained the 'Coade Stone Girl', the pair with the Charity School Boy, but about which nothing has been heard since the Asylum was evacuated to Cornwall. The Asylum was also taught by the Charity School head, Mr George Reynolds (see p. 126).

In 1873 part of the site was taken by J. Oakey & Sons for the manufacture of emery paper and blacking and called Wellington Mills. The remainder of the site was bought to build Christ Church in memory of Rowland Hill and his Chapel in Blackfriars Road. The Surrey Chapel Centenary Fund that came from the numerous branches of the church in the United States and from Rowland Hill's original collections supplied the money. The Church, Hawkstone Hall and other buildings were completed in 1876 and included a spire built to celebrate the anti-slavery movement of Wilberforce and other church members. The spire, which is still standing, has red brick stripes and white stone stars (stars and stripes) and is called the Lincoln Tower.

Past and present patrons include Admiral Nelson, Florence Nightingale, Queen Victoria, King Edward VII, Queen Elizabeth II and the Queen Mother.

The General Lying-in Hospital [w4.3]

Dr John Leake (1729-92) was particularly concerned with the welfare of women and the frequently fatal conditions in which childbirth took place in urban slums.[99] The huge influx of people into Lambeth Marsh that came with the building of the Thames bridges proved the total inadequacy of the parish and the later vestry systems of administering to the needs of those without money. When faced with the epidemics of cholera that were unheard of in the rural setting of just a few years earlier, the systems failed. If a family did not live literally all the time on the street, then they shared one room in an insanitary basement with two or three others. A woman in labour more often than not had nowhere to give birth other than a stinking alley.

Dr Leake set up his Charity Lying-in Hospital for the '. . . relief of those child-bearing women who are the wives of poor industrious Tradesmen or distressed house-keepers, and who either from unavoidable misfortunes or the expenses of maintaining large families are reduced to real want . . .' and himself became the first Physician Man-Midwife to the hospital. The Westminster New Lying-in Hospital opened in 1767 in Westminster Bridge Road, the road's first building after the bridge had opened. In 1830 both the words 'Westminster' and 'New' were dropped and the title 'The General Lying-in Hospital' was

Ill. 88 General Lying-in Hospital 1751

incorporated by Royal Charter. After only a few months parish officers of St Mary Lambeth were complaining that the hospital was delivering babies to unmarried women, and though the babies were a burden to the parish when the women then absconded, the hospital refused to ask for marriage certificates as a requirement for admission. In 1773 an Act was passed making it necessary by law for admissions to prove marriage; if patients were unmarried, notification had to be made to the parish.

Dr Leake's work was a milestone in changing the medical establishment to meet the needs of crowded urban living and it became a lifetime's work to establish the hospital and get medical treatment for those in need. The hospital was rarely a financial success and on several occasions came near to closing.

1765 First stone laid in Westminster Bridge Road.
1767 Opened.
1828 Old building demolished and the York Road building first opened.
1879 New floor and inscription added, still standing.
1907 Adjoining houses to the north taken for nurses' home.
1946 Became part of St Thomas's Hospital.
1971 Last patient admitted.

In the intervening 150 years well over 150,000 babies were delivered, and as many again in their own homes.

Ill. 89 General Lying-in Hospital 1992

Royal Waterloo Hospital for Children and Women [w3.8]

Originally the Royal Universal Infirmary for Children, this hospital moved in 1823 to its present site in Waterloo from St Andrew's Hill, Doctors Commons. The building on the bridge approach had two-storey basements, the lower accessed from Doon Street. The present building, rebuilt in 1903-5 and renamed the Royal Waterloo Hospital for Children and Women, is faced with specially designed glazed ware with the outpatient entrance panels in an unusual Art Nouveau style that was donated by Doulton's pottery.

Ill. 90 The Royal Waterloo Hospital

St George's Military Hospital Stamford Street 1916-20 [w3.9]

The HMSO building still standing in Stamford Street was completed in the middle of the 1914-18 war and was used as an army hospital, called St George's Military Hospital. It had a tunnel to Waterloo station which enabled emergency patients to be ferried direct from the trains to their beds, with the least public exposure. After the war the building was renamed Cornwall House and returned to its designed use as a book store.

St Thomas's Hospital [w4.16]

St Thomas's Spital, part of the priory of St Mary the Virgin, had existed before the Norman conquest for charitable work and the healing of the sick [Southwark Cathedral] and later moved to the corner between Borough High Street and the north side of St Thomas Street.[100]

Ill. 91 St Thomas's Hospital nurse's home, site of Astley's

Ill. 92 St Thomas's Hospital in 1871

When in 1847 the London Bridge railway gave notice of the compulsory purchase of their premises the hospital had to look for a new larger site. After numerous eviction orders the railway made the hospital move in 1862, temporarily, to the disused Surrey Zoological Gardens [1.11] at Manor Place, Walworth.[101] Between 1866 and 1869 the Albert Embankment was being built opposite the Houses of Parliament and it was decided that the large area of marsh and reclaimed river was suitable for the new hospital. The permanent new building with 569 beds and a nurses' school that the Committee and Florence Nightingale had designed was opened on 21 June 1871 by Queen Victoria. Matching the scale of the Parliament building opposite, the hospital had five large ward blocks, three of which still stand and now are fully restored after the devastating bombing the hospital received in the 1939-45 war. After the war new ward blocks and nurses' homes were built on extra land acquired towards the Archbishop's Palace gardens and the realigned Lambeth Palace Road.

Royal Eye Hospital [w2.40]

The Royal South London Ophthalmic Hospital opened in 1857, suitably positioned opposite the School for the Indigent Blind on St George's Circus. The present building was built in 1890-91 with the foundation stone, laid by Prince Edward, still visible on the otherwise derelict facade.

The School for the Indigent Blind [w2.31]

The School for the Indigent Blind was in 1799 the first of its kind in London, set up with others of the same foundation in Liverpool, Bristol and Edinburgh on the lines of a similar school in Paris. The school, another of Hedger's tenants, first opened at the Dog and Duck with 15 pupils but when the lease ran out in 1811 a new school was erected on two acres fronting on St George's Circus. In 1833 there were 55 males and 57 females and it became necessary to enlarge the premises. Extensive new buildings were completed between 1835 and 1838. The school trained pupils in mat-making, basket-weaving, knitting and so on, and was thus the predecessor to the Blind Employment Factory in Waterloo Road, south of Webber Row. In 1901 the school was compulsorily purchased for the marshalling yards of the present Bakerloo underground line and the school moved to Leatherhead.

King's Bench Prison [w4.51]

The King's Bench prison, always situated close to the King's Bench Courts in Borough High Street, was the debtors' prison for this High Court. Debtors' prisons were created not just to help the creditor to get his money back, but to protect the debtors from extortion and sometimes murder committed by their creditors. As with Dickens' father in the Marshalsea, the debtor did not always want to get out. The law accepted that some of the blame for debt could be put on the creditor, and reformists were always trying to make the life of the debtor in prison more humane. With this in mind and when the King's Bench required bigger and better premises than those that existed in the Borough, the new prison and its surrounding Rules were built on St George's Fields.

The prison building ran between Borough Road and Webber Street along Lancaster Road. Outside these buildings was a large area of circumscribed land controlled by the prison and inaccessible to creditors, called 'Within the Rules' of the King's Bench. This covered most of the land from the Borough to Kennington Road and enabled debtors to live relatively normal lives in rented properties with family and friends. The new prison opened in 1758 'situated in fine air', the Fields and Lambeth Marsh still being farm land.

'how many prisoners ... occupy rooms, keep shops, enjoy places of profit, or live on the rent of their rooms, a life of idleness; and being indulged with the use of a key, go out when they please, and thereby convert a prison ... into an almshouse.'

William Smith, 1776.

The prison was run on these lines till 1842, when fees were abolished and with them the privileges that fees could buy. In 1869 the prison was closed and for ten years the building was used for convicts in transit, a dubious reform that inflicted the debtor with the even harsher punishment of transportation to Australia, that is if he survived the ordeal of the journey round the world.

Philanthropic Society [w2.34]

The Philanthropic Society was founded in 1788 at a house in Cambridge Heath and in 1806 moved to purpose-built premises in St George's Road, in the triangle between Gladstone Street and Garden Row, then still the green St George's Fields. The Society was incorporated by Parliament to care for deserted and vagrant children who were either juvenile offenders or the children of convicted felons. The Society was supported by church collections and by selling the children's work, but following reform Acts in 1840 and restrictions on child labour the girls' side was forced to close and the boys' side was limited to the 'reformation' of criminal boys. In 1848 the site was sold and the chapel used for many years as the parish church of St Jude. The present church of St Jude is on the same site.

'Accommodation for lodging one hundred boys, workshops for carrying on the following trades, viz. printing, copper-plate printing, shoe making, tailor's work, rope-making and twine spinning ... The girls are placed in a building contiguous to the manufactory; but all intercourse between them and the boys is effectually prevented by a wall of considerable height ... The girls are brought up for menial servants: they make their own clothing, and shirts for the boys, and wash and mend for the manufactory: besides which, their earnings

Ill. 93 The Philanthropic Society by Rowlandson

in plain work have for the last three years been considerable. When of proper age they are placed out, at low wages, in respectable families, and receive rewards for good behaviour at the end of the first and third years of their service ... Objects [children] are admitted by the committee, at its weekly meetings, held at twelve o'clock on every Friday at the St Paul's coffee-house, in St Paul's churchyard. They are seldom taken younger than eight or nine, or older than twelve: no female has of late been received beyond that age.'

Ackermann's *Microcosm of London* 1808.

Archbishop Tenison's School [w4.31]

This school, at first in Lambeth Road near St Mary Lambeth, was endowed and built by the Archbishop for the education of twelve poor girls in 1715. Rebuilt twice, the building in Lambeth High Street dates from 1863 and really served Water Lambeth as opposed to Lambeth Marsh, which by then had its own parish of St John's Waterloo Road.

Ill. 94 Archbishop Temple School, now Marine Society

Change to Urban Living

Archbishop Temple's School [w4.32]
See page 126: The Parochial Boys' School and George Reynolds.

Surrey Institution, later the Rotunda [w3.19]
The Surrey Institution was founded in 1808.

'The entrance to this academic mansion is in Blackfriars Road, beneath an elegant portico of the Ionic Order . . . The vicinity of Blackfriars Bridge suggested the advantage of fixing on the south side of the river, in order to connect that district of increasing population with the southern part of London. The great encouragement expected from the county of Surrey, and the opportunity of engaging a convenient building already erected . . . induced the proprietors to denominate the establishment the Surrey Institution. Their object comprises a series of lectures, an extensive library, and reading rooms: a chemical laboratory and philosophical apparatus; together with a supplementary library, the books of which, under certain restrictions, may be perused at the houses of subscribers.'

Ackermann's *Microcosm of London* 1808.

'I was lately taken by Mr Edwards (my master) to the Surry Institution. They have a good library and they also take in the daily papers and Magazines and at night there are lectures upon the different Sciences. I heard one on Electricity which was both useful and amusing . . . he has offered me a ticket when I choose which I think good of him.'

John Reynolds' letter, 31 December 1808.

Ill. 95 Surrey Institute

It was perhaps on Reynolds' recommendation that Keats attended Hazlitt's lectures on English poetry here. In spite of its eminent membership and with Sir Ashton Lever's natural history collection containing Captain Cook's curios, the Society was not a success and survived only till 1823. The building was then used for many purposes and known as the Rotunda. At first it was a theatre, and in 1830 Richard Carlile (1790-1843), a free thinker, took it for rowdy public meetings that in 1832 led to public complaints and to his spending at various times a total of nine years in prison for the riots he caused. In 1833 it was opened as the Globe Theatre and in 1838 returned to concerts and as a penny gaff (see p. 113), being finally closed in 1855. Although the hall was bombed in the 1939-45 war, it survived without a roof till 1959, when it was demolished for an office block; a plaque detailing its history is displayed on the outside of the building.

PLACES OF WORSHIP

Lambeth Marsh, where a certain freedom from property exploitation already existed, was also a safe haven for progressive freedom seekers and individualists. Outspoken words could be heard here, the most famous being in 1780 when Lord George Gordon assembled sixty thousand Protestants in St George's Fields prior to the marching and riots that followed against Catholics.

'Terrible riots in London: & unprecedented burnings, & devastations by the mob.'

Gilbert White, 6 June 1780.

In 1802 Colonel Edward Desparte was arrested with other Irish labourers at the Oakley Arms [w2.24] on the corner of Frazier Street and convicted and hanged for plotting the downfall of the state, and the Lambeth Irish became a force to be reckoned with in the trade union movement. In the nineteenth century public speaking always drew massive crowds, whether at church, open-air pulpits, Kennington Common or the many local institutes and halls. The communication business as we now call it had taken off with an explosion of writing, public speaking and live entertainment. On Sundays Kennington Common regularly held twenty thousand people, coming to hear the hellfire and thunder preachers or to hear the Chartists and the political ranting of the day.

Before 1800 there were only three churches, all on the edge of Lambeth Marsh:

1. Parish church of St Mary Lambeth, now the Tradescant Trust, next to Lambeth Palace, first built in 1062.[102]
2. Christ Church, built in 1695 when Paris Garden Manor was developed as a parish (see p. 73).
3. Surrey Chapel, 1782-1881, of the Reverend Rowland Hill, in Blackfriars Road (see p. 110).

Then, between 1800 and 1872 over twenty-four new places of worship were built to keep up with the growth of the population and their search for knowledge and truth. Because of the depopulation since 1939, the number is now down to seven: St John's, Waterloo; St Andrew, Short Street; St George's

Ill. 96 St Mary Lambeth

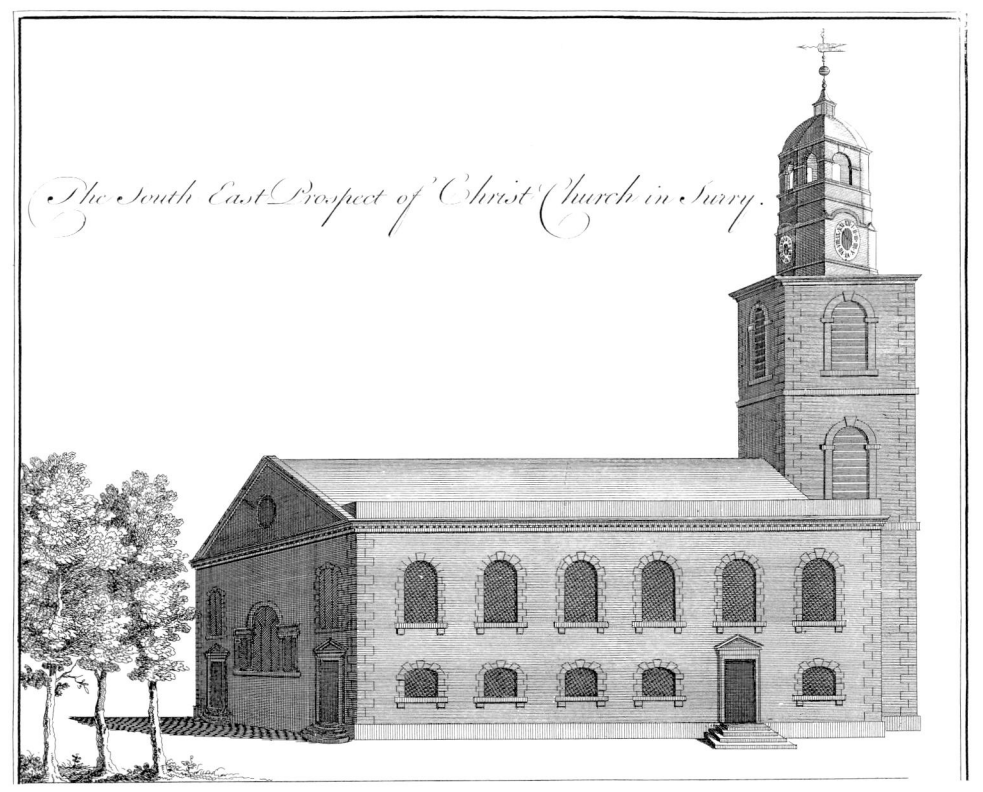

Ill. 97 Christ Church Blackfriars

Ill. 98 Christ Church and Upton Chapel

Ill. 99 St George's Cathedral

Cathedral; Christ Church, Blackfriars; Lambeth Methodist Mission, Lambeth Road; Mission Hall Ufford/Webber Street; Christ Church and Upton Chapel. (See Index for list and locations of places of worship.)

All Saints, Leake Street, and the York Road Chapel [w2.9]

Between 1844 and 1846 and before the railway, All Saints church was built at the Lower Marsh end of Leake Street with a tall spire rising over a Grecian portico. By 1899 the station had expanded, the church was demolished and the elaborate altar moved to the York Road Chapel [w4.4] that had been built in 1847-8 on the corner of Addington Street and York Road next to the Lying-in Hospital.

Christ Church and Upton Chapel [w4.57]
See Asylum for Girls p. 130.

St George's Cathedral [w2.30]

In 1788 the Catholic Relief Bill was passed and for the first time since Henry VIII's reign the Catholics were allowed to build. The chapel off the London Road was their first in the area and was finished in 1790 on a site that later became the South London Palace of Varieties. In 1848 the Roman Catholic Cathedral of St George's was opened to provide for the large numbers of Catholics that included the Lambeth Irish in the vicinity. The site in St George's Fields was ironically remembered as the place where the anti-Catholic Gordon riots started fifty years earlier. The Cathedral, designed by A. W. Pugin in the gothic style, provided for the three thousand standing worshippers and included a school and seminary buildings. Pugin's building was totally destroyed in the 1939-45 war, but afterwards it was rebuilt on the same foundations but in a very much economised gothic style.

St John's Waterloo [w3.7]

When South London's population started to grow the Church of England was worried by the competition from other churches and in 1818 persuaded

Ill. 100 St John's Waterloo 1992

Ill. 101 St John's Waterloo bombed in 1941, by Capa.

Parliament to allocate large sums of money for building some new ones. These churches became known as the Waterloo Churches and St John's Waterloo was one of the first to be built, opening in 1824. The church received a direct bomb hit in the 1939-45 war, when only the strength of the crypt saved the lives of those sheltering there. After the war the church was fully restored, and its crypt is now used as a refuge for those no longer helped by the Welfare State.[103]

St Thomas's Church and vicarage [w2.27]

St Thomas's Church, on the corner of Pearman Street and Westminster Bridge Road, was built in 1856. Over one hundred people sheltering in the church were killed when it was demolished by a direct hit in the 1939-45 war by a V2.

Holy Trinity, Carlisle Lane [w4.33]

The church of Holy Trinity was consecrated in 1839 and demolished in the 1950s after sustaining serious war damage. The church stood in Carlisle Lane [car park next to the Archbishop's Park] and the school and vicarage are still in use as the Holy Trinity Urban Centre down a small road that in early days was Rochester's right of way from Carlisle House to the Stangate ferry. At the time of the 1939-45 war the terracotta Doulton altarpiece by Tinworth was removed to Tisbury, where it still remains in pieces gathering dust on the floor.

St Andrew, Coin Street [w3.10]

The Duchy refused to sell the Church Commissioners their preferred site for this new church so finally land was bought from Richard Palmer Roupell. St Andrew, consecrated in 1856, was built of close-banded red and yellow brick with a tall slated spire and was on the corner of Coin Street and Palmer Street [Theed Street]. In the 1939-45 war the church was bombed, and later demolished when that end of Coin Street was closed to Palmer Street and the plot developed for light industry.

7
THE MARSH LIVES ON

The study of history has the advantage of being done with hind-sight and so is always available for reassessment. Received wisdom is open to amendment and if the preceding pages have raised as many questions as they answer then they will have served their purpose.

The correct locations for many buildings have been confirmed by the surprising accuracy of paintings or engravings, and as with the London Botanic Garden behind the Old Vic, locations are often different from those previously established. Buildings lasting over a hundred years frequently had more than one period of fashion or disrepute, for example, The Canterbury Arms operated as a music-hall long before Morton was supposed to have started it in 1848, and The Ring was a chapel long before boxing came to it. Places, like people, rarely fall neatly into categories or time periods, least of all in an area with a history as full as Lambeth Marsh.

Lambeth Marsh, as a living organism, reacts to human interference as if controlling it, as if its character is stronger and more resilient. Despite apparent changes and continual developments, the rise and fall of shops in Westminster Bridge Road today is identical to Dickens' description of them quoted on page 65. Today still sees the greedy landlords, whether councils, developers, or individuals, who wait for the tenant with more money than sense, but themselves go bankrupt. Lambeth Marsh continues to witness depressions when the infrastructure collapses, roads return to gravel lanes, ruined shops end with roofs falling in and basements run with rats or cockroaches. Maybe the present emptiness is Lambeth Marsh's way of taking time to recuperate.

Improvements require trial and error, and rapid changes, such as those caused by the Plague, the Industrial Revolution and the 1939-45 war, always seemed to spell disaster. Real improvements never arise from the action of one person; many have to pull, often in different directions, for any final outcome to be an improvement. Improvements in Lambeth Marsh were rarely planned or foreseen, and when they did occur it was in spite of people with power, rarely because of them. The horror of industrial pollution only finally ceased when there was no industry left: the squalor of disease-ridden slums stopped only when people voted with their feet and left the place a concrete desert, left the grass to grow in the centre of main roads and the hawks to nest on empty office blocks.

Lambeth Marsh had just two population peaks, one before the Fire and Plague in the 1660s and the other in the 1870s that led to the decline that still continues. Although Britain's population today is ten times that of a century ago it is spread more evenly, to everyone's benefit, and is housed in large areas of sub-urban or sub-rural estates. The desire for the future is that improvements will be gradual, with more deliberation, fewer dictatorial schemes and greater individual freedom. The character of Lambeth Marsh, like that of any other area, has to be respected by all concerned if it is to become sufficiently pleasant to attract people back to live, work and raise families.

Thus William Blake, who at first lived in Lambeth Marsh, then in the country, had this to say on his return to live in the metropolis, his Jerusalem:

> And now the time returns again:
> Our souls exult, & London's towers
> Receive the Lamb of God to dwell
> in England's green and pleasant bowers.

William Blake   selection from 'Jerusalem'

Ill. 102 The Oxo building comes to life with housing and workshops

APPENDIX
– John Evelyn – Wenceslas Hollar –
– Gilbert White – William Blake –
– Joyce Culpeper –

JOHN EVELYN

The quotations are taken, complete with original spellings, from *The Diary of John Evelyn*, editor William Bray (London, W. W. Gibbings, 1890).

10 June 1640:
London, and especially the Court, were at this period in frequent disorders, and great insolences were committed by the abus'd and too happy Citty; in particular the Bish. of Canterbury's Palace at Lambeth assaulted by a rude rabble from Southwark; my Lord Chamberlain imprison'd, and many scandalous libells and invectives scatter'd about the streetes, to the reproach of Government and the fermentation our since distractions.

19 September 1655:
Came to see me Sir Edw. Hales, Mr Ashmole, Harlakenton and Mr Thornhill.

17 September 1657:
I went to see Sir Robert Needham at Lambeth, a relation of mine; and thence to John Tradescant's Museum, in which the chiefest rarities were, in my opinion, the ancient Roman, Indian and other nations armour, shields and weapons: some habits of curiously-colour'd and wrought feathers, one from the Phoenix wing as tradition goes. Other innumerable things there were, printed in his catalogue by Mr Ashmole, to whom after the death of the widow they are bequeath'd, and by him design'd as a gift to Oxford.

3 July 1658:
To London, and dined with Henshaw, Mr Dorell, and Mr Ashmole, founder of the Oxford repository of rarities, with divers doctors of physic and virtuosos.

31 August 1663:
I was invited . . . to the ceremony performed at Lambeth . . . so going to visit my Lady Needham who lived in Lambeth, I went over to Lambeth.

19 September 1667:
When I saw these precious monuments miserably neglected and scattered up and down about the garden, and other parts of Arundel House, and how exceedingly the corrosive air of London impaired them, I procured him [Mr Henry Howard of Norfolk] to bestow them on the University of Oxford. This he was pleased to grant me, and now gave me the key of the Gallery [depicted in Hollar prints], with leave to mark all the stones, urns, alters, &c. and whatever I found had inscriptions on them, that were not statues. This I did, and getting them remov'd and pil'd together, with those that were encrusted in the garden-walls, I sent immediately letters to the Vice-Chancellor of what I had procured.

23 July 1678:
Went to see Mr Elias Ashmole's Library and curiosities at Lambeth. He has divers MSS, but most of them astrological, to which study he is addicted, tho' I believe not learned, but very industrious, as his History of the Order of The Garter proves. He shew'd me a toad included in amber. The prospect from a turret is very fine, it being neer London, and yet not discovering any house about the country. The famous John Tradescant bequeathed his Repository to this gentleman, who has given them to the University of Oxford, and erected a lecture on them, over the laboratorie, in imitation of the R. Society.

Appendix

2 February 1683/4:
   He [Captain Collins, cartographer] affirm'd, that of all the mapps put out since, there are non extant so true as those of Jo. Norden, who gave us the first in Qu. Elizabeth's time; all since are erroneous.

9 July 1685:
   I supp'd this night at Lambeth at my old friends, Mr Elias Ashmole's, with my Lady Clarendon, The Bishop of St Asaph, and were treated at a great feast.

6 July 1694:
   I dined at Lambeth, making my first visit to the Archbishop, where there was much company and great cheer. After prayers in the evening, My Lord made me stay to show me his house, furniture and garden, which were all very fine, and far beyond the usual Archbishops, not as affected by this, but being bought ready furnished by his predecessor.

1 June 1697:
   I went to Deptford to dispose of my goods, in order to letting the house for three years to Vice Admiral Benbow, with condition to keep up the garden. This was done soon after.

JOHN EVELYN BIOGRAPHY

Quotations referring to the area of Lambeth Marsh and North Southwark are from *John Evelyn and His World*, John Bowle (Routledge & Kegan Paul, 1981).

page 7 line 17:
   Charles also ordered the East India Company to import saltpetre in ballast from India, and during the personal rule of the late 1630s infuriated a widespread interest by allowing government contractors to carry off earth from pigeon houses without the owners' consent and to commandeer carts cheaply to carry the stuff to the King's main store at Southwark.

On p. 108 there are further references to lime kilns on Bankside near the Falcon and near Vauxhall.

WENCESLAS HOLLAR

The following have been used as references to Hollar's work and life:
- Denkstein, V. *Hollar drawings* (London, Orbis, 1979).
- Adams, Bernard. *London Illustrated: 1604-1851* (London, Library Association, 1983).
- Hodges, W. *Shakespeare's Second Globe* (London, Oxford University Press, 1973).
- Piper, David. *The Treasures of Oxford* (London, Paddington Press, 1977).
- Smith, Urwin. *Shakespeare's Blackfriars Playhouse: Its History and Design* (New York, New York University Press, 1964).

1607	Born 13 July in Prague; postal number 1195.
1613	Mother Marketa, née Lowe Von Lowengrun died.
1627-8	Worked in Stuttgart, Germany.
1629-30	Worked for printseller Jacob Van der Heyden, Strasbourg.
1636	Published his own work. In May met the Earl of Arundel in Cologne, entered the Earl's service as designer, travelled the Rhine to Prague in July. Also with Dr William Harvey.
1636-44	Living in Arundel House in the Strand.
1641	4 July married mistress Tracy, lady-in-waiting to Countess of Norfolk.
1642	Arundel moved to Antwerp. Hollar stayed in London and worked for Duke of York, future King James II, and lodged in Larkhall village near Tradescant and Ashmole.
1643	The four seasons series of prints.
1644-52	Hollar in Netherlands. Visited Arundel in Antwerp, copied more of the Earl's collection.
1646	Earl of Arundel died. Hollar continued work on collection.
1652	Second London visit. Arrested on arrival; William Dugdale bought his release. Hollar worked for Elias Ashmole, who married Elizabeth Dugdale, and also for William Dugdale. He illustrated Ashmole's *History of the Order of the Garter* and Dugdale's *Monisticon Anglicanum* (1655-73) and *History of St Paul's Cathedral* (1658), also praised by John Evelyn.
1655	Early in year wife died, then his gifted draughtsman son died of plague. Same year married Honora, a young girl he adopted during the Plague.
1665	Engraved the New River Islington.
1666	Year of the Fire, appointed Scenographer Royal.
1668-9	Expedition for the King to Tangier, part of the Queen's dowry.
1672	Travelled around England, drawing buildings.
1677	Died in poverty 25 March.

Appendix

———GILBERT WHITE———

The quotations are from the *Journals of Gilbert White*, edited by Walter Johnson (London, Routledge & Kegan Paul, reprint 1970).
N.B. White carefully distinguishes whether he visits South Lambeth or London, and also gives the period of his stay. His brothers Thomas and Ben lived on a country farm at South Lambeth in Tradescant's house, South Lambeth Road [w1.15].

1774
    November 22 (London). *footnotes*. When I came to town I found herrings were out of season ... The public papers here abounded with accounts of most severe & early frosts, not only in the more Northern parts of Europe, but on the Rhine. ... The news of severe weather usually reaches us some days before the cold arrives.

1776
    January 23 (London). Therm: in London areas 20. The ground covered with snow & everything frozen up.

    January 26. Snow very thick on the roofs & in areas.

    January 27. Snow all day, fierce frost at night.

    January 28 (South Lambeth). Fierce frost; ice under people's beds, & cutting winds. Therm at Selbourne: abroad, 7.

    January 29. (thermometer 6) As intense a frost usually befalls in Jan: our saxon fore-fathers call'd that month with no small propriety wolf-month; because the severe weather brought down those ravenous beasts out of the woods among the villages.

    January 31. Below zero!! 32 deg. below the freezing point. At eleven it rose to $16\frac{1}{2}$. Rime A most unusual degree of cold for S. E. England.

    February 1. Snow now lying on the roofs for 26 days! Thames frozen above and below bridge: crowds of people running about on the ice. The streets strangely encumbered with snow, which crumbles and treads and looks like bay salt – carriages run without any noise or clatter. Thaws, I have observed, take place immediately from intense freezing; as men in sickness frequently mend from a paroxysm.

1778
    March 3-12 (South Lambeth). Ben's Turkey-cock struts and gabbles.
    March 7. Rain, harsh and dark, much London smoke.
    March 10. Titlark in cages essay to sing. For want of rain hot-beds languish. Every matter in field & garden is very backward.

    March 12 (London). Dark and windy. Bright.

    March 13-25 (South Lambeth). Ice, bright sun. Full moon.
    March 14. The green woodpecker laughs in the fields of Vauxhall.
    March 22. Frogs spawn in ditches.

1778
    July 18. The thermometer belonging to my brother Thomas White of South Lambeth was in the most shady part of his garden on july the 5th and July 14th: up at 80, a degree of heat not very common even at Gibraltar! July 1st: therm. at Lyndon in Rutland 85.

1779
　　February 23-March 19 (South Lambeth).
　　February 26 Pilewort (Lessor celandine) Summer-like.
　　February 27 The gardener begins to mow my Brother's grass-walks.
　　February 28 Gossamer abound. Frogs swarm in the ditches. Spawn.
　　March 6 Radishes pulled in the cold ground.
　　March 13 The roads in a most dusty, smothering condition.
　　March 14 Small rain. Quick-set hedges begin to leaf. Dust is laid.
　　March 17 Tussilago Farfara (coltsfoot). Stellaria holostia (greater stitchwort).

1780
　　February 29-March 11 (South Lambeth).
　　February 29 (South Lambeth). Remarkable vivid Aurora borealis.
　　March 6 (London). Sky-larks mount and sing.
　　March 8 Mr Snooke died aged 86.

　June 6 Red valerian blows (later note) Terrible riots in London: & unprecedented burnings, & devastations by the mob (Gordon riots).

　June 19 (South Lambeth). Dust well-laid on the road. Barley in ear on the sands. Much upland hay mowed near London.
　June 20. Early pease abound. Strawberries, & cherries ill-ripened, & very small. Much wall-fruit. Roses blow.
　June 22. Gloomy and moist, rain. Sold my Saffron the 13th crop. Lighted a fire in the dining room. Rain at South Lambeth (32 hundredths of an inch).

　　June 25-9 (South Lambeth).
　　June 27. Swallows feed their young on the ground in Mr Curtis's botanic garden in George's Fields.
　　June 29. Jane White was married to Mr Clement.

　December 12. . . . The Barometer at South Lambeth was this day at 30-6-10: a sure token that South Lambeth is much Lower than Selbourne [Selbourne 10-1-10].

1782
　　February 19-March 15 (South Lambeth). Thomas kept account of the rain in my absence.
　　March 3 (London). Daffodil opens. Mistle thrush sings.
　　March 6. Almond tree in blossom.

　June 5. My brother Thomas nailed-up several large 'scallop shells under the eaves of his house at South Lambeth, to see if the house-martins would build in them. These conveniences had not been fixed half an hour, before several pairs settled upon them; &, expressing great complacency, began to build immediately. The shells were nailed on horizontally with the hollow side upward; & should, I think, have a hole drilled in their bottoms to let-off moisture from driving rains.

1784
　　February 25-April 1 (South Lambeth). Little snow on the road. Thomas Hoar kept an account of the rain at Selbourne in my absence.
　　March 1. Brother Thomas: found a grass-hopper lark dead in his outlet: it seamed to be starved. I was not aware that they were about in the winter.

1786
　　June 14-July 6 (South Lambeth). About Newton men were cutting their saffron: and all the way towards London their upland meadows, many of which, notwithstanding the draught, produce decent crops. We had a dusty fatiguing journey. Brother Thomas has made his hay; and his fields are much burnt-up.

Appendix

June 19. My brother's gardeners plant-out annuals. The ground is well moistened. They prick-out young cabbages, celery, &c.

June 20. On this day Miss Anne Blunt, by being married to Mr Edmund White, increased the number of my nephews & nieces to forty & five.

June 22 (London). Jasmine in warm aspects begins to blow.

June 24. Wheat is in bloom, & has had a fine, still, dry, warm season for blowing. Nights miserable hot, & sultry.

June 25. Cauliflowers, Coss-lettuce, marrow-fat pease, carrots, summer-cabbage, & small beans in great profusion, & perfection. Cherries begin to come in: artichokes for supper. Brother Ben's outlet swarms with *Scarabaeous solstitialis*, which appears at Midsummer. My two brothers gardens about with all sorts of kitchen crops.

June 27. Many of Brother Thomas's young fowls pine, & die; & so did last summer.

June 28. Brother Thomas's gardener stops his vines, & tacks them. Brother Ben's vines (those that come from Selbourne) have very weal scanty shoots. Brother Thomas's vines have good wood, & show for much fruit.

June 30. Brother Ben: cuts his Lucerne a second time: the second crop is very tall.

1789

September 12. . . . Sent 12 plants of *Ophrys spiralis* to Mr Curtis of Lambeth Marsh.

1790

June 7 (London). Went to London by Guildford & Epsom. Spring-corn & grass look well. Hay making near town.

June 17-July 1 (South Lambeth).

June 12. Cauliflowers abound. Pease sold for ten pence a peck.

June 13. Artichokes and chardons, come into eating. Cucumbers abound.

June 14. Sweet hay-making weather.

June 16. My brother finishes a large rick of hay in very nice order.

June 20. Muck laid on a gardener's field poisons my brother's outlet. A martin at Stockwell chapel has built its nest against the window: it seems to stick firmly to the glass, and has no other support. In former summers I remember similar instances.

June 21. Scarlet-straw-berries good. A small praecox melon. The longest day:

June 22. . . . My brother Thomas's thermometer in Blackfriars road against an eastern wall in the afternoon was 89 . . .

October 2. Brother Thomas, & his daughter Mrs Ben White left us, & went to London.

October 7 (Selbourne). Mr Edmund White, whilst he was at South Lambeth, this summer, kept for a time a regular journal of his Father's barometer, which, when compared to with a journal of my own for the same space, proves that the mercury at South Lambeth at an average stands full *three* tenths of an inch higher than at Selbourne . . . it plainly appears that the mercury at South Lambeth exceeds in height at an average the mercury at Newton by six tenths at least. Hence it follows, according to some calculations, that Newton vicarage house is 600 feet higher than the hamlet of South Lambeth, which, as may be seen by the tide coming-up the creek before some of the houses, stands but a few feet above high water mark.

1791

February 2. Prodigious high tide at London & its environs! it did much damage in various parts.

June 25 to July 18 (South Lambeth).

June 25. My brother's straw-berries well flavoured. The vines here in bloom, & smell very sweet.

June 26. Fifteen Whites dined this day at Brother Ben White's table; as did also Mr

Wells, a great, great, grandson of the Rev'd John Longworth, in old times vicar of Selbourne...

June 28. When the barometer is 30 at South Lambeth, it is 29-7 at Selbourne, and 29-4 at Newton. My brother cut a good Romagna melon.

June 29. Some swallows in the district, & only two pairs of swifts, and no martins. No wonder then that they overrun with flies, which swarm in the summer months, & destroy their grapes.

June 30. The Passion-flower buds for bloom: double flowering Pomegranate has had bloom.

July 3. My brother's cow, when there is no extraordinary call for cream, produces three pounds of butter each week. the footman churns the butter overnight, & puts it in water; in the morning one of my nieces beats it, & makes it up, & prints it. Mr M. black cluster-grapes in his pine-house seem to be well ripened.

July 5 (London). Rasps come in. Many Martins in the green park. In a fruit-shop near St James were set out to sale black cluster-grapes, pine apples, peaches, nectarines, & Orleans plums.

July 6. Many martins in Lincoln's Inn Fields.

July 7 (South Lambeth). Fine, showers, clouds.

July 8. Cut chardon-heads for boiling: artichokes dry, & not well flavoured. Roses in high beauty. My nieces make Rasp jam. Goose-berries not finely flavoured.

July 9. A cuckoo cries in my Brother's garden: some birds of that sort have frequented this place all the summer. Young swallows at Stockwell... Crops of pease go off. Some celerei trenched out from the seedling bed.

July 10. Grapes swell. New potatoes.

July 11. Chardons are usually blanched, & stewed like celery: but my Brother boils the head of his, which are very sweet, & in flavour like artichokes...

July 12. On this day My Brother Benjamin White began to rebuild his house in Fleet Street which he had entirely pulled to the ground. His grandson Ben White laid the first brick of the new foundation, & then presented the workmen with five shillings for drink. Ben, who is five years old, may probably remember this circumstance hereafter, & may be able to recite to his grandchildren the occurrences of the day.

July 13. My brother gathered a sieve of mushrooms: they come up in the flower-borders, which have been manured with the dung from the old hot beds.

July 14. A bat of the largest sort comes forth every evening, & flits about in front of my brother's house. This is a very rare species, & seldom seen. See my history of Selbourne.

July 17. Small Shower: heavy rain at Clapham, & Battersea. On this day Mrs Edmund White was brought to bed of a daughter, who increases my nephews & nieces to the number of 58.

July 31. "On the last day of this month my father Mr Ben White shot in his garden at South Lambeth, a Loxia curvirostra, or Cross Bill, as it was feeding on the cones of his Scotch firs. There were six, four cocks, & two hens: what he shot was a cock, which was beautifully variegated brown, & green, & a great deal of red: it answered very accurately to Willughby's description; & weighed rather more than 1 ounce & an half. In the evening, the five remaining birds were seen to fly over the garden, making a cheerful not." Thus far Mrs Ben White...

1792

June 17 (Selbourne). The thermometer at George's fields Surrey 82: on the 21, -51. Saffron fly, sphynx filipendulae, appears.

1793

March 13.... My Brother has a pigeon-house stocked with perhaps 50 pairs of birds, which have not yet begun to breed. He has in the yard Turkeys, a large breed of ducks, & fine fowls. On the ponds are geese, which begin to sit.

Appendix

WILLIAM BLAKE

1757	WILLIAM BLAKE, Born 28 November.
1779	First employed by bookseller J. Johnson.
1782	Married Catherine Bowcher, lived 23 Green Street, Leicester Fields.
1783	First published, *Poetical Sketches* helped by Flaxman and Mathew.
1784	Lived 27 Broad Street, Golden Square.
1786	The Albion Mills in Blackfriars road. First steam-powered flour mill.
1787	Lived 28 Poland Street.
1791	Albion Mills burned out and remains as a shell.
1791-1800	Lived at 13 Hercules Buildings, Lambeth (23 Hercules Row [Road]).
1789	*Songs of Innocence*, including *London*.
1790	*Marriage of Heaven and Hell* (engraving).
1793	*America: A Prophecy*.
1793	*Visions of the Daughters of Albion*.
1794	*Songs of Experience*.
1794	*Book of Urizon*.
1794	*Europe: A Prophecy*.
1794	*The Book of Los*.
1800-3	Lived under patronage of William Hayley at Felpham, Sussex, but not always happy there.
1802	Hayley's *Ballads* with Blake's illustrations.
1803	Started writing *Milton*

> I will not cease from Mental Fight,
> Nor shall my Sword sleep in my hand,
> Till we have built Jerusalem,
> In England's green & pleasant Land.

1803-27	Moved back to London, 17 South Molton Street.
1804-8	Published *Milton*.
1803	Albion Mills refurbished as housing.
1809	*The Canterbury Pilgrims* exhibited 28 Broad Street.
1804-20	Published *Jerusalem*.
1818	*The Everlasting Gospel* and *For the Sexes: The Gates of Paradise*.
1821	Moved to 3 Fountain Court, Strand.
1825-7	Illustrations for *The Book of Job* and *Dante's Inferno*.
1827	Died 12 August. Buried Bunhill Fields.

Blake has been labelled many things by many people, visionary, madman, prophet, the Interpreter, nationalist, and dreamer. Blake moved in a wide circle of society, was an avid reader, and was influenced by many diverse movements taking place at that time. He had most sympathy with the Swedenborg movement, but he wrote about many others such as the Naturists, new movements in the church, Rousseau, and Tom Paine. With his active imagination Blake's thoughts never stood still long enough to believe in any existing philosophy, but evolved to a point that:

'I have most at heart, more than life ... the interest of True Religion & Science ... I am under the direction of Messengers from Heaven, Daily and Nightly ...'
Letter to Thomas Butts 1808.

Blake was vociferously critical of nearly everyone, artists at the Royal Academy, religions in Lambeth, and even his best friends.

'Thy friendship oft has made my heart to ache:
Do be my enemy – for friendship's sake.'

His treatment of friends often turned them away from him and led him to become bitter at not receiving commissions. However, he was rarely put off his work, which he saw as a God-given task, and when he was unable to find a publisher, he engraved and printed his works with his wife's help. His very individualistic work is its own best expression, out of his time and out of all time, and best left for people to interpret in their own way.

Blake's work is concerned with spirits and souls and with the places and people these inhabit. The mythical name he gave each spirit may be looked at in several ways; as a convenient label for the many similar spirits and emotions that it propounds; as a human spirit that is manifest in people's actions and thoughts; or as an expression of the people or places that the soul inhabits. Thus the portrait of a Ghost of a Flea could be a portrait of a pure spirit, or an imagined portrait of a flea in man's form, or a literal caricature of a real person with a mean parasitic character. Thus Albion is the pure spirit of Eternal Man, a heavenly state where the spirit is free and at one with the universe, or simply a portrait of England as Blake saw it: Jerusalem may be the spirit of a rebuilt city, or at its most prosaic London as Blake saw it. Urizon, the worldly spirit, is false and sterile and 'your reason', Los is the spirit of time, working for the unity of spirit and reality, and Beulah the blissful marital state, or his home in Hercules Road.

Blake believed that peoples' imagination creates the real world in its own likeness, and seeing the horrors of the industrial revolution in Lambeth he was terrified by the minds that were creating it. Making the connection between the imagination and the real world, it is of interest here to read Blake's work as descriptions of real people and places, such as Lambeth Marsh.

'So spoke London, immortal Guardian! I heard in Lambeth's shades.
In Felpham I heard and saw the Visions of Albion.
I write in South Molton Street what I both see and hear
In regions of Humanity, in London's opening streets.'

Jerusalem, The Sickness of Albion

The changes happening in London and where he lived in Lambeth Marsh coincided exactly in time with the emotional changes in Blake's life. Hercules Road, when he first moved there in 1791, was a rural hamlet with a village green and school, a few new houses along country lanes, all with gardens, and with the fields, cows and sheep enclosed by hedgerows and open ditches.

'I love the oaken seat,
Beneath the oaken tree,
where all the old villagers meet,
And laugh our sport to see.'

Songs of Innocence the title to his first important work, sums up a rural life and his marital bliss, where on one occasion he and his wife, Kitty, opened the door to a friend whilst naked except for helmets, during the reading of Paradise Lost.

'There is a Grain of Sand in Lambeth that Satan cannot find
Nor can his Watch Fiends find it; 'tis translucent and has many Angles,
But he who finds it will find Oothoon's palace; for within
Opening into Beulah, every angle is a lovely heaven.
But should the watch Fiends find it, they would call it sin.'

Life did not stand still for Blake, and for Lambeth Marsh the changes took place faster than had ever been seen before or since. On his arrival industry was river based, and had been developing slowly for over a hundred years, with timber, coal and boat yards, and with breweries, windmills and cloth bleaching using clean running stream water.

Appendix

However, between 1791 and 1800 Lambeth Green was built-over, Carlisle house pottery started to belch chlorine gas from the salt glazing furnace, and ditches overflowed with sewage and brewery waste, as the tenfold increase of the population occurred whilst Blake lived here.

Blake's most famous lines are thought of as the Midlands' Black Country by millions that have sung them:

'And was Jerusalem builded here,
Among these dark Satanic Mills.'

However in Blake's real life they described the once famous flour-mill (Albion Mills) in the Blackfriars Road. The mill, opened in 1786, was London's first rotary steam-powered flour-mill, and used Boulton and Watt's engine and John Rennie's grinding gear. The mill attracted many visitors and, from the day of its opening, became London's symbol for the impending industrial revolution. In 1791 when Blake came to Hercules Road, a stones throw away, the mill had just been burnt down, supposedly by arsonists, and remained a blackened satanic shell till 1809 when it was rebuilt as housing, the rebuilding of Jerusalem. A coloured print of the fire was published by Ackerman and Rowlandson in *Microcosm of London*.

'Albion's Spectre from his Loins
Tore forth in all the pomp of War:
Satan his name: in flames of fire
He stretched his Druid Pillars far,

Jerusalem fell from Lambeth's Vale
Down thro' Poplar and Old Bow, . . . '

The Albion Mill was first seen as a blessing of the modern world, supplying cheap flour, but very soon put the miller tradesmen out of work by closing Lambeth's windmills. The mill employed the low waged country women and children who flocked to London into this and other undeveloped outskirts to live amongst the disease and death of urban poverty. The outcries against industrialisation came not only from those whose livelihoods were at stake but from a few artists who had the vision to see the horrors to come. Even fewer of them had the strength to make it their life's work, as did Blake, when each political, reform, religious or industrial solution was applied in turn but was found ineffective at righting injustices.

On returning to London in 1803 to South Molton Street, he refers to Lambeth in his poems as a place of spiritual events:

'Prepare the furniture, O Lambeth, in thy pitying looms,
The curtains, woven tears and sighs wrought into lovely forms
For comfort; there the furniture of Jerusalem's chamber
is wrought. Lambeth! the Bride, the Lamb's Wife, loveth thee.'

and:
'Return, return to Lambeth's Vale, O building of human souls!
                                                          . . . soft Oothoon
Pants in the Vale of Lambeth, weeping o'er her Human Harvest.'

CULPEPER FAMILY TREE

KEY

æt	Attained, derobed
bh	beheaded
b1600	born 1600
C	Colepeper or Culpeper
co.	County
cr	Title created
d1600	died 1600
da	daughter of
Dk	Duke
dsp	died without issue
H	Howard
l	living
m1600	married in 1600
res	Restored to previous title
sps	without surviving issue
sp	without issue
suc	succeeded (not always heir)
=	married
=1st	married firstly
1650'51	old new year April 1st

Colepepers of Preston Hall, over the Medway from Aylesford
current spelling CULPEPER

Thomas de Colepeper

Walter Colepeper d1327 = Joan

Thomas sp — Sir Jeffrey C., Sheriff of Kent 1366 & 1374 — John

William Colepeper

Sir John Colepeper of Oxenheath = Katherine
(Oxen Hoath)

Sir William Colepeper = Elizabeth d1460 mon St.Dunstan,
of Oxenheath, Sheriff   West Peckham
of Kent d1459

Sir John Colepeper of Oxenheath

Sir William Colepeper = da of Ferrers of Groby

Sir Richard C = Isabella co-heir of   William C.Esq of = Margaret   Jeffrey C.
of Preston Hall Otwell Worcely, of   Preston Hall   Pedwarden
Sheriff of Kent Stamworth   Thomas C.
11y ED.IV   Edward C. = Jane   John C. = Jane Whetenhall   of Bedgbury
d1485
              Anne C. = Smedley   da   Thomas C. d1578 = Margaret

              Sir Thomas C. controller = Mary   Anne   Mary
              to Qu. Elizabeth d1604
              mon St.Peter Aylesford   line died out 1723

JOHN LEIGH of Ridge, co. of Chester

John LEIGH 3rd son   Margaret   = William Cotton   JOYCE   Elizabeth
                                   heir to   3rd son Sir Thomas b 1485   = Henry Barham
                                   Oxenheath   Cotton of Lanwade   d 1531

Ralph LEIGH,   = Elizabeth Langley
of STOCKWELL   l. a widow 1471   Sir Thomas Cotton, alienated
l.1452   Oxenheath to John Chowne
d Aug 14--

Sir John   = Isabella heir   3-8 Margaret = Denny   Ralph LEIGH, 1st = JOYCE = 2nd Lord Edmund
LEIGH of   of Otwell Worsley John sp   Under-Sheriff   Howard
Stockwell   of Calais   Alicia, Allen, sp   London, heir   3rd child d1538
d 27 Aug 1523   d 18 apr 1524   Katherine = Quickley   to Stockwell
                                    Margaret   1523   Isabel   Henry Howard sp
Jane,   = 1st Frowick   Jocasa   Sir Charles Howard sp
Abbess of   2nd Walter Ford   Sir George Howard sp
St. Mary   Margaret
Convent   = Sir John LEIGH   Margaret = Sir Thomas Arundell
Winchester   Anne Leigh   æt 21 nov 1523   KATHERINE   HENRY VIII
                = 1st Thomas Paston   b 1521   5th WIFE
                = 2nd FitzGerrard   m 1540
                                                            bh 1542
                Margaret = Ralph LEIGH
                da Wm.   Mary = Henry Trafford
                Ireland
                                                            Joyce = Slanney
                Margery = John LEIGH   Isabell = BAYNTON
                dau & heir
                Sir Thomas West of Westwood
                co. Southampton

Family Tree showing how **JOYCE CULPEPER** joined by marriage the two great families of the Duke of Norfolk and the Leighs of Stockwell.

Appendix

SOURCES
1. St.Mary Lambeth Monuments (keyed mSt.M)
   Chapels built 1505 dedicated to Leigh (S),
   Howard (N) 1522
2. Pevsner Guide *West Kent*
3. Robinson *The Dukes of Norfolk*
4. Burke's *Extinct and Dormant Baronetcies*
5. Tanswell *History of Lambeth*
6. Hacket *Henry the Eighth*

KATHERINE'S LOVERS (l) & TRIAL WITNESSES (w)
Manox, music teacher (l)
Francis Derham a Norfolk relative (l)
Thomas Culpeper (l) NOT a true cousin
Edward Baynton sister-in-law (w)
Lady Rochford, Anne Boleyn's sister-in-law (w)

THE HOWARDS OF NORFOLK

Plantagenet Dukes of Norfolk, Earls of Surrey

Sir Robert Howard b circa 1420'22 d1436 = Margaret d1481 da Thomas (Mawbray) Dk
heir to Howards recreated 1st Dk of Norfolk, of Norfolk, her issue became coheirs
Earl Marshal Lord High admiral to her family 1482

Sir John H b1421'2 æt & slain 1485, Lord Howard 1466, Dk of Norfolk 1483 = Katherine Molyns d1465

Elizabeth Tilney = 1st Thomas Earl = 2nd Agnes Tilney, Dowager   Richard H   Henry H
d1497 m1472   of Surrey cr1483   Duchess m1497 d1545 mSt.M   d1517   d1513
sister to Agnes 2nd Dk of Norfolk 1514
                 b1443 d1524 mSt.M

William, b1510 d1578 = 1st Katherine Lady Effingham d1535 mSt.M
cr Baron of Effingham 1554 | da John Broughton & isssue mSt.M

Elizabeth   = Thomas Boleyn,   Anne da EDW IV 1st = Thomas 3rd Dk of Norfolk = m1512 separated 1534
d1538 mSt.M   Earl of   d1511 sps m1495   æt 1547, res 1553   Lady Elizabeth
Countess of   Wiltshire   b1473 d1554   Stafford d1558 mSt.M
Wiltshire   d1538   da Dk of Buckingham
                                    4 sons dsp   bh 1521

= ANNE BOLEYN   Mary b1503   George B.   Henry Howard b1517 bh1547   2nd son   Mary
  b1507 bh 1534   Ld. Rochford   Poet styled Earl of Surrey
  m1533   = William Carey   b1505 bh1534
                 | = Francis Vere
                 Henry VIII's   = Lady   d1577
                 illegitimate   Rochford
                 son, Dk of   bh1542
                 Richmond

HENRY VIII   Lady Mary FitzAlan = Thomas 4th Dk of Norfolk = 2nd Margaret da   Henry Howard
2nd WIFE   heir of Henry Earl   suc.grandfather 1554   Lord Audley,   Earl of Northampton
                 of Arundel   b1538 st & bh 1572   of Walden d1563   dsp 1603
ELIZABETH I
Queen   = 3rd m to Elizabeth
b1533   1567 sps   H. of Walden   H. of Naworth
suc 1558 d1603

         Philip Earl of Arundel = Anne coheir & sister of
         suc 1580 b1557 d1595   Lord Dacre b1556 d1639

Elizabeth   Thomas Howard res Earl of Arundel and Surrey = Lady Alathea Talbot heir of Gilbert
             in 1604 Earl of Norfolk 1644 d1646   7th Earl of Shrewsbury d1654

Henry Frederick Earl of Arundel = Elizabeth Stuart   William H. Baron Stafford = Mary Countess
Surrey and Norfolk d1652   d1673'4   1640 later Visc. Stafford   of Stafford d1694
                                                       æt 1678 bh 1680
         Heirs to current Dukes of Norfolk

NOTES

1. Barton, N. J. *Lost Rivers of London*, p.44.
2. Museum of London excavation. *Campbell buildings* (1984).
3. Curtis, William. *Proposals for Opening the London Botanic Garden*, Introduction: 'Peculiarly favourable to the growth of aquatic and bog plants, and all such as love a moist bottom'.
4. Allen, T. *History and antiquities of the Parish of Lambeth*, p. 357, including map and discussion of possible routes.
   Defoe, Daniel. *A tour through the whole island of Great Britain, 1778*, p. 69: 'They turn'd the channel of this great river Thames and made a new course for the waters . . . end houses in Newington; between which and Kennington Common, on the left road, as you go south, there is a very large pond or lake or water, part of the channel not filled up today'.
   Stow, John. *The survey of London, 1603* (London, Dent, Everyman edition, n.d.), p. 21: 'Canute, . . . on the south of the Thames caused a trench to be cast, through the which his ships were towed'.
5. Brazel, J. H. *London weather*, Appendix I, pp. 146-7.
6. Roebuck, Janet. *Urban Development in 19th century London; Lambeth, Battersea and Wandsworth 1838-1888*, p. 43: 'Notwithstanding the defects of sewers and drains, that the filth of privies are allowed to be pumped into the sewers . . . which filth runs into the River Thames near where the Lambeth Water Works supply the water drunk and consumed by the inhabitants'.
7. Gosse, Edmund: editor, Desmond Eyles. *Sir Henry Doulton*.
8. Bowle, John. *John Evelyn and His World*, p. 107, paragraph 2.
9. Wind-powered saw-mill. Hulton's 1731 map, also
   Short, Michael. *Windmills in Lambeth*, p. 19, site 1.
10. Walker, R. J. B. *Old Westminster Bridge*.
11. Ibid, p. 84: 'Sir George Oxenden and the secretary of the Admiralty, Josiah Burchett, commissioned Labelye (d. 1782) to carry out a survey of "The Downs and the coast between the North and South Forelands" that was published 1738.'
12. *Church Commissioners Records A/C 1693*:
    Ye Flower Pot tavern [Red Lion].
    1730-40 Lease to Lady Cooke at £13 /annum.
    sub-let to Mr Higgins rent s18 3s.
13. Boswell, James. *Boswell's London Journal 1762-1763*,
    Tuesday 10 May 1763:
    'At the bottom of the Haymarket I picked up a strong, jolly young damsel, and taking her under the arm I conducted her to Westminster Bridge, and then in armour complete did I engage her upon this noble edifice. The whim of doing it there with the Thames rolling below us amused me much. Yet after the brutish appetite was sated, I could not but despise myself for being so closely united with such a low wretch.'
14. Searle, Mark. *Turnpikes and Toll-bars*.
15. Local Act 49, George III, cap. 191, 'Strand Bridge Company'.
16. Preston, H. *London and the Thames: Paintings of Three Centuries*, paintings number 49, 50, 51.

17. Searle, Mark. *Turnpikes and Toll-bars*.
18. Robertson, Kevin. *150 Years of the L&SWR*, p. 3.
19. Sims, George R. *Living London*, p. 85.
20. *Treasury receipts miscellaneous books* no. 168, p. 64, 5Edward VI: 'Robert Aylward holds . . . one tenement with wharf'.
21. LCC. *Survey of London : St Mary Lambeth, part I, north*, pp. 12-13: 'Land disputed between the King, Duchy of Cornwall and the Archbishop of Canterbury.'
22. Petitions for Kennington Leases. *Reports Vol.B* (1660), pp. 127-32.
23. Goldman, Paul. *Sporting Life: an Anthology of British Sporting Prints*, p. 85, print 153: 'aquetint by Henry Pyall published by W. Lyon the boat builders 1831'.
24. MBW 1862 survey, number 125.
25. The spelling of Belvidere with an i appears on the 1806 Enclosure Survey map referring to this brewery, maybe to differentiate this place from the Belvedere House site nearer the river.
    Allen, T. *History and antiquities of the Parish of Lambeth*, p. 295.
26. Church Commissioners: Deeds, 1837, 54670, 'part of Seven Acres from Henry Warbourton'.
27. Whitaker, W. *Memoirs of the Geological Survey. The Geology of London*, vol. 2.
28. 28 January 1756, letter from Vinegar yard; but not till 1762 was Beaufoy granted a 20-year lease.
29. Hodskinson and Middleton. *Survey of the property of Messrs. Beaufoy etc*, 21 May 1788.
30. Kerr, Barbara. *The Dispossessed. An Aspect of Victorian social history*, pp. 81-5.
31. Robert Henley 1721 lease (Cumbria record office, Carlisle), DRC/2/216 and 7.
32. British Museum. *Etchings of Coade's artificial stone manufacture*. Catalogues 1777-1779.
33. Freestone, I. C, Bimson, M and Tite. *Some Recent Research on Coade Stone*.
    Newbery, Christopher. 'Coade artificial stone: finds from the site of the Coade manufactory at Lambeth', *Collectianea Londiniensia studies*.
34. Clowes, W. B. *Family Business: William Clowes*.
    Jennet, Sean. *The Making of Books*.
    Plant, Marjorie. *The English Book Trade*.
35. LCC. *Survey of London: St Mary Lambeth, part I, north*, p. 133. 'Augustus Applegarth lived at 239 Kennington Road in 1791-99, brother-in-law and partner of Edward Cowper'.
36. Clowes, W. B. *Family Business: William Clowes*, p. 41.
37. Plant, Marjorie. *The English Book Trade*, p. 379: 'The Combination Acts'.
38. Prothero, I. *Artisans and Politics*.
39. Mayhew, Henry. *Mayhew's London. 1st edition 1851, being selections from London Labour and London Poor*.
40. Harris, Judy. *The Roupell Story*.
41. Gilbert, K. R. *Henry Maudslay: Machine Builder*.
42. Sturt, George. *The Wheelwright's Shop*.
43. Development Plan. *South Bank Redevelopment Area* (London County Council Development Plan, 1943).
44. Hodskinson and Middleton. *Survey Executed for the Surveyor General, Duchy of Cornwall* (1785).
45. Clowes, R. L. *The History of the Manor of Kennington*.
46. Adams, Bernard. London Illustrated: 1604-1851, ref. 82/3. Also Lambeth Palace Library, ref. TD 191.
47. Owen, Dorothy. Lambeth Palace Charters. *Lambeth Manuscripts 889 to 901 (Carte antique et miscellanee)*: XII 40, Exemplification, 28 Jan. 1572-3, 'of a case heard since 17th nov. 1572, concerning lands of the Duke of Norfolk in Southwark and Lambeth'.
48. Hackett, Francis. *Henry the Eighth*, pp. 431-51.

49. Tanswell. *History and antiquities of Lambeth*, p. 40.
50. LCC. *Survey of London: St George's Fields*.
51. Colvin, Ransome, Summerson. History of the King's Works, vol. 3, 1485-1660 pt. 1, admin, pp. 156-9.
52. Clowes, R. L. *The History of the Manor of Kennington*, p. 93, also Hodskinson and Middleton Survey map 1785-6, plot no. 129 that also contains the tavern the Rose with large stable yard.
53. Wroth, Warwick. *The London Pleasure Gardens of the Eighteenth Century*.
54. Pepys, Samuel. *The Diary of Samuel Pepys. Complete unabridged 1659-1669*. Wheatley Edition.
    28 May 1668: 'over to Fox Hall, and there fell into the company of Harry Killigrew, a rogue newly come back out of France ... and young Newport and others ... who were ready to take hold of every woman that come by them ... Harris telling how it was ... and with Lady Bennet and her ladies; and their dancing naked, and all the roguish things in the world.'
55. Price, Rebecca, *1681 record of recipes*; gives this recipe for a tansy.
    26 eggs less 8 whites
    nutmeg
    1 lb of sugar
    poringerfull of spinach juice
    a little Tansy
    One and a half pints of thick cream. Stirred and placed in a well buttered dish and covered. Set over gentle coals until done and turn out. Serve with sliced lemons on it.
56. Adams, Bernard. *London Illustrated: 1604-1851*, ref. 113/13.
    Allen, T. *History and antiquities of the Parish of Lambeth*, p. 381.
    Tanswell. *History and antiquities of Lambeth*, p. ?.
    Walford, Edward. *Old and New London*, Vol. 6, p. 415.
    Map of 1806, Enclosure Survey of the Manor of Kennington.
57. Robinson, Martin. *The Dukes of Norfolk*.
58. Hodges, W. *Shakespeare's Second Globe*.
59. Wroth, Warwick. *The London Pleasure Gardens of the Eighteenth Century*, p. 248: 'There was a back way to the gardens leading from St George's Fields, and watchmen were appointed.'
60. Nichols, J. *History and antiquities of Lambeth*, 'John Cuper [maybe another alias for Boydel Cuper] sold some statuary in 1717 for £75'.
61. LCC Records. *1760 minutes of Surrey and Kent sewer commission*, 'Application to arch over pipes or ditches'.
62. Coxe, A. H. *The lesser-known circuses of London, Theatre Notebook vol. 13, Spring 1959*, p. 89.
63. George, Dorothy. *London life of the 18th century*, p. 81.
64. LCC. Survey of London: *St George's Fields (the parishes of St George the martyr and St Mary Newington)*, pp. 52-6, Dog and Duck references.
    Also the Greater London Record Office. *Rendle Collection*. Newspaper cuttings.
65. Barty-King, Hugh. *Scratch a Surveyor*.
66. Pepys, Samuel. *The Diary of Samuel Pepys. Complete unabridged 1659-1669*. Wheatley Edition, vol. 7,
    13 April 1668: 'Spent at Michel's, 6d.; in the Folly, 1s.; oysters, 1s.'
67. Walford, Edward. *Old and New London*, vol. 3, p. 290.
68. Adams, Bernard. *London Illustrated: 1604-1851*, ref. 131/153-154.
69. Curtis, William. *Proposals for Opening the London Botanic Garden. Plan and Catalogue*.
70. Brazel J. H. *London Weather*.
71. Gibberd, Graham. 'The location of William Curtis's London Botanic Garden in Lambeth', *Garden History*.

Notes

72. Allen, T. *History and antiquities of the Parish of Lambeth*, p. 303.
    Walford, Edward. *Old and New London*, vol. 5, p. 389, paragraph 3: 'Curtis's botanical gardens, on the spot where in the old times had stood a Lazar-house'.
73. Edwards, James. *A Companion from London to Brighthelmstone*.
74. This painting, now in the Hunt Botanical Museum, Pittsburgh, USA, is reproduced in the Horniman Museum.
75. Nichols, J. *History and antiquities of Lambeth*, p. 84.
76. Wroth, Warwick. *The London Pleasure Gardens of the Eighteenth Century*, p. 263.
    Also maps depicting the site are:
    as Spring Garden, Robert Hulton map 1731.
    as Restoration Garden, Stow Survey map 1755.
77. Ford, E. B. *Butterflies*, p. 13 and plate 1.
78. Howard, Diana. *London Theatres and Music halls 1850-1950*.
79. Newton, Chance. *The Old Vic. and Its Associations*.
80. Richardson, Joanna. *Letters from Lambeth*, p. 55: letter dated 1 August 1810.
81. Coxe, A. H. *A Seat at the Circus*.
82. Speaight, George. *Astley's Amphitheatre; Theatre Notebook, vol. 42 no. 2, 1988*, pp. 75-8.
83. Disher, M. Willson. *Pleasures of London*.
84. Walford, Edward. *Old and New London*, Vol. 6, p. 375, paragraph 2.
85. Bell, Leslie. *Bella of Blackfriars*.
86. Goldman, Paul. *Sporting Life: an Anthology of British Sporting Prints*, p. 34, print number 38:
    'Lunardi had arranged to take up Mrs Letitia Anne Sage, a famous Beauty, and George Biggin from St George's Fields on 29 June 1785. However, the balloon proved incapable of lifting more than two people so Biggin and Mrs Sage ascended alone, needless to say the print (number 38) shows Lunardi also aboard'. The two landed on Harrow Common and may have broken a height record, except that Mrs Sage had carelessly broken the barometer.
87. Mayhew, Henry. *Mayhew's London. 1st edition 1851, being selections from London Labour and London Poor*, p. 37: 'The London Street markets on a Saturday night.'
88. Ibid, p. 499: 'The penny-gaff clowns.'
89. Sala, George. *Twice Round the Clock 1st.ed. 1858*, p. 269.
90. Morice, G., and Speaight, G. *New light on the juvenile drama. Theatre Notebook, vol. 26, Spring 1972*, newly found interview of Mayhew with West, pp. 115-21: References to Astley's, *Blood Red Knight*, The Surrey theatre, Grimaldi and a great deal more. Also:
    The Jonathan King Collection of juvenile drama, a reference collection of prints of actors, performances and scenery from all the Surreyside theatres.
91. Ashton, John. *Varia, including Childhood Drama*.
92. Also told by Peter Acroyd in *Dressing Up: Transvestism and Drag*.
93. Manvell, Roger. *The Trial of Annie Besant and Charles Bradlaugh*. Also
    Longford, E. *Eminent Victorian Women*.
94. Richards, Denis. *Offspring of the Vic*.
95. Williams, Marguerite. *Charlotte Sharman: The Romance of a Great Faith*.
96. Darley, Gillian. *Octavia Hill, a Life*.
97. Pearce, S. B. P. *An Ideal in the Working; The Magdalen Hospital 1758-1958*.
98. Account of the Asylum . . . for orphan girls within the *Bills of Mortality . . . 1773*.
99. Rhodes, Philip. *Dr John Leake's Hospital*.
100. Graves, Charles. *The Story of St Thomas's, 1106-1947*.
101. McInnes, E. M. *St Thomas' Hospital*, pp. 104-5.
102. LCC. *Survey of London: St Mary Lambeth, part I, north*.
103. Forbes-Robertson: photos by Capa. *The Battle of Waterloo Road*.

BIBLIOGRAPHY

Ackermann, see Rowlandson & Pugin delt. et sculpt.
Acroyd, Peter. *Dressing Up: Transvestism and Drag* (London, Thames & Hudson, 1979).
Adams, Bernard. *London Illustrated: 1604-1851* (London, Library Association, 1983).
Allen, T. *History and antiquities of the Parish of Lambeth* (London, 1826 edition).
Ashton, John. *Varia, including Childhood Drama* (London, Ward and Downey, 1879).
Baldwin & Cradock. *Register of 1835*.
Barker, F & P. Jackson. *London: 2000 years of a City and Its People* (London, Cassell, 1974).
Barton, N. J. *Lost Rivers of London* (London, Phoenix House Ltd, for Leicester University Press, 1962).
Barty-King, Hugh. *Scratch a Surveyor: Drivers, Jonas* (London, Heinemann, 1979).
Bell, Leslie. *Bella of Blackfriars* (London, Odhams, 1961).
Besant, Walter. *London* (London, Chatto & Windus, 1904).
Besant, Walter. *South of the Thames* (London, Chatto & Windus, 1912).
Boswell, James. *Boswell's London Journal 1762-1763* (London, Heinemann, 1950).
Bowle, John. *John Evelyn and His World* (Routledge & Kegan Paul, 1981).
Bray, William (editor). *The Diary of John Evelyn* (London, W. W. Gibbings, 1890).
Brazel, J. H. *London Weather* (London, HMSO, 1968).
Brown, Ivor. *London, An Illustrated History* (London, Studio, 1965).
Bugler, Caroline (editor). *The Image of London; views by travellers and emigrés 1550-1920* (London, Trefoil Publications Ltd for Barbican Art Gallery, 1987).
Chamberlain, Mary. *Growing Up in Lambeth* (London, Virago Press Ltd. 1989).
Clowes, R. L. *The History of the Manor of Kennington* (MS, Minet Archive Library, 1916).
Clowes, W. *Quarterly Review vols. 71, 87, 107* (London, Murray, 1843, 1850).
Clowes, W. B. *Family Business: William Clowes* (London, William Clowes & Sons, 1969).
Cobb, Gerald. *The Old Churches of London* (London, B. T. Batsford, 1948).
Colvin, Ransome, Summerson. *History of the King's Works* (7 vols.,London, HMSO, 1973), vol. 3, 1485-1660, part 1, admin.
Cooper, Lynden. *Carlisle Lane (Waterloo site F) SE11: preliminary report on the archaeological excavations* (London, The Museum of London, 1990).
Coxe, A. H. *A Seat at the Circus* (London, Evans, 1951).
Curtis, William. *Proposals for Opening the London Botanic Garden: Plan and Catalogue* (London, Curtis, 1778).
Darley, Gillian. *Octavia Hill, a Life* (London, Constable, 1990).
Davey, Dolly. *A Sense of Adventure* (SE1 People's History Project, ISBN 0 9506880 0 2, 1980).
Davies, W. H. *The Autobiography of a Super-tramp* (London, Jonathan Cape, 1908).
Davis, A. *Post Office London Directory* (38th edition, London, F. Kelly 1834).
Defoe, Daniel. *A Tour through the Whole Island of Great Britain* (London, J. M. Dent, facsimile 1974).
de Maré, Eric. *Wren's London* (London, The Folio Society, 1975).
Denkstein, V. *Hollar Drawings* (London, Orbis, 1979, 1st edition Odeon, Prague, 1977).
Dickens, Charles. *Sketches by Boz: Illustrative of Every-day life and Every-day People* (London, Chapman and Hall, n. d).
Dicks, O. L. *Aubrey's Brief Lives* (London, Martin Secker & Warburg, 1949).
Disher, M. Willson. *Pleasures of London* (London, Robert Hale Ltd, 1950).

Ellmers, Christopher: editor, Mike Seaborne. *George Reid River Thames: in the late twenties and early thirties* (London, Dirk Nishen Publications, 1987).
Evans, Charles. *The Grand Panorama of London* (London, Charles Evans, The Pictorial Times, 1844).
Evelyn, John: editor, Bray, William. *The Diary of John Evelyn* (London, W. W. Gibbings, 1890).
Festival of Britain. *South Bank Exhibition, catalogue* (London, 1951).
Forbes-Robertson: photos by Capa. *The Battle of Waterloo Road* (New York, Random House, 1943).
Ford, E. B. *Butterflies* (London, Collins, 1945).
Forster, E. M. *Marianne Thornton* (London, Butler, 1956).
Freestone, I. C, Bimson, M and Tite. *Some Recent Research on Coade Stone* (English Ceramic Circle *transactions*, 1986).
George, Dorothy. *London Life of the 18th century* (London, Kegan, 1925).
Gibberd, Graham. 'The location of William Curtis's London Botanic Garden in Lambeth', *Garden History* (London, Garden History Society, Spring 1985).
Gilbert, K. R. *Henry Maudslay: Machine Builder* (London, Science Museum, HMSO 1971).
Gladwin, D. D. *Passenger Boats: Inland Waterways* (Oakwood, 1979).
Godfrey, Richard T. *Printmaking in Britain* (Oxford, Phaidon, 1978).
Goldman, Paul. *Sporting Life: an Anthology of British SportingPrints* (London, British Museum Publications Ltd, 1983).
Gosse, Edmund: editor, Desmond Eyles. *Sir Henry Doulton* (London, Hutchinson & Co, 1970).
Gottheiner (trans.). *Canaletto's View of London* (London, Spring Books, 1961).
Graves, Charles. *The Story of St Thomas's, 1106-1947* (London, Faber & Faber, 1947).
Harris, Judy. *The Roupell Story* (Southwark and Lambeth Archaeological Society, No. 58, June 1985).
Harrison, Michael. *London Beneath the Pavement* (London, Peter Davies, 1961).
Hartnoll, Phyllis. *The Oxford Companion to the English theatre* (London, Oxford University Press, 1957).
Hill, Thomas. *The Gardener's Labyrinth* (London, Oxford University Press, 1987).
Hodges, W. *Shakespeare's Second Globe* (London, Oxford University Press, 1973).
Howard, Diana. *London Theatres and Music Halls 1850-1950* (London, The Library Association, 1970).
Huggett, F. E. *How It Happened* (Oxford, Blackwell, 1971).
Imber, Donald. *Lambeth lost and found* (London, Southwark and Lambeth Archaeological Excavation Committee, 1979).
Jackson, Peter. *Tallis's London Street Views. 1838-1840* (London, London Topographical Society, 1969).
Jeffries, R. *Nature Near London* (1st published 1893) (London, John Clare, 1980 edition).
Johnson, Walter. *Journals of Gilbert White* (London, Routledge, 1931 edition).
Kerr, Barbara. *The Dispossessed.* An Aspect of Victorian social history (London, Baker, 1974).
LCC. *Survey of London: St George's Fields* (London County Council, 1955).
LCC. *Survey of London: Bankside* (London County Council, 1950).
LCC. *Survey of London: St Mary Lambeth, part I, north* (London County Council, 1951).
LCC. *Survey of London: St Mary Lambeth, part II, south* (London County Council, 1956).
Links, J. G. *Canaletto* (London, Phaidon, 1982).
Longford, E. *Eminent Victorian Women* (London, Weidenfeld & Nicolson, 1981).
Long, J. C. *George III: a biography* (London, MacDonald, 1962).
Marsdon, Colin, J. *This Is Waterloo* (Shepperton, Ian Alan, 1981).
Manning, Owen and Bray, William. *The History and antiquities of the County of Surrey* (London, John Nichols and Son, 1804-14).

Manvell, Roger. *The Trial of Annie Besant and Charles Bradlaugh* (New York, Horizon Press, 1976).
Mayhew, Henry. *Mayhew's London. 1st edition 1851, being selections from London Labour and London Poor* (London, Spring Books edition).
McInnes, E. M. *St Thomas' Hospital* (London, George Allen and Unwin, 1963).
Milne, Gustave. *Medieval Waterfront Development* (London, Museum of London, 1982).
Munby, Arthur: editor Derek Hudson. *Munby, Man of Two Worlds* (London, Sphere books Ltd, Abacus edition, 1974).
Nash, Aileen Denise. *Living in Lambeth* (London, Lambeth Borough Council, 1950).
Newbery, Christopher. 'Coade artificial stone: finds from the site of the Coade manufactory at Lambeth', *Collectianea Londiniensia studies* (London and Middlesex Archaeological Society, Special Papers no. 2, 1978).
Newton, Chance. *The Old Vic and Its Associations* (London, Fleetwood, n.d).
Nichols, J. *History and antiquities of Lambeth* (London, 1786).
Ollard, Richard. *Pepys, a Biography* (London, Hodder, 1974).
Ordish, T. F. *Early London Theatres* (London, Elliot Stock, 1894).
Owen, Dorothy M. *A Catalogue of Lambeth Manuscripts 889 to 901: Carte Antique et Miscellanee* (London, Lambeth Palace Library, 1968).
Parker, K. T. *The Drawings of Hans Holbein* (London, Phaidon, 2nd edition 1945).
Pearce, S. B. P. *An Ideal in the Working; the Magdalen Hospital 1758-1958* (London, Skinner H. B. Ltd, 1958).
Pepys, Samuel. *The Diary of Samuel Pepys*. Latham edition (10 vols., London, Bell and Hyman, 1983).
Pepys, Samuel. *The Diary of Samuel Pepys. Complete unabridged, 1659-1669*. Wheatley edition (9 vols., London, George Bell, 1904).
Pevsner, Nikolas. *The Buildings of England. London, except the Cities of London and Westminster, BE6* (London, Penguin 1952).
Pevsner, Nikolas. *The Buildings of England. London, volume 1, BE12* (London, Penguin 1957).
Pevsner, Nikolas. *The Buildings of England. West Kent* (London, Penguin, 1969).
Phillips, Geoffrey. *Thames Crossings: Bridges, Tunnels and Ferries* (London, David & Charles, 1981).
Phillips, Hugh. *The Thames about 1750* (London, Collins, 1951).
Piper, David. *The Treasures of Oxford* (London, Paddington Press, 1977).
Plant, Marjorie. *The English Book Trade* (London, Allen & Unwin, 1965).
Preston, H. *London and the Thames: Paintings of Three Centuries* (National Maritime Museum, 1977).
Prothero, I. *Artisans and Politics* (London, Dawson, 1979).
Rawlinson, W. G. *The Watercolours of J. M. W. Turner* (The Studio Spring, 1909).
Reid, George. *River Thames; In the Late Twenties & Early Thirties* (London, Dirk Nishen Publishing, photo-library 1).
Rhodes, Phillip. *Dr John Leake's Hospital* (London, Davis-Poynter, 1977).
Richards, Denis. *Offspring of the Vic* (London, Routledge Kegan, 1958).
Richardson, J. *Letters from Lambeth* (Suffolk, for Royal Society of Literature by Boydell Press, 1981).
Roberts, Jane. *Master Drawings in the Royal Collection, from Leonardo da Vinci to the present day* (London, Collins Harvill, 1986).
Robertson, Kevin. *150 Years of the L&SWR* (Herefordshire, Amber Graphics, n.d).
Robinson, Martin. *The Dukes of Norfolk* (Oxford University Press, 1982).
Roebuck, Janet. *Urban Development in 19th century London; Lambeth, Battersea and Wandsworth 1838-1888* (London & Chichester, 1979).
Rothwell, Stanley. *Lambeth at War* (London, SE1 Press 1981).
Rowlandson & Pugin delt. et sculpt. *The Microcosm of London* (London Pub. 1808 at R. Ackermann's repository of Arts).

Russel, Ronald. *Guide to Topographical Prints* (David & Charles, 1979).
Sala, George. *Twice Round the Clock. 1st edition 1858* (Leicester University Press, facsimile, 1971).
Searle, Mark. *Turnpikes and Toll-bars* (2 vols., London, Hutchinson, c. 1922).
Shephard, Leslie. *The Broadside Ballad* (London, Legacy 1978).
Shephard, Thomas. *London in the 19th Century* (Bracken facsimile, 1983).
Short, Michael. *Windmills in Lambeth* (London, Lambeth Borough Council, 1971).
Sims, George, R. *Living London* (Cassel, 1902).
Smith, Urwin. *Shakespeare's Blackfriars Playhouse: Its History and Design* (New York, New York University Press, 1964).
Speaight, George. *Astley's Amphitheatre; Theatre Notebook, vol. 42 no. 2, 1988* (London, The Society for Theatre Research, 1988).
Stow, John. *The Survey of London, 1603* (London, Dent, Everyman edition n.d).
Sturdy, David. *The Tradescants at Lambeth. Reprint vol. 2, no. 1 1982. Journal of Garden History* (Taylor and Francis Ltd, 1982).
Sturt, George. *The Wheelwright's Shop* (Cambridge University Press, 1923).
Survey of London, see LCC.
Tallis, John. *Tallis's London Street Views, 1838-40* (London, London Topographical Society, 1969).
Tanswell. *History and antiquities of Lambeth* (London, 1858).
Taylor, Jeremy. *The architectural Medal* (London, British Library, 1978).
The Grand Panorama of London, Seen from the River (London, Charles Evans, 1844).
Thomas, Alan, G. *Great Books and Book Collections* (London, Weidenfeld, 1975).
Trease, Geoffrey. *London, A Concise History* (London, Thames and Hudson, 1975).
Walford, Edward. *Old and New London* (6 vols., London, Cassell Petter and Galpin, n. d), Vol. 3 and Vol. 6.
Walker, R. J. B. *Old Westminster Bridge* (London, David & Charles 1979).
White, Antonia. *The Memoirs of Chevalier D'Eon, with an introduction by Robert Baldick* (London, Anthony Blond, 1969).
Williams, Marguerite. *Charlotte Sharman: The Romance of a Great Faith* (London, Religious Tract Society, n. d.).
Williams, Neville. *Thomas Howard fourth Duke of Norfolk* (London, Barrie & Rockliff, 1964).
Wroth, Warwick. *The London Pleasure Gardens of the Eighteenth Century* (London, Macmillan & Co. Ltd, 1896).

REFERENCES TO PAINTINGS, DRAWINGS AND PHOTOGRAPHS

Capon, William, 1757-1827. *A View from a Gentleman's Seat in Lambeth Marsh 1804* (London, Greater London Record Office).
Chapuis, drawing. A. Appert, engraver. *Aspect général de Londres, 1857* (London, Guildhall Library), showing Hungerford Suspension Bridge and no Big Ben clock.
Daubigny, Charles-François. *St Paul's from the Surrey side* (London, National Gallery, Postcard no. 1710), canvas 44 × 81.3 cm.
Fenton, Roger. Photograph. *Houses of Parliament Under Construction*. London between late 1857 and early 1859.
Hungerford Suspension Bridge. Calotype c. 1845 (Science Museum, published by The Arts Council of Great Britain).
Lambert, W. H. (Lydia Dreams). *Popularity, music-hall artist Waterloo Rd, 1901-3* (London, The Museum of London: Postcard set of four, 1986).
Sandby, Paul. *Lambeth Marsh c. 1770* (London, Minet Archive Library, London Borough of Lambeth).
Sowerby, James 1757-1822. *William Curtis's London Botanic Garden* (copy at Horniman Museum, London).

INDEX

A
academy, *see* schools
Adelphi, 110
Agnes, Dowager Duchess of Norfolk d.1545, 72, 156
Albemarle, Duke of, General Monk 1608-70, 67, 76, 78, 102
Albert Embankment [w4.22], 2, 69, 79, 134
Albion mills [w3.20], 47, 153, 155
almshouses, 62
amphitheatre *see* entertainment
Angell, William, 73, 88
Apollo Gardens [w2.26], 16, 85
Applegarth, William 1788-1871 [w3.28], 60, 61, 63, 159
Archbishop Temple School [w4.32], 137
Archbishop Tenison School [w4.31], 136
Archbishop's garden, 45
Archives, French National, 118
Armourers' barge house, 55
Art Deco warehouse [w3.15]
Artichoke, Streets' public house, 77, 95
artificial stone, Coade, 59
Arundel & Surrey: collector Earl -1646, 25, 72, 81, 83, 84, 146, 148
Ashburton marble, 66
Ashmole, Elias 1617-92; house [w1.15], 80-1, 83, 84, 146-148
asparagus gardens [w3.43]
Astley, John, 29, 106-8
Astley, Philip 1742-1814, 29, 35, 38, 106-8
Astley's amphitheatre [w4.15]102, 106-8, 117-8
asylum: for full list *see* hospitals
Atkins, Robert, 112
Auralian, the, 94
Aylesford, 156
Aylward, Robert, 54
Ayres Street, 123

B
bakers, xii
Baldwin, 69
Balloon, 113, 161
Bankside, 147
barber surgeons, 55
Barge House Stairs [w3.24], 18, 22, 55, 73
barge houses [w4.24], 18, 22, 55, 73
barges, 33, 44, 55, 71
Barker, Henry Aston, panorama, 58
Battersea, 90, 152, 158
Baylis, Lilian 1874-1937, 18, 36, 106
Baylis Road, 64, 83
Bazalgette, 43
Beaufoy, Mark 1718-82, 84
Beaufoy's Wine and Vinegar Works, [w3.34], 54, 58, 98
Beddington, 38, 130
Bedlam, *see* Bethlem Hospital
Bell, Dr Andrew 1753-1832, 127
Belvedere Gardens, 25
Belvedere House [w3.38], 57
Belvedere Road, 43, 54, 77, 85
Belvidere Brewery [w3.6], 57, 98
Benevolent Society for St Patrick [w3.12], 62
Bermondsey, 21, 40, 80
Bermondsey Abbey [w1.21], 40
Besant, Annie 1847-1937 and Frank, 121
Besant, Sir Walter 1836-1901, 121
Bethlem Hospital [w4.54], 120, 124
Biggin, 133, 161
Bishop
  Bonner, 13, 14, 79
  Carlisle, 35, 71
  London, 13
  Rochester, 29, 33, 45, 67, 69, 71
Blackfriars Bridge [w3.21], 40, 47-8, 66, 129, 137
Blake, William 1757-1817 [w4.39], 35, 127, 144, 153-5
Bligh, William 1753-1817
  house [w4.52], 101
  tomb [w4.28]
blind workshops, 103, 104, 134
blue houses, 90

Index

boatyards
  Roberts', 55
  Searle's, 55
Boleyn, Anne, 72, 157
Bonner, Bishop 1500-69: House [w2.12], 79
Booth, Charles 1840-1916, 5, 101
Borough High Street, 36, 45, 47, 77, 123, 133, 135
Borough Road, 135
Boscom, Charles, 85
Boswell, James 1740-95, 158
Boundary Row [w2.43], 40, 73
Bowaters, 22, 65
Bower Saloon [w4.13], 102, 109
Boz, Sketches by, houses standing [w2.20], 65, 105, 107-8, 113
breweries
  Beaufoy's Wine and Vinegar Works [w3.34], 58, 98
  Belvidere Brewery, Vine Street [w3.6], 57
  Brewery at King's Arms Stairs [w3.41], 56-7
  Horn Brewery, windmill, tap house pub [w2.49], 57, 98
  Lion Brewery [w3.38], 58
  Union Brewery [w2.25], 57
  Vineyard (Cornwall Road) [w3.1]
bridges
  Blackfriars Bridge [w3.21], 47
  Cuper's Bridge [w3.34], 40, 45, 49, 54-5
  Fleet Bridge, 45
  Hungerford [3.40], 50
  Lambeth Marsh bridges, 45
  Lock Bridge, 45
  Strand Bridge, 49
  Westminster Bridge [w4.21], 45-6
  Waterloo Bridge [w3.32], 49
Bridge House Estates, 16, 74, 86-7
Brixton, 67, 112
Broadwall, 40
Brook Drive, the Neckinger [w4.50], 40, 75, 77, 86, 123
Brookwood cemetery, Woking, 53
brothel, Holland's Leaguer [w3.18], 18, 22, 88
Brunel, Isambard Kingdom 1806-59, 26, 50
Burge, Bella of Blackfriars 1877-1969 and Dick Burge, 15, 18, 112
By, John 1779-1836: house [w4.25], 55

C

Camberwell Beauty, 81, 94
canal, 43
Canaletto, Antonio Canale 1697-1768, 44, 55
candle factory [w4.36], 35
Canterbury, the Archbishop of, 5, 33, 51, 58, 69, 71, 146
Canterbury, The; Canterbury Arms [w4.11], 78, 108-9, 143
Canute, 43, 158
Capon, William 1757-1827, painting by; 'View from Gentleman's Seat...' [w4.7], 95, 98
Carlile, Richard 1790-1843, 138
Carlisle, Bishop of, 35, 71
Carlisle House [w4.35], 29, 34, 35, 45, 58, 69, 71
Carlisle Lane, 35, 58, 62, 108, 142
Caron House [w1.15]
Carter and Housten, 64
cemetery
  Brookwood Necropolis, Woking [w2.19], 53
  Norwood, 62
Channel Tunnel Terminus, 53
chapels see places of worship
Chaplin, Charlie, 123
Chapman's Garden, 87
Charing Cross, 26, 50-1, 60
Charity Boys' School [w4.41], 126
Charlotte, Sophia, Queen to George III 1744-1818, 118
Charlotte Sharman school see schools
Chelsea, 43, 90
Chevalier, Albert, 104
Chevalier D'Eon [w4.9], 29, 118
Chicheley Street, 66
cholera, 5, 43, 57, 131
Christ Church, Blackfriars [w3.16], 20, 73, 92, 99, 100, 138
Christ Church, Westminster Bridge Road [w4.57], 112, 130, 138, 141
Christ Church workhouse [w2.47], 123
Church Commissioners, 142
churches, see places of worship
Circus, St George's, 47
circus
  Astley's [w4.15], 106-8
  Frazier's [w2.6], 113
  Royal Circus and Equestrian Philharmonic Society [w2.39], 112
City of London, 47, 49, 54
civil war forts [w2.35], 16, 77

Claggat 1788-98; Apollo gardens [w2.26], 85
Clapham, 152
Clifton suspension bridge, 26, 50
Clowes, William 1779-1847
   printing works [w3.26], 54, 60-2, 65, 66
Coade, 25, 31, 35, 36, 38, 54, 57, 59-60, 101, 124, 128, 130
   Mrs Eleanor senior 1708-96
   Mrs Eleanor junior 1732-1821
   stone factory [w3.38]
   showroom and lion [w4.20]
Coal, 44, 60, 62, 64
Coburg, the Royal [w2.53], 104, 117
Coffee Hall Music Company, 106
Coin Street housing, 60, 120, 142
Cole, Mrs Marie, 118-9
Collector Earl *see* Surrey, Earl of
colleges *see* schools
Collinge, Charles, 63
Commissioner of Sewers, 43
Commonwealth, 69, 71
comprehensive redevelopment area, South Bank, 66
Congregational Church, Christ Church [w4.57], 112
Cons, Emma 1838-1912, 5, 18, 36, 106, 121-2
Constable, John 1776-1837, 49
Cook, Captain, 22, 138
Cooke, William, 14, 108
Cool (Cold) Harbour Lane, 94
Cooper *see* Cuper
Cornwall, Duchy of, 5, 75, 86
Cornwall, Duke of, 69, 71
Cornwall House, 133
Cornwall Road [w3.1], 105
Cosser Street, 107
Cottesloe, theatre [w3.31], 116
Council
   Lambeth Borough, 4, 5
   London County [w4.17], 66
   Southwark Borough, 4, 5
County Gaol, 123
County Hall [w4.17], 44, 54, 66, 110
County of Surrey, 77, 137
Cowper *see* Applegarth
Cox's bridge, 45
Cranmer, 13
cricket, 77
Cromwell, Oliver 1599-1658, 69
Crown and Cushion, New [w2.18]
Cruikshank, 115

Crystal Palace, 40
Culpeper, Joyce 1485-1531, 72, 73, 120, 143, 145, 156
Cuming Museum, 86
Cunningham, J. W, 64
Cuper (Cooper), Boyden (Boydel) d.1718 [w3.34]
Cuper's Bridge [w3.46], 40, 45, 49, 54-5
Cupid's Garden *see* gardens
Curtis, William 1746-99, 88-94
Curtis' garden, Bermondsey [w1.19], 88
Curtis' London Botanic Garden [w2.51], 80, 88-94, 150
Cut, The, 177

D

Dance, George, the Younger 1741-1825, 87
Davenant, Killigrew and, 102
Davey, Dolly, 123
Davis's Amphitheatre [w4.15], 108
Defoe, Daniel 1660-1731, 43
de Fortibus, 67
D'Eon, Chevalier 1728-1810 [w4.9], 118
Deptford, 10, 40, 43, 77, 78
Derham, Francis, 72, 157
Despard, Colonel Edward 1751-1803, 16
Dibden, 113
Dickens, Charles 1812-1870, 60, 65, 101, 107, 108, 113, 135, 143
Dingley, Robert, 129
dispensary, London [4.53]
Dodd, William 1729-77, 129-30
Dodson Street, 126
Dog and Duck [w4.47], 40, 86, 87, 102, 124, 134
Dog and Pot [w2.46], 64
Doggett, Thomas 1670-1721; Doggett's Arms [w3.22]
Domesday, 67, 69
Doulton, Sir Henry 1820-97, 21, 33, 43, 132, 142
Dovaston, J. M, 126
Dowager Duchess of Norfolk, 72, 157
drainage, 40, 74, 90, 102
drama, 106, 161
Dreams, Lydia, 104
Driver, Samuel 1692-1741, 87
Duchy of Cornwall, 5, 75, 86
Ducrow, Andrew, 31, 108
Duke's Arms, 109
Duke's Head, 29
Dunlop, Frank, 106
Dyster, 25

Index

E
Earl of Surrey, 67, 71, 83
Edward the Confessor, 67, 69,
Edwards, James, 90, 94
Edwards, Mrs, brewery, 57
Effra, river, 43
elected representatives, 101, 119-20
Elephant and Castle [w1.10]
Elliston, 113
embankment *see* Albert Embankment
Enclosure Survey and Act, 57, 69
English (England), Mr, 85
entertainment
   Astley's Amphitheatre [w4.15], 106-8
   Bower Saloon, Duke's Arms [w4.13], 109
   Canterbury, The (Arms) [w4.11], 108-9
   Dog and Duck, [w4.47], 86-7
   Folly, the [w3.46], 87
   Frazier's penny gaff [w2.6], 113
   Gatti's Palace of Varieties [w4.8], 110
   Hayward Gallery [w3.35], 116
   Museum of the Moving Image [w3.45], 115
   National Film Theatre [w3.45], 115-6
   National Theatre, the Lyttleton, the Olivier, the Cottesloe [w3.31], 116
   Old Vic, Royal Coburg, Royal Victoria, Royal Victoria Tea and Coffee House [w2.53], 104-6
   Queen Elizabeth Hall and Purcell Room [w3.44], 116
   Ring, The, the Surrey Chapel [w2.45], 110-1
   Royal Festival Hall [w3.38], 115
   South London Palace of Variety [w1.9], 110
   Surrey Music-hall, now the Winchester [w1.8], 110
   Surrey Theatre, the Royal Circus and Cinema [w2.39], 112-3
   Upstream Theatre [w2.50], 104
   Young Vic [w2.48], 106
Erith, sewer outfall, 43
Escheat, Vauxhall, 6, 9, 80, 94
Evans, Widow, 25, 26, 58, 84, 120
Evelyn, John 1620-1706 [w1.16], 44, 80, 81, 83, 84, 145-8, 146
Eye Hospital, Royal [w2.40], 16, 134

F
Fabian Society, 121
Feathers, the [w3.33], 58, 80, 84, 85

Female Orphan Society, asylum [w4.57], 130
ferry
   Horseferry [w4.26], 71
   Stangate [w4.23] 55, 69, 71, 142
Festival of Britain, 25, 26, 60, 66, 115
Field, Joshua 1757-1863, 64
Field's soap factory [w4.37], 62
film *see* National Film Theatre
Finch's Grotto [w1.6], 88
fire of
   London, 54
   Albion mills [w3.20], 47, 153, 155
fire engine manufactory [w4.6], 63
fire station [w3.3]
First Trade Society of Compositors, 62
flag pole, Festival of Britain [w3.42], 60
Flaxman, John 1755-1826, 29, 127, 153
flood, 40, 43, 98
Flora Tea Gardens [w4.59], 85
Flora, Temple of [w2.21], 86
flour, Albion Mills [w3.20], 47, 153, 155
Folly, the [w3.46], 87, 160
ford, 45
Fore Street, 79
forts, Civil War [w2.35], 77
Frazier's penny gaff [w2.6], 113-5
Frazier Street [w2.6], 53, 58, 138
Freemasons' School for Girls [w2.29], 126
Friends Row, 25, 58
Frost Fair, 31

G
gardens, 80
   Apollo Gardens [w2.26], 85
   asparagus gardens [w3.43]
   Belvedere Gardens [w3.38], 86
   Cuper's Gardens, Cupid's garden [w3.34], 58, 71, 80, 81, 83-4, 98, 116
   Dog and Duck [w4.47], 86
   Finch's Grotto [w1.6], 88
   Flora Tea Gardens [w4.59], 85
   Hercules Gardens and House [w4.58], 107
   Holland's Leaguer [w3.18], 88
   Lambeth Wells [w1.13], 87
   London Botanic Garden [w2.51], 88
   Pye gardens, Southwark [w1.4]
   Restoration Gardens, Spring Gardens [w2.51], 92-3
   St George's Spa [w4.47], 86
   Temple of Flora [w2.21], 86
   Tradescant's Garden [w1.15], 80

Vauxhall Gardens; Spring Gardens [w1.14], 77
gas lamp [w2.54]
Gatti's-in-the-Road [w4.8], 110, 112
General Lying-in Hospital [w4.3], 131
Glagget, Walter, 85
Goding, 57
Goldsmith, 25, 67, 88
Gordon, Lord George 1751-93; riots, 138, 141, 150
Granby Place [w2.7], 65, 99
Gravel Lane, Great Suffolk Street, 40, 69, 73, 77, 88, 123
Gray Street, 78, 90
Grimaldi, Joseph 1779-1837, and home [w4.34], 117

H

Halfpenny Hatch [w3.14], 107
Halfway House, Lambeth Marsh [w2.52], 78
Halfway House, Redriff [w1.17], 77
Handel, water music, 84
Hardicanute, 69
Hatfields, 73
Hawksmoor, Nicholas 1661-1736, 77
Hayward Gallery [w3.35], 116
health, 90, 120
Hedger, family, 86-7, 126
Henley, Robert, 58
Henry VIII, 22, 55, 71-3, 141
Hercules Road, 45, 58, 71, 83, 107, 126-7
Hercules Tavern and Hall [w4.58], 107
Hill, Octavia 1838-1912, 6, 90, 123
Hill, Rowland 1744-1833; preacher, 5, 18, 110-2, 130-1, 138
Hollar, Wenceslas 1607-77, 6, 9, 54, 81, 83, 148
Horn's Brewery [w2.49], 58
Horseferry [w4.26], 45, 55, 71
hospitals and asylums
   Asylum for Female Orphans [w4.57], 130
   Bethlem Hospital [w4.54], 120, 124
   Churchill Clinic [w4.53]
   General Lying-in Hospital [w4.3], 131
   Lambeth Hospital [w1.12]
   Lambeth Marsh private madhouse, 126
   Lazer Hospital [w2.51], 90
   London Dispensary [w4.53]
   Magdalen Hospital [w2.41], 129
   Philanthropic society [w2.34], 135
   Royal Eye Hospital [w2.40], 134
   Royal Waterloo Hospital for Women and Children [w3.8], 132
   St George's Military Hospital [w3.9], 133
   St Thomas's Hospital [w4.16], 133
   School for the Indigent Blind [w2.31], 134
   Tower clinic [w4.49]
Housing, 87, 88, 90, 95, 101, 102, 106, 107, 121, 123, 130
Howard see Surrey, Earl of
Howard, Katherine 1521-42 [w4.30], 71-3, 156
Hungerford Bridge and market [w3.40], 26, 40, 49-51, 60

I

Imperial War Museum [w4.54], 48, 59, 124
Indigent Blind, School for [w2.31], 134
ink, Stephens [w3.27], 60, 62
inns see pubs
institutes
   general, 123
   Southwark [w2.47]
   Surrey [w3.19], 137
islands, 40, 43, 66, 110

J

Jonas, Harold Driver 1879-1953, 87, 129
Jones, Inigo 1573-1652; treasure in Lambeth Marsh, 76

K

Kennington Common, 43, 138
Kennington Manor, 2, 55, 58, 67
Kennington Road, 22, 61, 77, 101, 104, 106-7, 135, 159
Killigrew and Davenant, 102
King's Arms and stairs [w4.19]
King's Bench Prison [w4.50], 85, 120, 135
Knott, Ralph, 66

L

Labelye, 31, 33, 46
Lactarium [w2.35], 77
Lambeth Asylum for Girls [w4.57], 130
Lambeth Council, 95
Lambeth Green [w4.40], 107, 126
Lambeth High Street [w4.29], 93
Lambeth Hospital [w1.12]
Lambeth Manor, 67, 69
Lambeth Marsh [w2.1], 2, 13, 119, 126

Lambeth Palace [w4.26], 43, 45, 47, 55, 71, 83, 119, 134, 138
Lambeth Road, 45, 47, 58, 72, 83, 86, 94, 101, 104, 122, 124, 136, 141
Lambeth Walk, 87
Lambeth Wells [w1.13], 82, 102
Lane, Mrs, 78
Langley, Batty, 31, 46
Langton, 69
Lawrence, Richard d.1671, 35, 126
Lazar hospital *see* hospitals and asylums
LCC, 31, 44, 66, 95, 108, 116
Leaguer, Holland's [w3.18], 88
Leake, Dr John 1729-92, 131-2
Leake Street [w4.2], 53, 98, 141
Leigh, 73, 156
Leno, Dan, 104, 112
leper *see* hospitals and asylums
Lett's, timber yard, 61
Library, North Lambeth [w2.55]
lime kilns, 5, 44, 147
Lincoln Tower [w4.57], 131
Lion Brewery [w3.38], 57, 85
Lion & Co, boatyard, 55
London, Bishop of, 13
London Botanic Garden [w2.51], 88
London Bridge, 31, 36, 43-7, 51, 54, 71, 78, 83, 134
London County Council [w4.17], 66
London Necropolis Railway [w2.19], 53
London School of Printing [w3.12], 62
London Weekend television [w3.30], 62, 116
Lower Marsh, 2
Lunardi, 113
Lydia Dreams, 104

M

Magdalen Hospital [w2.41], 76, 90, 99, 120, 129, 130
Manor House, 69, 73, 88
Manox, 72
manufactory, general, 29, 31, 63
Marshalsea, 13, 123, 135
Marshgate [w2.15], 46
Maudslay, Henry 1771-1831; works [w4.60], 64
Mayhew, Henry 1812-87, 1, 5, 13, 101, 103, 115
Meymot Street, 62
Middleton, 25, 69, 80, 95
mills
    Albion Mill, flour mill [w3.20], 47, 153, 155
    water mill, Paris Garden [w2.44]
    Water Works, Lambeth [w3.38]
    mill stone, Coade stone [w3.39], 60
    windmills *see* windmill
Monk, General *see* Albemarle
Monument, the [w1.24], 98, 100
Morley, Robert 1822-94; College [w4.55], 106, 121-2
Morton, 108-9, 143
Munby, Arthur Joseph 1828-1910, 48
Mylne, Robert, 47

N

Narrow Wall [w3.23], 54
National Film Theatre [w3.45], 66, 104, 115-6
National Theatre [w3.31], 104, 116
Neckinger, the road [w1.20], 40
Neckinger river [w1.8] and [w4.50], 40, 43, 45, 55, 75, 86
Nelson Square, 43
neolithic settlement [w2. 22], [w4.6], 43, 54
New Crown and Cushion [w2.18]
New Cut, 1, 77
Nightingale, Florence 1820-1910, 31, 131, 134
Norden, 79
Norfolk, Dukes of, 67, 71-3, 81, 83, 149, 156
Norfolk House [w4.30], 71, 72, 81
North, Richard, 87
Northumberland, 60
Norwood, 62

O

Oakey [w4.57], 130
Oakley Arms [w2.24], 138
obelisk [w2.33], 47-8, 107
oil jars [w2.8]
Old Dover Castle [w2.16]
Old House, Bonner's house [w2.12], 60, 78-9, 121
Old King's Head [w2.42], 78
Old Vic [w2.53], 38, 90, 104, 106, 121, 123, 143
Oxo Tower [w3.25], 22, 55, 73, 144

P

Page, Thomas, 33, 47
paper, Bowater's factory, 60-2, 117, 121, 130
Paris Garden Manor [w2.44], 22, 40, 55, 67, 73, 78, 88, 123, 138

parochial school *see* schools
Pearman Street, 16, 85, 142
Peckham, 40
Pedlar's Acre, 66
Pepys, Samuel 1633-1703, 43, 44, 55, 76-80, 87
    Elizabeth, wife 1640-69
Philanthropic Society [w2.34], 135
Physic Garden, 90
pigeon houses, 147, 152
plague, 54, 55, 90
plantagenet, 67, 71
pottery, 16, 35, 54, 58-60, 71, 132
Prince's Meadow, 53
printing, 60-3, 66, 117, 135
prisons
    New Bridewell, 123
    King's Bench, rules of [w4.51], 135
    Surrey County Gaol, 123
public houses, taverns, inns
    Artichoke, Streets' [w2.7], 98
    Bell [w2.11], 77
    Black Bull, or the Bull [w2.3]
    Bonner's House or 'the Old House' [w2.12], 79
    Bower Saloon [w4.13], 109
    Canterbury Arms [w4.11], 108
    Crown, the [w4.10]
    Crown and Cushion [w2.17], 85
    Dog and Duck [w4.47], 86
    Dogget's Arms [w3.22]
    Dover Castle [w2.16]
    Dukes Head, Bower Saloon [w4.13], 109
    Feathers, the [w3.33], 84
    Flower Pot, Ye, *see* Red Lion
    Folly, the [w3.46], 87
    Grapes *see* Surrey Music-hall
    Halfway House, Redriff, or Brady's [w1.17], 77
    Halfway House, the Stage Door [w2.52], 78
    Hatch House tavern, now White Hart [w3.14], 107
    Hercules Hall and Tavern [w4.58], 106
    Holland's Leaguer [w3.18], 86, 88
    Horse and Groom [w2.23]
    King's Arms, King's Arms stairs [w4.18], 54
    Mitre, Stangate [w4.23]
    New Crown and Cushion [w2.18], 85
    Oakley Arms [w2.24], 138
    Old Dover Castle *see* Dover Castle
    Old King's Head [w2.42], 78
    Pear Tree [w3.6]
    Pineapple [w4.38], 115
    Queen's Head [w4.12]
    Red Lion [w2.13]
    Rose, The [w2.14]
    Rose and Crown [w3.17]
    Royal George [w4.34], 117
    Royal Saloon *see* Canterbury Arms
    Royal Theatre, Westminster *see* Canterbury Arms
    St George's Tavern [w2.30]
    Spanish Patriot [w2.2]
    Stage Door *see* Halfway House
    Streets' *see* Artichoke
    Three Compasses [w2.4]
    Three Mariners, 79
    Three Stags [w4.46]
    Tower, the [w2.28]
    Watch House *see* Bonner's House
    White Hart [w2.4]
    Windmill, the [w2.49], 58
    York, The, 106
Pugin, Augustus 1812-52, 16, 141

Q
Queen Elizabeth Hall [w3.44], 62, 116
Queen's Head [w4.12]

R
railways, 51, 64
Red Cross Hall [w1.5], 123
Red Lion [w2.13], 46, 78
Redriff, Rotherhithe stairs [w1.18], 40, 43, 77, 78
Restoration Gardens [w2.51], 92
Reynolds, George 1765-1835, 126-7, 130
    John 1796-1852, 107, 117, 137
    Charlotte, 127
river wall, 22, 54
rivers, 40, 44, 46, 54
Roberts' boatyard, 55
Rochester, 29, 33, 35, 45, 67, 69, 71, 142
Roman boat [w4.17], 54
Roman pottery *see* pottery
Rotherhithe *see* Redriff
Rotunda [w3.19], 115, 137-8
Roupell Street [w3.13], 142
Roupell, William 1831-1909, 62-3
Royal Botanical Society, 93
Royal Circus [w4.15], 112
Royal Coburg [w2.53], 104
Royal Festival Hall [w3.38], 55, 57, 60, 62, 104, 115-6

Index

Royal Grove [w4.15], 108
Royal Saloon [w4.15], 108
Royal Street, 117
Royal Victoria Coffee Hall [w2.53], 106
Royal Waterloo Hospital for Women and Children [w3.8], 132
Rules of the King's Bench [w4.51], 135

S

St Andrew, Coin Street [w3.10], 99, 138, 142
St George's Cathedral [w2.30], 141
St George's Circus [w2.38], 47-8
St George's Fields [w2.32], 74-5
St George's Road, 135
St George's Tavern, 16
St John's, Waterloo Road [w3.7], 141
St Mary Lambeth [w4.27], 2, 45, 46, 72-3, 80-1, 88, 101, 119, 132, 136, 138
St Paul's Cathedral [w1.2], 99
St Paul's Westminster Bridge Road [w2.29]
St Thomas's Hospital [w4.16], 133
Sala, Augustus, 101-3, 105, 181
Sancroft, 71
sand-bank [w3.46], 40-3
Sandby, Paul 1730-1809, 95, 98
Sanger, George 1765-1911, 108
Saw-mill, 44, 55
Sayes Court, Evelyn's house [w1.16]
schools and colleges
    Addington Street Primary School [w4.5]
    Archbishop Temple School [w4.32], 137
    Archbishop Tenison School [w4.31], 137
    Benevolent Society of St Patrick [w3.12], 62
    Blind, School for Indigent [w2.31], 134
    Carlisle Academy of Young Gentlemen [w4.35], 71
    Charity Boys School [w4.41], 126-8
    Female Orphan Society, Asylum for Girls [w4.57], 130-1
    Freemasons' School for Girls [w2.29], 126
    King Edward's School [w2.37]
    London School of Printing [w3.12], 62
    Morley College [w4.55], 121-2
    Seamens' Mission School [w3.12], 62
    Sharman, Charlotte, Orphanage [w2.36], 122

Southwark Institute [w2.47]
    Yorkshire Society's School for Boys [w4.55], 121
Scott, Thomas, 71
Searle's boatyards [w4.24], 33, 55
sewers, 43, 86, 90
Sharman, Charlotte 1832-1929, orphanage [w2.36], 122
Short Street, 138
shot tower, round [w3.36], 62
shot tower, square [w3.29], 62, 98, 99
soap manufacture
    Field's [w4.37], 62
    Phelp's [w3.37]
South Bank, 65-6, 77, 103-4, 115-6
South London Dwellings Company, 106
South London Palace of Variety [w1.9], 110
Southwark, 1, 40, 44, 62, 64, 73, 75, 83, 88, 110, 119, 123
Sowerby, James 1757-1822, and house [w4.56], 76, 92-3, 95
spires
    All Saints, Leake Street [w2.9], 141
    Christ Church, Westminster Bridge Road [w4.57], 141
    St Andrew, Coin Street [w3.10], 142
Spring Gardens, 32, 92
Stage Door [w2.52], 78
Stamford Street, 49, 60, 62, 65, 94, 133
Stangate [w4.14], 45, 55, 69, 71, 78, 109, 117, 127, 142
Stangate ferry [w4.232], 55, 69, 71, 142
Stephens ink works, 100
Stockwell, 73, 104, 121, 156
Stow, 85, 87
Strand Bridge Company, 45, 49-50, 58, 76, 83, 110
Stratford Place, 59
Streatham, 62, 63, 130
Sudrey Street housing, Octavia Hill [w1.7], 123
Surrey Chapel [w2.45], 110-2, 131, 138
Surrey, Earl of, 71-3, 83
Surrey Docks, 40, 47
Surrey Institution [w3.19], 137
Surrey Lodge, Emma Cons [w4.44], 87, 106
Surrey Music-hall [w1.8], 110
Surrey Theatre [w2.39], 107, 112, 117
Surrey Zoological Gardens [w1.11], 134

T
tansy, recipe, 78, 160
taverns *see* public houses
Temple of Flora [w2.21], 86
Theatre Royal, Westminster; Astley's [w4.15], 108
Theed Street, 142
Thomas, Edward, 53
Three Compasses [w2.4]
Three Mariners, 79
Three Stags [w4.46], 77
Tinworth, George 1843-1913, 142
Tradescant, John the elder d.1638, 65, 80-3, 94, 119, 138
   John the younger 1608-62
     House [w1.15]
     Tomb [w4.28]
Trusson's, menswear shop [w2.5], 64
Trustee Savings Bank [w4.45]
turnpikes
   Kennington Road/Westminster Bridge Road [w4.57], 90
   Lambeth Road [w4.42]
   Marshgate [w2.15], 46
   St George's Circus [w2.38]

U
Ufford Street, 90, 92, 123, 141
Union brewery [w2.25], 58
Union Jack Club [w3.5], 53
Unitarian Chapel [w3.11]
Upper Ground, 54
Upper Marsh, 2, 13, 51, 78, 108, 109

V
Vauxhall, 40, 43, 45, 51, 58, 69, 80, 94
Vauxhall Gardens [w1.14], 77
vineyard and Vine Street [w3.1], 57

W
Walter, Hubert, 69
Walworth, 77, 86, 87, 123, 134
Warehouse, Art Deco [w3.15]
Warren, Earl of Surrey and, 67, 71
water mill, 18, 40
water works, 25, 85
Waterloo Bridge [w3.32], 40, 49, 66, 83, 103, 115, 116
Waterloo Road, 51, 62, 65, 83, 104, 123, 134, 136
Waterloo station [w3.6], 51-3, 57, 98, 133
Webber Street, 64, 78, 83, 90, 92, 104, 123, 135, 141

Wellington Mills [w4.37], 130
wells
   artesian, 58
   Lambeth Wells [w1.13], 87
Westminster Abbey [w1.1], 2
Westminster Bridge [w4.21], 45
White, Ben, 9, 94, 138, 149, 151, 152
White, Gilbert 1720-93, 9, 76, 80, 149
White, Thomas, 149
Widow Evans, 25, 58, 84, 120
William de Fortibus, 67
willow copses, withers [w3.43], 54
Windmill public house and street [w2.49], 58
windmills
   Horn's Brewery [w2.49], 58, 98
   saw-mill [w3.38], 44, 55
workhouse
   Lambeth [w1.12], 123
   Christ Church [w2.47]
workshops, 135
worship, places of
   general, 138
   All Saints, Leake Street [w2.9], 141
   Bermondsey Abbey [w1.21], 40
   Bible Christian Chapel, Waterloo Road [w3.2]
   Catholic Chapel, London Road [w1.9]
   Christ Church, Blackfriars Road [w3.16], 138
   Christ Church, and Hawkstone Hall [w4.57], 73, 130, 131, 138
   Congregational Chapel, York Road [w4.4], 141
   Gospel Hall, The Cut
   Holy Trinity, Carlisle Lane [w4.33], 142
   Lambeth Chapel (Wesleyan Methodist) [w4.43]
   Metropolitan Tabernacle, Spurgeon's Tabernacle [w1.10]
   Methodist Chapel, Waterloo Road [w3.4]
   Mission Hall, Short Street [w2.50], 141
   Mission Room, Roupell Street
   St Andrew's, Coin Street [w3.10], 99, 138, 142
   St Bride's Fleet Street [w1.3], 92
   St George's Cathedral, [w2.30], 141
   St John's Church, Waterloo [w3.7], 141
   St Jude's Church, St George's Road [w2.34], 135

St Margaret Pattens, Rood Street [w1.23], 98
St Mary Lambeth [w4.27], 2, 45, 46, 72-3, 80-1, 101, 119, 132, 136, 138
St Michael, Cornhill [w1.25], 10, 98, 100
St Paul's Cathedral [w1.2], 92
St Paul's, Westminster Bridge Road [2.29]
St Thomas's Church, Westminster Bridge Road [w2.27], 142
Surrey Chapel, Blackfriars Road [w2.45], 110
Unitarian Chapel, Stamford Street [w3.11]
Upton Chapel, Lambeth Road [w4.53]
Verulam Chapel, Kennington Road [w4.48]
Westminster Abbey [w1.1], 2
Zion Methodist Chapel, Waterloo Road [w3.4]
Wyatt, Sir James 1746-1827 [w4.44]
Wyndham Road, 128

Y

York, Frederick Duke of, 1763-1827, 49, 148
York Hotel, 104
York Road, 65-6, 98, 104, 132, 141
Yorkshire Society's School For Boys [w4.54], 121
Young Vic theatre [w2.48], 106